Frommer's®

PORTABLE

Puerto Rico

5th Edition

by John Marino

Here's what critics say about Frommer's:

"Amazingly easy to use. Very portable, very complete."
—**BOOKLIST**

"Detailed, accurate, and easy-to-read information for all price ranges."
—**GLAMOUR MAGAZINE**

WILEY
Wiley Publishing, Inc.

ABOUT THE AUTHOR

John Marino is the former editor of the *San Juan Star* and has written about Puerto Rico and the Caribbean for Reuters, *The Washington Post*, *The New York Times*, *Gourmet*, and other publications. He lives in San Juan with his wife, Jova, and son, Juan Antonio, who both provided valuable research and insight for this book.

Published by:

WILEY PUBLISHING, INC.

111 River St.
Hoboken, NY 07030

ISBN 978-0-470-47403-7

Editor: Stephen Bassman
Production Editor: Heather Wilcox
Cartographer: Guy Ruggiero
Photo Editor: Richard Fox
Production by Wiley Indianapolis Composition Services

For information on our other products and services or to obtain technical support, please contact our Customer Care Department within the U.S. at 877/762-2974, outside the U.S. at 317/572-3993 or fax 317/572-4002.

Wiley also publishes its books in a variety of electronic formats. Some content that appears in print may not be available in electronic formats.

Manufactured in the United States of America

5 4 3 2 1

CONTENTS

LIST OF MAPS

AN INVITATION TO THE READER

In researching this book, we discovered many wonderful places—hotels, restaurants, shops, and more. We're sure you'll find others. Please tell us about them, so we can share the information with your fellow travelers in upcoming editions. If you were disappointed with a recommendation, we'd love to know that, too. Please write to:

Frommer's Portable Puerto Rico, 5th Edition
Wiley Publishing, Inc. • 111 River St. • Hoboken, NY 07030-5774

AN ADDITIONAL NOTE

FROMMER'S STAR RATINGS, ICONS & ABBREVIATIONS

Every hotel, restaurant, and attraction listing in this guide has been ranked for quality, value, service, amenities, and special features using a **star-rating system.** In country, state, and regional guides, we also rate towns and regions to help you narrow down your choices and budget your time accordingly. Hotels and restaurants are rated on a scale of zero (recommended) to three stars (exceptional). Attractions, shopping, nightlife, towns, and regions are rated according to the following scale: zero stars (recommended), one star (highly recommended), two stars (very highly recommended), and three stars (must-see).

In addition to the star-rating system, we also use **seven feature icons** that point you to the great deals, in-the-know advice and unique experiences that separate travelers from tourists. Throughout the book, look for:

(Finds)	Special finds—those places only insiders know about
(Fun Facts)	Fun facts—details that make travelers more informed and their trips more fun
(Kids)	Best bets for kids, and advice for the whole family
(Moments)	Special moments—those experiences that memories are made of
(Overrated)	Places or experiences not worth your time or money
(Tips)	Insider tips—great ways to save time and money
(Value)	Great values—where to get the best deals

The following **abbreviations** are used for credit cards:

AE	American Express	**DISC**	Discover	**V**	Visa
DC	Diners Club	**MC**	MasterCard		

FROMMERS.COM

Now that you have this guidebook to help you plan a great trip, visit our website at **www.frommers.com** for additional travel information on more than 4,000 destinations. We update features regularly to give you instant access to the most current trip-planning information available. At Frommers.com, you'll find scoops on the best airfares, lodging rates, and car rental bargains. You can even book your travel online through our reliable travel booking partners. Other popular features include:

- Online updates of our most popular guidebooks
- Vacation sweepstakes and contest giveaways
- Newsletters highlighting the hottest travel trends
- Podcasts, interactive maps, and up-to-the-minute events listings
- Opinionated blog entries by Arthur Frommer himself
- Online travel message boards with featured travel discussions

The Best of Puerto Rico

It's only the size of Connecticut, but Puerto Rico pulsates with more life than any other island in the Caribbean. Whether it's the beat of *bomba y plena,* salsa, or reggaeton, there's a party going on here 24/7.

Puerto Rico is blessed with towering mountains, rainforests, white sandy beaches along Caribbean shores, and a vibrant culture forged from a mix of Caribbean, Hispanic, African, and U.S. influences. History buffs will get more ancient buildings and monuments here than anywhere else in the Caribbean, many of them dating back some 500 years to the Spanish conquistadors. Add some of the best golf and tennis in the West Indies, posh beach resorts, tranquil country inns or guesthouses, and a great nightlife, and you've got a formidable attraction.

Here are our picks for the best Puerto Rico has to offer.

1 THE BEST BEACHES

White sandy beaches put Puerto Rico and its offshore islands on tourist maps in the first place. Many other Caribbean destinations have only jagged coral outcroppings or black volcanic-sand beaches that get very hot in the noonday sun. The best beaches are labeled on the "Puerto Rico" map on p. 9.

- **Best Beach for Singles:** Sandwiched between the Condado and Isla Verde along San Juan's coast, **Ocean Park** beach offers a more laid-back experience and attracts a younger, more progressive crowd. The wide beach, lined with palm and sea grape trees, fronts a residential neighborhood of beautiful homes, free of the high-rise condos that line other San Juan beaches. A favorite for swimming, paddle tennis, and kite surfing, the beach is also a favorite spot for young and beautiful sanjuaneros to congregate, especially on weekends. Area guesthouses cater to young urban professionals from the East Coast, both gay and straight. So there is something of a South Beach–Río vibe here, with more than a fair share of well-stuffed bikinis and other beach outfits, but it's decidedly more low-key and Caribbean. It's a good spot for tourists and locals to mix.

- **Best Beach for Families: Luquillo Beach,** 30 miles (48km) east of San Juan, attracts both local families, mainly from San Juan, and visitors from Condado and Isla Verde beaches in San Juan. Beach buffs heading for Luquillo know they will get better sands and clearer waters there than in San Juan. The vast sandy beach opens onto a crescent-shaped bay edged by a coconut grove. Coral reefs protect the crystal-clear lagoon from the often rough Atlantic waters that can buffet the northern coast, making Luquillo a good place for young children to swim. Much photographed because of its white sands, Luquillo also has tent sites and other facilities, including picnic areas with changing rooms, lockers, and showers.

- **Best for Swimming: Pine Grove Beach,** which stretches between the Ritz-Carlton and the Marriott Courtyard at the end of Isla Verde near the airport, is a crescent, white-sand beach, whose tranquil, rich blue waters are protected by an offshore reef from the often rough Atlantic current. By the Ritz-Carlton and the Casa Cuba social club to the west, the water is completely sheltered, and a long sandbar means shallow water stretches way offshore. There's more of a surf to the east, which is a popular spot for surfing, boogie boarding, and bodysurfing. The waves are well formed but never too big, which makes it a perfect spot to learn to surf.

2 THE BEST GOLF & TENNIS

- **Río Mar Beach Resort & Spa, A Wyndham Grand Resort** (Río Grande; ℂ **787/888-6000**): Two world-class golf courses are located here in the shadow of El Yunque rainforest along a dazzling stretch of coast. The entire length (6,782 yards/6,201m) of Tom and George Fazio's Ocean Course has seaside panoramas, breezes, and fat iguanas scampering through the lush grounds. The other course, a 6,945-yard (6,351m) design by golf pro Greg Norman, follows the flow of the Mameyes River through mountain and coastal vistas. The resort is a 30-minute drive from San Juan on the northeast coast. Wind is often a challenge here. See p. 124.

- **Dorado Beach Resort & Club** (Dorado; ℂ **787/796-8961** or 626-1006): With 72 holes, Dorado has the highest concentration of golf on the island. The legendary Dorado Beach and Cerromar hotels run by Hyatt are now gone, but the four courses and other facilities—spectacular tennis courts, pools, and beaches—live on. Of the courses, Dorado East is our favorite. Designed by Robert Trent Jones, Sr., it was the site of the Senior PGA Tournament of Champions throughout the 1990s. True tennis buffs head here, too. The Dorado courts are the best on the island.

- **Trump International Golf Club** (Río Grande; © 787/657-2000): Located on 1,200 acres (486 hectares) of glistening waterfront, this recently improved 36-hole golf course designed by Tom Kite allows you to play in the mountains, along the ocean, among the palms, and in between the lakes. Its bunkers are carved from white silica sand. Real estate magnate Donald Trump announced plans in conjunction with local developer Empresas Díaz, Inc., to develop 500 luxury residences here. The first phase, announced in March 2008, consists of 56 villas, with starting prices of $1.4 million, that have access to private jet, yacht, and limousine service. See p. 122.

3 THE BEST NATURAL WONDERS

- **El Yunque** (© 787/888-1880): A half-hour east of San Juan in the Luquillo Mountains, El Yunque is Puerto Rico's greatest natural attraction, the only tropical rainforest in the United States National Forest System. It sprawls across 28,000 acres (1,133 hectares) of the rugged Sierra de Luquillo mountain range, covering areas of Canóvanas, Las Piedras, Luquillo, Fajardo, Ceiba, Naguabo, and Río Grande. The area is named after the Indian spirit Yuquiye, which means "Forest of Clouds," who local Taínos thought protected the island from disaster in times of storms. Originally established in 1876 by the Spanish Crown, it's one of the oldest reserves in the region. There are some 240 species (26 endemic) of trees and plants found here and 50 bird species, including the rare Puerto Rican Parrot (scientific name: *Amazona vitatta*), which is one of the 10 most endangered species of birds in the world. Some 100 billion gallons of rain fall annually on this home to four forest types. Visitors can explore dozens of trails that wind past waterfalls, dwarf vegetation, and miniature flowers, while the island's colorful parrots fly overhead. See "El Yunque" in chapter 7.
- **Río Camuy Caves** (© 787/898-3100): Some 2½ hours west of San Juan, visitors board a tram to descend into this forest-filled sinkhole at the mouth of the Clara Cave. They walk the footpaths of a 170-foot-high (52m) cave to a deeper sinkhole. Once they're inside, a 45-minute tour helps everyone, including kids, learn to differentiate stalactites from stalagmites. At the Pueblos sinkhole, a platform overlooks the Camuy River, passing through a network of cave tunnels. See "Arecibo & Camuy" in chapter 7.
- **Las Cabezas de San Juan Nature Reserve** (© 787/722-5882): This 316-acre (128-hectare) nature reserve about 45 minutes from San Juan encompasses seven different ecological systems, including

forestland, mangroves, lagoons, beaches, cliffs, and offshore coral reefs. It also has one of the finest phosphorescent bays in the world. See the box, "To the Lighthouse: Exploring Las Cabezas de San Juan Nature Reserve," in chapter 10.

4 THE BEST FAMILY RESORT

• **El Conquistador Resort & Golden Door Spa** (Las Croabas; $\textcircled{C}$ **866/317-8932** or 787/863-1000): Located 31 miles (50km) east of San Juan, this resort offers Camp Coquí on Palomino Island for children 3 to 12 years of age. The hotel's free water taxi takes kids to the island for a half- or full day of watersports and nature hikes. The Coquí Waterpark also adds to the family appeal. Boasting several pools (including its main 8,500-sq.-ft. main pool, several slides, a rope bridge, and a winding river attraction), this resort has some of the best facilities and restaurants in eastern Puerto Rico and all of the Caribbean. See p. 183.

5 THE BEST HONEYMOON RESORTS

• **El San Juan Hotel & Casino** (Isla Verde; $\textcircled{C}$ **787/791-1000**): Newlyweds will find themselves at the heart of San Juan's vibrant nightlife scene, yet they will be ensconced in luxury along a beautiful stretch of beachfront. In fact, the hotel boasts probably the best nightlife and entertainment, as well as fine dining, of any property in San Juan—and the competition is fierce. There's live music at the casino or adjacent nightclubs. Its elegant lobby, with wooden paneling and a sprawling, opulent chandelier, is a magnet for the young, beautiful, and moneyed visitors. Set on 12 lush acres (4.9 hectares) of prime beachfront, the rooms are as light and airy as the setting. Honeymooners might want to try an Ocean Front Lanias room or one of the resort's villas. See p. 58.
• **Hotel El Convento** (Old San Juan; $\textcircled{C}$ **800/468-2779** or 787/723-9020): Newlyweds can sleep in and spend their afternoons wandering the Old City or lolling around the rooftop splash pool, with its sweeping vistas of San Juan Bay and the bluff overlooking the Atlantic Ocean. There are bougainvillea and tropical flowers hanging

from seemingly every window and terrace, as well as colorful, restored Spanish colonial architecture everywhere you turn. You'll feel spoiled by your room's marble bathroom and elegant bed. Explore Old San Juan; it's chock-full of galleries, historic fortresses and churches, wonderful cafes, and funky shops. The Romantic Memories of San Juan package will get you fresh flowers, champagne, and chocolates in your room, but all guests get a world-class wine-and-cheese tasting every early evening on one of the hotel's many spectacular terraces. There are also pre- and post-cruise packages. See p. 44.

- **Horned Dorset Primavera** (Rincón; ✆ **800/633-1857** or 787/ 823-4030): The most romantic place for a honeymoon on the island (unless you stay in a private villa somewhere), this small, tranquil estate lies on the Mona Passage in western Puerto Rico, a pocket of posh where privacy is almost guaranteed. Accommodations are luxurious in the Spanish neocolonial style. The property opens onto a long, secluded beach of white sand. There are no phones, TVs, or radios in the rooms to interfere with the soft sounds of pillow talk. This is a retreat for adults only, with no facilities for children. Seven-night packages, with all meals included and round-trip transfers from the airport, are featured. See p. 166.

6 THE BEST BIG RESORT HOTELS

- **Ritz-Carlton San Juan Spa & Casino** (San Juan; ✆ **800/241-3333** or 787/253-1700): At last Puerto Rico has a Ritz-Carlton, and this truly deluxe, oceanfront property is one of the island's most spectacular resorts. Guests are pampered in a setting of elegance and beautifully furnished guest rooms. Hotel dining is second only to that at El San Juan, and a European-style spa features 11 treatments "for body and beauty." See p. 58.
- **El Conquistador Resort & Golden Door Spa** (Las Croabas; ✆ **866/317-8932** or 787/863-1000): The finest resort in Puerto Rico, this is a world-class destination—a sybaritic haven for golfers, honeymooners, families, and anyone else. Three intimate "villages" combine with one grand hotel, draped along 300-foot (91m) bluffs overlooking both the Atlantic and the Caribbean at Puerto Rico's northeastern tip. The 500 landscaped acres (202 hectares) include tennis courts, an 18-hole Arthur Hills–designed championship golf course, and a marina filled with yachts and charter boats. There's a water park and an island beach just offshore for guests. See p. 183.

7 THE BEST MODERATELY PRICED HOTELS

- **Gallery Inn at Galería San Juan** (San Juan; © 787/722-1808): The most whimsically bohemian hotel in the Caribbean sits on a coastal bluff at the edge of the historic city. Once the home of an aristocratic Spanish family, it is today filled with verdant courtyards and adorned with sculptures, silk screens, and original paintings of artist Jan D'Esopo, who along with husband Manuco Gandia owns the inn. Many of the rooms have dramatic views of the coast, with two historic Spanish forts framing the view. Staying in one of the comfortable rooms here is like living in an art gallery. See p. 45.
- **At Wind Chimes Inn** (San Juan; © 800/946-3244 or 787/727-4153): This renovated and restored Spanish manor house, a favorite with families, is one of the best guesthouses in the Condado district. The inn, which offers spacious rooms with kitchens, lies only a short block from one of San Juan's best beaches. There's also a pool and a nice restaurant/bar catering exclusively to guests. The nearby sister property **Acacia Sea Side Inn** is another good option, and guests at the Acacia can use the pool at the Wind Chimes and get access to its bar/restaurant. See p. 53.

8 THE BEST ATTRACTIONS

- **The Historic District of Old San Juan:** There's nothing like it in the Caribbean. Partially enclosed by old walls dating from the 17th century, Old San Juan was designated a U.S. National Historic Zone in 1950. Some 400 massively restored buildings fill this district, which is chockablock with tree-shaded squares, monuments, and open-air cafes as well as shops, restaurants, and bars. If you're interested in history, there is no better stroll in the Caribbean. It continues to be a vibrant cultural center and enclave of the arts and entertainment, as well as one of the region's culinary capitals. See "Seeing the Sights," in chapter 6.
- **Castillo de San Felipe del Morro** (Old San Juan): In Old San Juan and nicknamed El Morro, this fort was originally built in 1540. It guards the bay from a rocky promontory on the northwestern tip of the old city. Rich in history and legend, the site covers enough territory to accommodate a 9-hole golf course. See p. 89.

- **The Historic District of Ponce:** Second only to Old San Juan in terms of historical significance, the central district of Ponce is a blend of Ponce Creole and Art Deco building styles, dating mainly from the 1890s to the 1930s. One street, Calle Isabel, offers an array of Ponceño architectural styles, which often incorporate neoclassical details. The city underwent a massive restoration preceding the celebration of its 300th anniversary in 1996. See p. 136.

Planning Your Trip to Puerto Rico

This chapter discusses the where, when, and how of your trip to Puerto Rico—everything required to plan your trip and get it on the road. Here we've concentrated on what you need to do *before* you go.

1 VISITOR INFORMATION

For information before you leave home, visit **www.gotopuertorico. com** or contact the **Puerto Rico Tourism Company** offices at La Princesa Building, Paseo La Princesa 2, Old San Juan, PR 00902 (© **800/866-7827** or 787/721-2400). There are several tourism-related websites on Puerto Rico, including the **Tourism Association of Rincón** (www.rincon.org), **Insider's Guide to South Puerto Rico** (www.letsgotoponce.com), the Vieques website **Enchanted Isles** (www.enchanted-isle.com), **Discover Culebra** (www.culebra-island. com), and **Puerto Rico Travel Maps** (www.travelmaps.com).

2 ENTRY REQUIREMENTS & CUSTOMS

ENTRY REQUIREMENTS

DOCUMENTS Because Puerto Rico is a commonwealth, **U.S. citizens** coming from mainland destinations do not need any documents to enter Puerto Rico. It is the same as crossing from Georgia into Florida. They do not need to carry proof of citizenship or to produce documents. However, because of new airport security measures, it is necessary to produce a government-issued photo ID (federal, state, or local) to board a plane; this is most often a driver's license.

Be sure to carry plenty of documentation. You might need to show a government-issued photo ID (federal, state, or local) at various airport checkpoints. Be sure that your ID is *up-to-date:* An expired driver's license or passport, for example, might keep you from boarding a plane.

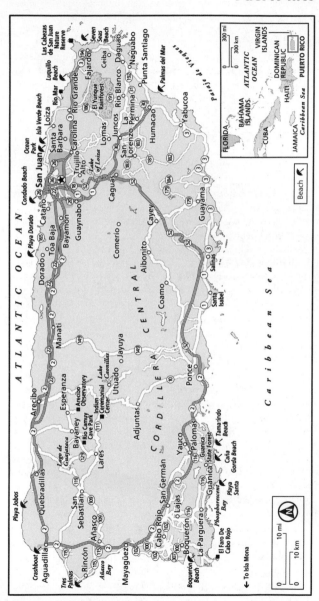

Visitors from other countries, including Canada, need a valid passport to land in Puerto Rico. For those from countries requiring a visa to enter the U.S., the same visa is necessary to enter Puerto Rico.

CUSTOMS

U.S. citizens do not need to clear Puerto Rican Customs upon arrival by plane or ship from the U.S. mainland. All non-U.S. citizens must clear Customs and are permitted to bring in items intended for their personal use, including tobacco, cameras, film, and a limited supply of liquor (usually 40 oz.).

What You Can Take Home

U.S. CUSTOMS   On departure, U.S.-bound travelers must have their luggage inspected by the U.S. Agriculture Department because laws prohibit bringing fruits and plants to the U.S. mainland. Fruits and vegetables are not allowed, but otherwise, you can bring back as many purchased goods as you want without paying duty.

Download the invaluable free pamphlet *Know Before You Go* online at **www.cbp.gov**. (Click on "Travel," and then click on "Know Before You Go! Online Brochure" for more specifics.)

For a clear summary of **Canadian** rules, write for the booklet *I Declare,* issued by the **Canada Border Services Agency** (© **800/461-9999** in Canada, or 204/983-3500; www.cbsa-asfc.gc.ca). Canada allows its citizens a C$750 exemption, and you're allowed to bring back duty-free one carton of cigarettes, one can of tobacco, 40 imperial ounces of liquor, and 50 cigars. In addition, you're allowed to mail gifts to Canada valued at less than C$60 a day, provided they're unsolicited and don't contain alcohol or tobacco (write on the package "Unsolicited gift, under $60 value"). All valuables should be declared on the Y-38 form before departure from Canada, including serial numbers of valuables you already own, such as expensive foreign cameras. *Note:* The C$750 exemption can only be used once a year and only after an absence of 7 days.

U.K. citizens returning from **a non-E.U. country** have a Customs allowance of 200 cigarettes; 50 cigars; 250 grams of smoking tobacco; 2 liters of still table wine; 1 liter of spirits or strong liqueurs (over 22% volume); 2 liters of fortified wine, sparkling wine or other liqueurs; 60cc (mL) of perfume; 250cc (mL) of toilet water; and £145 worth of all other goods, including gifts and souvenirs. People 16 and under cannot have the tobacco or alcohol allowance. For more information, contact **HM Revenue & Customs** at © **0845/010-9000** (from outside the U.K., 020/8929-0152), or consult their website at www.hmrc.gov.uk.

The duty-free allowance in **Australia** is A$900 or, for those under 18, A$450. Citizens can bring in 250 cigarettes or 250 grams of loose tobacco, and 2.25 liters of alcohol. If you're returning with valuables you already own, such as foreign-made cameras, you should file form B263. A helpful brochure available from Australian consulates or Customs offices is *Know Before You Go.* For more information, call the **Australian Customs Service** at ✆ **1300/363-263,** or log on to www.customs.gov.au.

The duty-free allowance for **New Zealand** is NZ$700. Citizens 18 and over can bring in 200 cigarettes, 50 cigars, or 250 grams of tobacco (or a mixture of all three if their combined weight doesn't exceed 250g); plus 4.5 liters of wine and beer, or 1.125 liters of liquor. New Zealand currency does not carry import or export restrictions. Fill out a certificate of export, listing the valuables you are taking out of the country; that way, you can bring them back without paying duty. Most questions are answered in a free pamphlet available at New Zealand consulates and Customs offices: *New Zealand Customs Guide for Travellers, Notice no. 4.* For more information, contact **New Zealand Customs Service,** The Customhouse, 17–21 Whitmore St., Box 2218, Wellington (✆ **04/473-6099** or 0800/428-786; www.customs.govt.nz).

3 MONEY

CURRENCY   The U.S. dollar is the coin of the realm. Keep in mind that once you leave Ponce or San Juan, you might have difficulty finding a place to exchange foreign money (unless you're staying at a large resort), so it's wise to handle your exchange needs before you head off into rural parts of Puerto Rico.

ATMS   ATMs are linked to a network that most likely includes your bank at home. Cirrus (✆ **800/424-7787;** www.mastercard.com) and PLUS (✆ **800/843-7587;** www.visa.com) are the two most popular networks in the U.S.

CURRENCY EXCHANGE   The currency exchange facilities at any large international bank within Puerto Rico's larger cities can exchange non-U.S. currencies for dollars. You can also exchange money at the Luis Muñoz Marín International Airport. Also, you'll find foreign-exchange facilities in large hotels and at the many banks in Old San Juan or Avenida Ashford in Condado. In Ponce, look for foreign-exchange facilities at large resorts and at banks such as Banco Popular.

Note: The "What Things Cost in Puerto Rico" box in this section uses an exchange rate of £1 = $1.40, though the pound has fluctuated wildly recently. Check www.xe.com for the latest rates.

What Things Cost in Puerto Rico	US$	UK£
Taxi from airport to Condado	15.00	10.75
Average taxi fare within San Juan	12.00	8.50
Typical bus fare within San Juan	0.75	0.55
Local telephone call	0.50	0.35
Double room at the Condado Plaza (very expensive)	650.00	465.00
Double room at Numero Uno Guesthouse (moderate)	175.00	125.00
Double room at El Canario Inn (inexpensive)	109.00	78.00
Lunch for one at Amadeus (moderate)	23.00	16.50
Lunch for one at Bebos (inexpensive)	12.00	8.50
Dinner for one at Pikayo (very expensive)	50.00	35.75
Dinner for one at Ostra Cosa (moderate)	26.00	18.50
Dinner for one at La Bombonera (inexpensive)	15.00	10.75
Bottle of beer in a bar	3.50	2.50
Glass of wine in a restaurant	5.00	3.50
Roll of ASA 100 color film (36 exposures)	8.50	6.00
Movie ticket	6.50	4.60
Theater ticket	15.00–125.00	10.75–90.00

---

4 WHEN TO GO

CLIMATE

Puerto Rico has one of the most unvarying climates in the world. Temperatures year-round range from 75° to 85°F (24°–29°C). The island is wettest and hottest in August, averaging 81°F (27°C) and 7 inches (18cm) of rain. San Juan and the northern coast seem to be cooler and wetter than Ponce and the southern coast. The coldest

The Hurricane Season

The hurricane season, the curse of Puerto Rican weather, lasts—officially, at least—from June 1 to November 30. But there's no cause for panic. In general, satellite forecasts give adequate warnings so that precautions can be taken. The peak of the season, when historically the most damaging storms are formed and hit the island, is in August and September.

If you're heading to Puerto Rico during the hurricane season, you can call your local branch of the **National Weather Service** (listed in your phone directory under the U.S. Department of Commerce) for a weather forecast or check out their website.

Average Temperatures in Puerto Rico

	Jan	Feb	Mar	Apr	May	June	July	Aug	Sept	Oct	Nov	Dec
Temp. (°F)	75	75	76	78	79	81	81	81	81	81	79	77
Temp. (°C)	24	24	25	26	26	27	27	27	27	27	26	25

THE "SEASON"

In Puerto Rico, hotels charge their highest prices during the peak winter period from mid-December to mid-April, when visitors fleeing from cold northern climates flock to the islands. Winter is the driest season along the coasts but can be wet in mountainous areas.

If you plan to travel in the winter, make reservations 2 to 3 months in advance. At certain hotels it's almost impossible to book accommodations for Christmas and the month of February.

A second tourism high season, especially for hotels and destinations outside San Juan, does take place in July, when most islanders take vacation.

Saving Money in the Off Season

Puerto Rico is a year-round destination. The island's "off season" runs from late spring to late fall, when temperatures in the mid-80s Fahrenheit (about 29°C) prevail throughout most of the region. Trade winds ensure comfortable days and nights, even in accommodations without air-conditioning. Although the noonday sun may raise the temperature to around 90°F (32°C), cool breezes usually make the morning, late afternoon, and evening more comfortable here than in many parts of the U.S. mainland.

Dollar for dollar, you'll spend less money by renting a summer house or fully equipped unit in Puerto Rico than you would on Cape Cod, Fire Island, Laguna Beach, or the coast of Maine.

The off season in Puerto Rico—roughly from May through November (rate schedules vary from hotel to hotel)—amounts to a summer sale. In most cases, hotel rates are slashed from 20% to a startling 60%. It's a bonanza for cost-conscious travelers, especially families who like to go on vacations together. In the chapters ahead, we'll spell out in dollars the specific amounts hotels charge during the off season.

But the off season has been shrinking of late. Many hotels, particularly outside of San Juan, will charge full price during the month of July and summer holiday weekends. Some properties, particularly guesthouses and small hotels in vacation towns like Vieques and Rincón, have dispensed with off-season pricing altogether.

In San Juan, a trend among smaller properties is to charge higher rates on weekends and holidays than during the week, rather than seasonal fluctuations in price.

HOLIDAYS

Puerto Rico has many public holidays when stores, offices, and schools are closed: New Year's Day, January 6 (Three Kings Day), Washington's Birthday, Good Friday, Memorial Day, July 4th, Labor Day, Thanksgiving, Veterans Day, and Christmas, plus such local holidays as Constitution Day (July 25) and Discovery Day (Nov 19). Remember, U.S. federal holidays are holidays in Puerto Rico, too.

PUERTO RICO CALENDAR OF EVENTS

JANUARY

Three Kings Day, islandwide. On this traditional gift-giving day in Puerto Rico, there are festivals with lively music, dancing, parades, puppet shows, caroling troubadours, and traditional feasts. January 6.

San Sebastián Street Festival, Calle San Sebastián in Old San Juan. Nightly celebrations with music, processions, crafts, and typical foods, as well as graphic arts and handicraft exhibitions. For more information, call © 787/721-2400. Mid-January.

FEBRUARY

Coffee Harvest Festival, Maricao. Folk music, a parade of floats, typical foods, crafts, and demonstrations of coffee preparation in Maricao, a 1-hour drive east of Mayagüez. For more information, call © 787/838-2290 or 267-5536. Second week of February.

Carnival Ponceño, Ponce. The island's Carnival celebrations feature float parades, dancing, and street parties. One of the most vibrant festivities is held in Ponce, known for its masqueraders wearing brightly painted horned masks. For more information, call © **787/284-4141.** Mid-February.

Casals Festival, Performing Arts Center in San Juan. The Caribbean's most celebrated cultural event, named after renowned cellist Pablo Casals, who founded the festival and the Puerto Rico Symphony Orchestra to foster musical development when he moved to the island in 1957. For more information, contact the **Puerto Rico Symphony Orchestra** in San Juan (© **787/721-7727**), the **Luis A. Ferré Performing Arts Center** (© **787/620-4444**), **Ticket Center** (© **787/792-5000**), and **Casals Festival** (© **787/721-8370;** www.festcasalspr.gobierno.pr). The festivities take place from late February to early March.

MARCH

Emancipation Day, islandwide. Commemoration of the emancipation of Puerto Rico's slaves in 1873, held at various venues. March 22.

APRIL

Good Friday and Easter, islandwide. Celebrated with colorful ceremonies and processions. April 10 to April 12, 2009.

José de Diego Day, islandwide. Commemoration of the birthday of José de Diego, the patriot, lawyer, writer, orator, and political leader who was the first president of the Puerto Rico House of Representatives under U.S. rule. April 17.

MAY

Heineken JazzFest, San Juan. The annual jazz celebration is staged at Parque Sixto Escobar. Each year a different jazz theme is featured. The open-air pavilion is in a scenic oceanfront location in the Puerta de Tierra section of San Juan, near the Caribe Hilton. For more information, check out the website www.prheinekenjazz.com, which has schedules and links to buy tickets and package information. End of May through the beginning of June.

JUNE

San Juan Bautista Day, islandwide. Puerto Rico's capital and other cities celebrate the island's patron saint with weeklong festivities. At midnight, sanjuaneros and others walk backward into the sea (or nearest body of water) three times to renew good luck for the coming year. June 24.

Aibonito Flower Festival, at Road 721 next to the City Hall Coliseum, in the central mountain town of Aibonito. This annual flower-competition festival features acres of lilies, anthuriums, carnations, roses, gardenias, and begonias. For more information, call © **787/735-3871.** Last week in June and first week in July.

Constitution Day, islandwide. A celebration commemorating the birth of the Puerto Rico Constitution and its political status as a commonwealth with the United States. July 25.

Loíza Carnival. This annual folk and religious ceremony honors Loíza's patron saint, John *(Santiago)* the Apostle. Colorful processions take place, with costumes, masks, and *bomba* dancers (the *bomba* has a lively Afro-Caribbean dance rhythm). This jubilant celebration reflects the African and Spanish heritage of the region. For more information, call ✆ **787/876-1040.** Late July through early August.

August

International Billfish Tournament, at Club Náutico, San Juan. This is one of the premier game-fishing tournaments and the longest consecutively held billfish tournament in the world. Fishermen from many countries angle for blue marlin that can weigh up to 900 pounds (408kg). For specific dates and information, call ✆ **787/722-0177.** Late August to early September.

October

La Raza Day (Columbus Day), islandwide. This day commemorates Columbus's landing in the New World. October 12.

National Plantain Festival, Corozal. This annual festivity involves crafts, paintings, agricultural products, exhibitions, and sale of plantain dishes; *neuva trova* music and folk ballet are performed. For more information, call ✆ **787/859-3060.** Mid-October.

November

Start of Baseball Season, in Hiram Bithorn Park in San Juan and throughout the island. Six Puerto Rican professional clubs compete from November to January. Professionals from North America also play here.

Jayuya Indian Festival, Jayuya. This fiesta features the culture and tradition of the island's original inhabitants, the Taíno Indians, and their music, food, and games. More than 100 artisans exhibit and sell their works. There is also a Miss Taíno Indian Pageant. For more information, call ✆ **787/828-2020.** Second week of November.

Puerto Rico Discovery Day, islandwide. This day commemorates the "discovery" by Columbus in 1493 of the already inhabited island of Puerto Rico. Columbus is thought to have come ashore at the northwestern municipality of Aguadilla, although the exact location is unknown. November 19.

Bacardi Artisans' Fair, San Juan. The best and largest artisans' fair on the island features more than 100 artisans who turn out to exhibit and sell their wares. The fair includes shows for adults and children, a Puerto Rican troubadour contest, rides, and typical food and drink—all sold by nonprofit organizations. It is held on the grounds of the world's largest rum-manufacturing plant in Cataño, an industrial suburb set on a peninsula jutting into San Juan Bay. For more information, call ☎ **787/788-1500.** First two Sundays in December.

Las Mañanitas, Ponce. A religious procession that starts out from Lolita Tizol Street and moves toward the city's Catholic church, led by mariachis singing songs to honor Our Lady of Guadalupe, the city's patron saint. The lead song is the traditional Mexican birthday song, *Las Mañanitas.* There's a 6am Mass. For more information, contact **Ponce City Hall** (☎ 787/284-4141). December 12.

Hatillo Masks Festival, Hatillo. This tradition, celebrated since 1823, represents the biblical story of King Herod's ordering the death of all infant boys in an attempt to kill the baby Jesus. Men with colorful masks and costumes represent the soldiers, who run or ride through the town from early morning, looking for the children. There are food, music, and crafts exhibits in the town square. For more information, call ☎ **787/898-4040.** December 28.

YEAR-ROUND FESTIVALS

Many of Puerto Rico's most popular events are during the **Patron Saint Festivals** *(Fiestas patronales)* in honor of the patron saint of each municipality. The festivities, held in each town's central plaza, include religious and costumed processions, games, local food, music, and dance, and often feature some of the island's top musical acts performing at free outdoor concerts.

For more information, contact the **Puerto Rico Tourism Company** (☎ **800/866-7827** or 787/721-2400), La Princesa Building, Paseo La Princesa 2, Old San Juan, PR 00902.

5 THE ACTIVE VACATION PLANNER

There are watersports opportunities throughout Puerto Rico, from San Juan's waterfront hotels to eastern resorts and the offshore islands of Vieques and Culebra, all the way to the Rincón on the west coast and Cabo Rojo in the south.

BOATING & SAILING

The waters off Puerto Rico provide excellent boating in all seasons. Winds average 10 to 15 knots virtually year-round. Marinas provide facilities and services on par with any others in the Caribbean, and many have powerboats or sailboats for rent, either crewed or bareboat charter.

Puerto Rico is ringed by marinas. In San Juan alone, there are three large ones: **Club Nautico de San Juan** (② 787/722-0177), **San Juan Bay Marina** (② 787/721-8062) and the **Cangrejos Yacht Club** (Rte. 187, Piñones; ② 787/791-1015).

Fajardo, on Puerto Rico's northeast corner, boasts seven marinas, including the Caribbean's largest, the **Puerto del Rey Marina** (Rte. 3 Km 51.4; ② **787/860-1000** or 801-3010). Others include **Villa Marina Yacht Harbour** (Rte. 987 Km 1.3; ② **787/863-5131** or 863-5011), **Puerto Chico** (Rte. 987 Km 2.4; ② **787/863-0834**), and **Puerto Real** (Playa Puerto Real; ② **787/863-2188**).

Along the south coast, there's the **Ponce Yacht & Fishing Club** (La Guancha, Ponce; ② **787/842-9003**) and in the southwest, **Club Nautico de Boquerón** (② **787/851-1336**) and **Club Nautico de La Parguera** (② **787/899-5590**).

Several sailing and ocean racing regattas are held in Puerto Rico annually. The east of Puerto Rico and the southwest are particularly attractive for sailors. Fajardo is the start of a series of ports, extending from Puerto Rico's own offshore islands through the U.S. and British Virgin Islands to the east, which is probably the Caribbean's top sailing destination.

The easiest way to experience the joys of sailing is to go out on a day trip leaving from one of the Fajardo marinas (with transportation from San Juan hotels often included). The trips usually take place on large luxury catamarans or sailing yachts, with a bar serving drinks and refreshments, a sound system, and other creature comforts. Typically, after a nice sail, the vessel weighs anchor at a good snorkeling spot, then makes a stop on one of the beautiful sand beaches on the small islands off the Fajardo coast. Operators include **Traveler Sailing Catamaran** (② 787/853-2821), **East Island Excursions** (② 787/860-3434), **Catamaran Spread Eagle** (② 787/887-8821), and **Erin Go Bragh Charters** (② 787/860-4401).

San Juan Water Fun on Isla Verde Beach in back of the El San Juan Hotel and Casino, Avenida Isla Verde in Isla Verde, San Juan (② **787/644-2585**), rents everything from a two-seater kayak for $30 per hour to a banana boat that holds eight passengers and costs $15 per person for a 20-minute ride.

CAMPING

Puerto Rico abounds in remote sandy beaches, lush tropical forests, and mountain lakesides that make for fine camping.

Some of the nicest campgrounds, as well as the best equipped and safest, are those run by the government **Compañia de Parques Nacionales** (Av. Fernández Juncos 1611, Santurce; © 787/622-5200). Six of the eight campsites it operates are located on the coast—at Luquillo, Fajardo, Vieques, Arroyo, Añasco, and Vega Baja. It also runs two fine campgrounds in the mountain town of Maricao and in Camuy's Cave Park.

Some of these are simple places where you erect your own tent, although they are outfitted with electricity and running water; some are simple cabins, sometimes with fireplaces. Showers and bathrooms are communal. To stay at a campsite costs between $15 and $25 per night per tent.

Many sites offer very basic cabins for rent. Each cabin is equipped with a full bathroom, a stove, a refrigerator, two beds, and a table and chairs. However, most of your cooking will probably be tastier if you do it outside at one of the on-site barbecues. In nearly all cases, you must provide your own sheets and towels.

The agency, the National Parks Company in English, also operates more upscale "vacation centers," which feature rustic cabins and more tourist-ready "villas," on par with many island inns.

State forests run by the **Departamento de Recursos Naturales y Ambientales** also allow camping with permits. Except for cabins at Monte Guilarte State Forest, which cost $20 per night, camping sites are available at $5 per person. For further information about permits, contact the DRNA at (Rte. 8838 Km 6.3, Sector El Cinco, Río Piedras; © 787/999-2200).

There are seven major on-island camping sites in the following state forests: **Cambalache State Forest,** near Barceloneta; **Carite State Forest,** near Patillas; **Guajataca State Forest,** near Quebradillas; **Monte Guilarte State Forest,** near Adjuntas; **Susua State Forest,** near Yauco; **Río Abajo State Forest,** near Arecibo; and our favorite, **Toro Negro Forest Reserve,** near Villaba, where you can camp in the shadow of Puerto Rico's highest peaks.

It's also possible to camp at either of two wildlife refuges, **Isla de Mona Wildlife Refuge,** lying some 50 miles (80km) off the west coast of Puerto Rico surrounded by the rough seas of Mona Passage, and at **Lago Lucchetti Wildlife Refuge,** a beautiful mountain reservoir between Yauco and Ponce.

Meanwhile, visitors can also camp at **El Yunque National Forest** (© 787/888-1810), which is under the jurisdiction of the U.S. Forest Service. There is no cost, but permits are required. They can be

Take Me Out to the *Beisbol* Game

Baseball has a long, illustrious history in Puerto Rico. Imported around the turn of the 20th century by plantation owners as a leisure activity for workers, *beisbol* quickly caught fire, and local leagues have produced such major-league stars as Roberto Alomar, Bernie Williams, and the late great Roberto Clemente. Current stars include Carlos Delgado, Jorge Posada, Iván Rodríguez, Carlos Beltrán, and the Molina brothers. A top-notch league of six teams—featuring many rising professionals honing their skills during the winter months—holds its season November through January and plays in ballparks throughout Puerto Rico. This is a chance to see good baseball in a more intimate setting than is afforded in the U.S. Major Leagues.

Puerto Rico is also host to the World Baseball Classic, held in 2006 and 2009, an international baseball tournament, where top-notch regional teams from the Dominican Republic, Venezuela, and Cuba play against the Puerto Rico team.

obtained in person at the Catalina Service Center (Rte. 191 Km 4.3) daily from 8am to 4:30pm and weekends at the Palo Colorado Visitor Center (Rte. 191 Km 11.9) from 9:30am to 4pm. It's primitive camping within the rainforest.

DEEP-SEA FISHING

Deep-sea fishing is top-notch throughout the island. Allison tuna, white and blue marlin, sailfish, wahoo, dolphin (mahimahi), mackerel, and tarpon are some of the fish you can catch in Puerto Rican waters, where 30 world records have been broken. While fishing is good year-round, the winter season from October to early March is among the best. Blue marlin can be caught all summer and into the fall, and renowned big-game fish tournaments take place in August and September.

Charters are available at marinas in major cities and tourism areas. Most boats range between 32 and 50 feet; fit six passengers; can be chartered for a half- or full day; and usually include bait, crew, and equipment.

Big game fish are found close to shore across Puerto Rico, so you won't waste time traveling to fishing spots. A mile off the San Juan coast, the ocean floor drops 600 feet (183m), and the awesome Puerto Rico Trench, a 500-mile-long (805km) fault that plunges to a depth of 28,000 feet (8,354m), lies about 75 miles (121km) directly north. It's a 20-minute ride to where the big game fish are biting, so it's possible to leave in the morning, make the catch of the day, and be back at the marina in the early afternoon.

A half-day of deep-sea fishing (4 hr.) starts at around $550, while full-day charters begin at around $900. Most charters hold six passengers in addition to the crew.

In San Juan, experienced operators include Capt. Mike Benítez at **Benítez Fishing Charters** (© 787/723-2292), as well as **Castillo Fishing Charters** (© 787/726-5752), which has been running charters out of the **Caribbean Outfitters** (© 787/396-8346).

Rincón also has a number of deep-sea fishing charters, like **Makaira Fishing Charters** (© 787/823-4391 or 299-7374) and **Moondog Charters** (© 787/823-3059).

GOLF

With nearly 30 golf courses, including several championship links, Puerto Rico is rightly called the "Scotland" or the "golf capital" of the Caribbean, especially since they have been designed by the likes of Robert Trent Jones, his son Rees Jones, Greg Norman, George and Tom Fazio, Jack Nicklaus, Arthur Hills, and Puerto Rico's own Chi Chi Rodriguez.

Many of the courses are jewels of landscape architecture, running through verdant tropical forest and former coconut groves, or winding in dramatic switchbacks aside a breathtaking stretch of coast. Year-round summer weather and mostly gentle breezes add to the joy of playing here.

The bad news is it's often quite expensive to tee off in Puerto Rico, with prices starting at $120 and ranging up to nearly $200.

There are some bargains, however, particularly the **Berwind Country Club** (© 787/876-5380) in **Loiza** and the **Punta Borinquén Golf Club,** Rte. 107 (© 787/890-2987), 2 miles (3.2km) north of Aguadilla's center. Berwind is the closest to San Juan, in a breathtaking setting on a former coconut plantation, while the Aguadilla course struts across a beautiful patch of coast.

The legendary Dorado courses are 35 minutes west of San Juan at the **Dorado Beach Resort & Club** (© 787/796-8961; p. 127), the scene of world championships and legendarily difficult holes, making it among the most challenging in the Caribbean still. Jack Nicklaus rates the challenging 13th hole at the Dorado as one of the top 10 in the world.

Río Grande, however, is becoming as important a center for golf as Dorado. The **Wyndham Río Mar Beach Resort** golf offerings (© 787/888-7060) have world-class rainforest and coastal courses, designed, respectively, by Greg Norman and Tom and George Fazio. The **Trump International Golf Club** (© 787/657-2000) is actually four different 9-hole courses sprawled out across 1,200 acres (486 hectares) of coast. Each course is named after its surrounding environment: the Ocean, the Palms, the Mountains, and the Lakes. Also in town is the **Bahia Beach** course (© 787/957-5800), recently renovated as part of a new St. Regis resort development.

Also on the east coast, crack golfers consider holes 11 through 15 at the **Palmas del Mar Country Club** (p. 186) to be the toughest five successive holes in the Caribbean. At **El Conquistador Resort & Golden Door Spa** (p. 183), the spectacular $250-million resort at Las Croabas east of San Juan, you play along 200-foot (61m) changes in elevation that provide panoramic vistas.

There are now golf courses along the south coast, in Coamo and Ponce, as well as the southwest in Cabo Rojo. These are a needed complement to the north-coast courses. The **Costa Caribe Golf & Country Club** (© 787/848-1000 or 812-2650) commands views of the ocean and mountains, while the **Club Deportivo del Oeste,** Hwy. 102 Km 15.4, Barrio Jogudas, Cabo Rojo (© 787/851-8880 or 254-3748), is more no-frills.

HIKING

The mountainous interior of Puerto Rico provides ample opportunities for hill climbing and nature treks. These are especially appealing because panoramas open at the least-expected moments, often revealing spectacular views of the distant sea.

The most popular, most beautiful, and most spectacular trekking spot is **El Yunque,** the sprawling "jungle" maintained by the U.S. Forest Service and the only rainforest on U.S. soil.

El Yunque is part of the **Caribbean National Forest,** which is a 45-minute drive east of San Juan. More than 250 species of trees and some 200 types of ferns have been identified here. Some 60 species of birds inhabit El Yunque, including the increasingly rare Puerto Rican parrot. Such rare birds as the elfin woods warbler, the green mango hummingbird, and the Puerto Rican lizard-cuckoo live here.

Park rangers have clearly marked the trails that are ideal for walking. See "El Yunque" in chapter 7 for more details.

A lesser forest, but one that is still intriguing to visit, is the **Maricao State Forest,** near the coffee town of Maricao. This forest is in western Puerto Rico, east of the town of Mayagüez.

Ponce is the best center for exploring some of the greatest forest reserves in the Caribbean Basin, notably **Toro Negro Forest Reserve** with its **Lake Guineo** (the lake at the highest elevation on the island), the **Guánica State Forest,** ideal for hiking and bird-watching, and the **Carite Forest Reserve,** a 6,000-acre (2,428-hectare) park known for its dwarf forest. For more details, see "Ponce" in chapter 8.

Equally suitable for hiking are the protected lands (especially the **Río Camuy Cave Park**) whose topography is characterized as "karst"—that is, limestone riddled with caves, underground rivers, and natural crevasses and fissures. Although these regions pose additional risks and technical problems for trekkers, some people prefer the opportunities they provide for exploring the territory both above and below its surface. See "Arecibo & Camuy" in chapter 7 for details about the Río Camuy Caves.

Aventuras Tierra Adentro (*©* **787/766-0470;** www.aventuraspr.com) offers the best island adventure tours, focusing on hiking through virgin forests, rock climbing, or cliff jumping. Four different adventures are offered, costing $150 per person, which includes transportation from San Juan. Most of the jaunts take place on weekends.

SCUBA DIVING

The continental shelf, which surrounds Puerto Rico on three sides, is responsible for an abundance of coral reefs, caves, sea walls, and trenches for scuba diving and snorkeling.

Open-water reefs off the southeastern coast near **Humacao** are visited by migrating whales and manatees. Many caves are located near Isabela on the west coast. A large canyon, off the island's south coast, is ideal for experienced open-water divers. Caves and the sea wall at **La Parguera** are also favorites. **Vieques** and **Culebra islands** have coral formations. **Mona Island** offers unspoiled reefs at depths averaging 80 feet (24m), with an amazing array of sealife. Uninhabited islands, such as **Icacos,** off the northeastern coast near Fajardo, are also popular with both snorkelers and divers.

These sites are now within reach because many of Puerto Rico's dive operators and resorts offer packages that include daily or twice-daily dives, scuba equipment, instruction, and excursions to Puerto Rico's popular attractions.

Introductory courses for beginners range between $90 and $130, and two-tank dives for experienced divers run up to $150.

In San Juan, try **Caribe Aquatic Adventures,** Normandie Hotel San Juan, Calle 19 1062, Villa Nevarez (*©* **787/281-8858**), or **Ocean Sports** (Av. Isla Verde 77; *©* **787/268-2329**).

We recommend diving off the east, west, or south coasts, however.

In Rincón, there's **Taíno Divers,** Black Eagle Marina at Rincón (© 787/823-6429), which offers trips to the waters surrounding Desecheo island natural reserve.

The ocean wall in the southwest is famous, with visibility ranging from 100 to 120 feet (30–37m) and reefs filled with abundant sea life. **Paradise Scuba Center,** Hotel Casa Blanca Building, at La Parguera (© 787/899-7611), and **Mona Aquatics,** Calle José de Diego, Boquerón (© 787/851-2185), are two good operators in the area.

In Guánica, there's **Sea Venture Dive Copamarina** (© 787/821-0505, ext. 729), part of the Copamarina Beach Resort.

The Dive Center at the Wyndham Río Mar Beach Resort (© 787/888-6000) is one of the largest in Puerto Rico.

Elsewhere on the island, several other companies offer scuba and snorkeling instruction. We provide details in each chapter.

SNORKELING

Because of its overpopulation, the waters around San Juan aren't the most ideal for snorkeling. In fact, the entire north shore of Puerto Rico fronts the Atlantic, where the waters are often turbulent.

Yet there are some protected areas along the north coast that make for fine snorkeling, even in surf capitals like Rincón and Aguadilla. Many of the best surfing beaches in winter turn into a snorkeler's paradise in summer when the waves calm down.

The most ideal conditions for snorkeling in Puerto Rico are along the shores of the remote islands of **Vieques** and **Culebra.**

The best snorkeling on the main island is found near the town of **Fajardo,** to the east of San Juan and along the tranquil eastern coast (see chapter 10).

The calm, glasslike quality of the clear Caribbean along the south shore is also ideal for snorkeling. The most developed tourist mecca here is the city of Ponce. Few rivers empty their muddy waters into the sea along the south coast, resulting in gin-clear waters offshore. You can snorkel off the coast without having to go on a boat trip. One good place is at **Playa La Parguera,** where you can rent snorkeling equipment from kiosks along the beach. This beach lies east of the town of Guánica, to the east of Ponce. Here tropical fish add to the brightness of the water, which is generally turquoise. The addition of mangrove cays in the area also makes La Parguera more alluring for snorkelers. Another good spot for snorkelers is **Caja de Muertos** off the coast of Ponce. Here a lagoon coral reef boasts a large number of fish species (see chapter 8).

Even if you are staying in San Juan and want to go snorkeling, you are better off taking a day trip to Fajardo, where you'll get a real Caribbean snorkeling experience, with tranquil, clear water and stunning reefs teaming with tropical fish. Several operators offer day trips (10am–3:30pm) leaving from Fajardo marinas, but transportation to and from your San Juan hotel can also be arranged. Prices start at around $99 (see "Boating & Sailing," earlier in this chapter.)

SURFING

Puerto Rico's northwest beaches attract surfers from around the world. Called the "Hawaii of the East," Puerto Rico has hosted a number of international competitions. October through February are the best surfing months, but the sport is enjoyed in Puerto Rico from August through April. The most popular areas are from Isabela to Rincón—at beaches such as Wilderness, Middles, Jobos, Crashboat, Las Marías, and the Spanish Wall.

There are surf spots across the entire north coast from San Juan to the northwest, including Los Tubos in Vega Baja.

San Juan itself has great surfing spots, including La 8, just outside of Old San Juan in Puerta de Tierra, near Escambrón Beach, which has some of the largest waves. Pine Grove in Isla Verde is a great spot to learn because of the small, steady, well-formed waves there.

International competitions held in Puerto Rico have included the 1968 and 1988 World Amateur Surfing Championships and the annual Caribbean Cup Surfing Championship. Currently, Corona sponsors an annual competition circuit taking place in Isabela and Rincón.

If you want to learn to surf or perfect your technique while in Puerto Rico, it's quite easy.

Operating right near the Ritz-Carlton and Courtyard Marriott hotels in Isla Verde, the best surf lessons are given by professional surfer William Sue-A-Quan at his **Walking on Water Surfing School** (© 787/955-6059; www.gosurfpr.com). He and a few associates work right on the beach at Pine Grove and also offer lessons through the Ritz-Carlton. He's a great teacher and takes on students as young as 5 and as old as 75.

Rincón also has many surf schools, some of which book packages including lodgings.

The **Rincón Surf School** (P.O. Box 1333, Rincón; © 787/823-0610) offers beginners lessons and weeklong packages. **Puntas Surf School** (P.O. Box 4319, HC-01 Calle Vista del Mar; © 787/823-3618 or 207/251-1154) is another good option run by Melissa Taylor and Bill Woodward.

Lessons start at around $50 per hour.

Board rentals are available at many island surf shops, with prices starting at $25 a day. We list them in subsequent chapters.

TENNIS

Puerto Rico has approximately 100 major tennis courts. Many are at hotels and resorts; others are in public parks throughout the island. Several *paradores* also have courts. A number of courts are lighted for nighttime play. See "Paradores," later in this chapter.

In San Juan, the **Caribe Hilton** and the **Condado Plaza Hotel & Casino** have tennis courts. Also in the area are the **public courts** at the San Juan Central Municipal Park. The **Hyatt Dorado Beach Resort & Country Club** maintains a total of 21 courts. (*Note:* The property is closing as we go to print, but the golf courses and tennis courts will remain open.)

WINDSURFING

The best windsurfing is found at Punta Las Marias in the Greater San Juan metropolitan area. Other spots on the island for windsurfing include Santa Isabel, Guánica, and La Parguera in the south; Jobos and Shacks in the northwest; and the island of Culebra off the eastern coast.

Kite-boarding is becoming increasingly popular as well. Watch them flying through the choppy waters off Ocean Park in San Juan.

Lessons, advice, and equipment rental are available at **Velauno,** Calle Loíza 2430, Punta Las Marias in San Juan (© 787/728-8716).

6 HEALTH & SAFETY

STAYING HEALTHY

Puerto Rico poses no major health problem for most travelers. Finding a good doctor in Puerto Rico is easy, and most speak English. See the appendix for the location of the hospital.

It's best to stick to **bottled mineral water** here. Although tap water is safe to drink, it gives some visitors diarrhea. The **sun** can be brutal here. **Mosquitoes** are a nuisance, and although they do not carry malaria, some do carry dreaded dengue fever, which has returned to Puerto Rico. The disease, transmitted by the Aede mosquito, causes fever, headaches, pain in the muscles and joints, skin blisters, and hemorrhaging.

Puerto Rico has been especially hard hit by **AIDS.** Exercise *at least* the same caution in choosing your sexual partners, and in practicing safe sex, as you would at home.

STAYING SAFE

The U.S. State Department issues no special travel advisories for the Commonwealth of Puerto Rico. And while violent crime is on the rise, tourists are generally safe. Caution in handling valuables and money is called for as it would be in any metropolitan area. Don't leave valuables unattended on the beach, and don't go wandering down dark city streets alone at night.

---

7 SPECIALIZED TRAVEL RESOURCES

TRAVELERS WITH DISABILITIES

Most disabilities shouldn't stop anyone from traveling. There are more options and resources out there today than ever before. The Americans with Disabilities Act is enforced as strictly in Puerto Rico as it is on the U.S. mainland. The U.S. National Park Service offers a Golden Access Passport that gives free lifetime entrance to U.S. national parks, including those in Puerto Rico, for persons who are blind or permanently disabled, regardless of age. For more information, go to www.nps.gov/fees_passes.htm or call © 888/467-2757. Many travel agencies offer customized tours and itineraries for travelers with disabilities. Try **Flying Wheels Travel** (© 507/451-5005; www.flyingwheelstravel.com) or **Accessible Journeys** (© 800/846-4537 or 610/521-0339).

GAY & LESBIAN TRAVELERS

Puerto Rico is the most gay-friendly destination in the Caribbean, with lots of accommodations, restaurants, clubs, and bars that actively cater to a gay clientele.

The **International Gay & Lesbian Travel Association (IGLTA;** © 800/448-8550 or 954/776-2626; www.iglta.org) links travelers up with gay-friendly hoteliers, tour operators, and airline and cruiseline representatives. There are also a number of gay and lesbian tour operators like **Above and Beyond Tours** (© 800/397-2681; www.abovebeyondtours.com) and **Now, Voyager** (© 800/255-6951; www.nowvoyager.com). **Gay.com Travel** (© 800/929-2268 or 415/644-8044; www.gay.com/travel or www.outandabout.com) provides regularly updated information about gay-owned, gay-oriented, and gay-friendly lodging, dining, sightseeing, nightlife, and shopping establishments in every important destination worldwide.

SENIOR TRAVEL

All major airlines and many Puerto Rican hotels offer discounts for seniors. The best source of information for seniors is the Puerto Rico Tourism Company (see "Visitor Information," earlier in this chapter), or, if you're staying in a large resort hotel, talk to the activities director or the concierge. Members of **AARP,** 601 E St. NW, Washington, DC 20049 (© **888/687-2277** or 202/434-4277; www.aarp.org), get discounts on hotels, airfares, and car rentals. The **U.S. National Park Service** offers a **Golden Age Passport** that gives seniors 62 years or older lifetime entrance to U.S. national parks for a one-time processing fee of $10. For more information, click onto www.nps.gov or call © **888/467-2757.**

8 GETTING THERE & GETTING AROUND

Puerto Rico is by far the most accessible of the Caribbean islands, with frequent airline service. It's also the major airline hub of the Caribbean Basin.

GETTING THERE
By Plane

American Airlines (© 800/433-7300; www.aa.com), backed up by the likes of **JetBlue** (© 800/538-2583; www.jetblue.com), **Delta** (© 800/221-1212; www.delta.com), **United Airlines** (© 800/241-6522; www.united.com), **Continental Airlines** (© 800/525-0280 or 787/890-2990; www.continental.com), and others, provides frequent service between San Juan and most major points in the East Coast and Central United States, and connecting flights to just about everywhere. Canadians can fly **Air Canada** (© 800/426-7000; www.air canada.com) from either Montreal or Toronto to San Juan.

Puerto Rico is the major transportation hub of the Caribbean, with the best connections for getting anywhere in the islands. American Airlines' **American Eagle** is the leader of the short-haul carriers, offering service to 37 destinations in the Caribbean and The Bahamas. Other small airlines providing inter-island service include **Cape Air** (© 800/352-0714 or 787/253-1121; www.flycapeair.com), **Seaborne Airlines** (© 888/FLY-TOUR [359-8687]; www.flyseaborne.com), and **LIAT** (© 787/791-0800).

GETTING AROUND
By Plane

Cape Air flies from Luis Muñoz Marín International Airport to Mayagüez, Ponce, and Vieques several times a day. They also offer many flights daily to St. Thomas, St. Croix, and Tortola.

By Rental Car

Puerto Rico offers some of the most scenic drives in all the Caribbean. Driving around and discovering its little hidden beaches, coastal towns, mountain villages, vast forests, and national parks is reason enough to visit the island. And you'll need a car to explore it well.

Local drivers can be maddening though, as can the legendary traffic jams around cities, and some of the roads, especially in the mountainous interior, are just too narrow or poorly maintained for comfort.

Avis (© 800/331-1212 or 787/791-2500; www.avis.com), Budget (© 800/472-3325 or 787/791-3685; www.budget.com), and Hertz (© 800/654-3131 or 787/791-0840; www.hertz.com) are located here, and reputable local outfits include Charlie Car Rental (© 800/ 289-1227 or 787/728-2418; www.charliecar.com) and Target Car Rental (© 787/782-6380; www.targetrentacar.com). Added security comes from an antitheft double-locking mechanism. Distances are often posted in kilometers rather than miles (1km = 0.62 mile), but speed limits are displayed in miles per hour.

GASOLINE   In Puerto Rico, gasoline is sold by the liter, not by the gallon (there are 3.78 liters to the gallon). The cost of gasoline is often somewhat cheaper than in the United States.

DRIVING RULES   Speed limits are given in miles per hour.

BREAKDOWNS & ASSISTANCE   Make arrangements ahead of time with your rental agency about what to do in an accident or breakdown, and ask for backup emergency services and numbers.

By Public Transportation

Cars and minibuses known as *públicos* provide low-cost transportation around the island. Their license plates have the letters "P" or "PD" following the numbers. They serve all the main towns of Puerto Rico; passengers are let off and picked up along the way, both at designated stops and when someone flags them down. Rates are set by the Public Service Commission. *Públicos* usually operate during daylight hours, departing from the main plaza (central square) of a town. There are several operators listed under Lineas de Carros in the local Yellow Pages. It costs about $25 from San Juan to just about anywhere on the island.

9 TIPS ON ACCOMMODATIONS

HOTELS & RESORTS

There is no rigid classification of Puerto Rican hotels. The word "deluxe" is often used—or misused—when "first class" might be a more appropriate term. We've presented fairly detailed descriptions of the hotels in this book, so you'll get an idea of what to expect once you're there.

Puerto Rico has had a bum rap for bad service, but our experience is that service in hotels and restaurants has been on a dramatic upswing over the last decade. There is still the slow tropical pace, what folks mean when they talk about "island time," however.

Ask detailed questions when booking a room. Entertainment in Puerto Rico is often alfresco, so light sleepers obviously won't want a room directly over a band. In general, back rooms cost less than oceanfront rooms, and lower rooms cost less than upper-floor units. Always ascertain whether transfers (which can be expensive) are included. And make sure that you know exactly what is free and what costs money. Some resorts seem to charge every time you breathe and might end up costing more than a deluxe hotel that includes most everything in the price.

Also factor in transportation costs, which can mount quickly if you stay 5 days to a week. If you want to go to the beach every day, it might be wise to book a hotel on the Condado and not stay in romantic Old San Juan, from which you'll spend a lot of time and money transferring back and forth between your hotel and the beach.

Most hotels in Puerto Rico are on the windward side of the island, with lots of waves, undertow, and surf. If a glasslike smooth sea is imperative for your stay, you can book on the leeward (eastern shore) or Caribbean (southeast coast) sides, which are better for snorkeling. The major centers in these areas are the resort complex of Palmas del Mar and the "second city" of Ponce.

PUERTO RICAN GUESTHOUSES

A unique type of accommodations is the guesthouse, where Puerto Ricans themselves usually stay when they travel. Ranging in size from 7 to 25 rooms, they offer a familial atmosphere. Many are on or near the beach; some have pools or sun decks, and a number serve meals.

In Puerto Rico, however, the term "guesthouse" has many meanings. Some guesthouses are like simple motels built around pools. Others have small individual cottages with their own kitchenettes, constructed around a main building in which you'll often find a bar and a restaurant serving local food. Some are surprisingly comfortable, often with private bathrooms and swimming pools. You may or may not have air-conditioning. The rooms are sometimes cooled by ceiling fans or by the trade winds blowing through open windows at night.

For value, the guesthouse can't be topped. If you stay at a guesthouse, you can journey over to a big beach resort and use its seaside facilities for only a small fee. Although bereft of frills, the guesthouses we've recommended are clean and safe for families or single women. However, the cheapest ones are not places where you'd want to spend a lot of time because of their modest furnishings.

For further information on guesthouses, contact the **Puerto Rico Tourism Company** (© **800/866-7827** or 787/721-2400), La Princesa Building, Paseo La Princesa 2, Old San Juan, PR 00902.

PARADORES

In an effort to lure travelers beyond the hotels and casinos of San Juan's historic district to the tranquil natural beauty of the island's countryside, the Puerto Rico Tourism Company offers *paradores puertorriqueños* (charming country inns), which are comfortable bases for exploring the island's varied attractions. Vacationers seeking a peaceful idyll can also choose from several privately owned and operated guesthouses.

Using Spain's parador system as a model, the Puerto Rico Tourism Company established the paradores in 1973 to encourage tourism across the island. Each of the paradores is situated in a historic place or site of unusual scenic beauty and must meet high standards of service and cleanliness.

Some of the paradores are located in the mountains and others by the sea. Most have pools, and all offer excellent Puerto Rican cuisine. Many are within easy driving distance of San Juan.

Properties must meet certain benchmark standards of quality to be admitted to the program, so tourists feel comfortable staying at the property. One complaint about the program is that variances in quality still range widely from one property to the next. For more information call © **800/866-7827** or check out www.gotoparadores.com.

Our favorite paradores are all in western Puerto Rico (see chapters 8 and 9). **Parador Posada Porlamar** in La Parguera gives you a taste of the good life in a simple fishing village. For a plantation ambience and an evocation of the Puerto Rico of colonial times, there is the

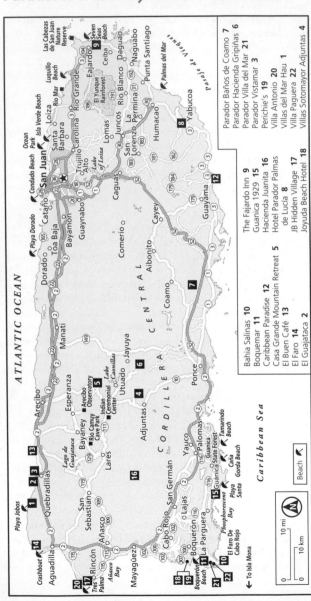

Parador Baños de Coamo **7**
Parador Hacienda Gripiñas **6**
Parador Villa del Mar **21**
Parador Vistamar **3**
Perichie's **19**
Villa Antonio **20**
Villas del Mar Hau **1**
Villa Paguera **22**
Villas Sotomayor Adjuntas **4**

The Fajardo Inn **9**
Guanica 1929 **15**
Hacienda Juanita **16**
Hotel Parador Palmas
de Lucia **8**
JB Hidden Village **17**
Joyuda Beach Hotel **18**

Bahia Salinas **10**
Boquemar **11**
Caribbean Paradise **12**
Casa Grande Mountain Retreat **5**
El Buen Café **13**
El Faro **14**
El Guajataca **2**

Beach ◤

Parador Hacienda Gripiñas at Jayuya, some 30 miles (48km) south-west of San Juan; it was a former coffee plantation. **Parador Vista-mar,** at Quebradillas, one of the largest paradores in Puerto Rico, is located on a coastal bluff with beautiful gardens of tropical flowers.

The Tourism Company also operates a similar program which promotes local restaurants called *mesones gastronómicos* (© **800/ 981-7575**). Restaurants in this program also have to pass muster with the Tourism Company for inclusion.

VILLAS & VACATION HOMES
You can often secure good deals in Puerto Rico by renting privately owned villas and vacation homes.

Almost every villa has a staff, or at least a maid who comes in a few days a week. Villas also provide the essentials of home life, including bed linens and cooking paraphernalia. Condos usually come with a reception desk and are often comparable to life in a suite at a big resort hotel. Nearly every condo complex has a swimming pool, and some have more than one.

Private apartments are rented either with or without maid service. This is more of a no-frills option than the villas and condos. An apartment might not be in a building with a swimming pool, and it might not have a front desk to help you. Among the major categories of vacation homes, cottages offer the most freewheeling way to live. Most cottages are fairly simple, many opening in an ideal fashion onto a beach, whereas others may be clustered around a communal pool. Many contain no more than a simple bedroom together with a small kitchen and bathroom. For the peak winter season, reservations should be made at least 5 or 6 months in advance.

RENTAL AGENCIES
Agencies specializing in renting properties in Puerto Rico include:

- **VHR, Worldwide,** 235 Kensington Ave., Norwood, NJ 07648 (© **800/633-3284** or 201/767-9393; www.vhrww.com), offers the most comprehensive portfolio of luxury villas, condominiums, resort suites, and apartments for rent in the Caribbean, including complete packages for airfare and car rentals.
- **Hideaways Aficionado,** 767 Islington St., Portsmouth, NH 03801 (© **800/843-4433** or 603/430-4433; www.hideaways. com), provides a 144-page guide with illustrations of its accommodations so that you can get an idea of what you're renting. Most villas come with maid service. You can also ask this travel club about discounts on plane fares and car rentals.

3

Getting to Know San Juan

San Juan, Puerto Rico's capital city, is the political, economic, and cultural center of the island. It's home to about one-third of all Puerto Rico residents.

Most resort hotels, restaurants, shops, galleries, and clubs are located in Old San Juan and the Isla Verde and Condado tourism sectors on the coast.

1 ORIENTATION

ARRIVING BY PLANE

Visitors from overseas arrive at **Luis Muñoz Marín International Airport,** the major transportation center of the Caribbean, which is located east of the city near major tourist districts. It has such amenities as a tourist-information center, restaurants, hair stylists, coin lockers for storing luggage, bookstores, banks, currency-exchange kiosks, and bars. There are also a number of shops selling souvenirs and local rums and coffees for last-minute shopping for gifts for folks back home.

Getting from the Airport to the City

BY TAXI   The island's **Puerto Rico Tourism Company (Transportation Division; ℭ 787/999-2100** or 253-0418) establishes flat taxi fares between the Luis Muñoz Marín International Airport and major tourist zones: From the airport to Isla Verde, the fee is $10; to the Condado district, the charge is $15; and to any hotel in Old San Juan, the cost is $19. Taxi service from the airport is quite well regulated, with a dispatcher handing you a ticket detailing your costs. These also include baggage costs (50¢ for each of the first three bags, then $1 per bag), and a 10% to 15% tip is expected.

BY LIMOUSINE   There are more than enough reputable limousine rental companies to choose from, but arrangements must be made beforehand. Limousines don't sit at the airport like taxis. You must arrange pickup in advance or call once you get in. A simple pickup from the airport to your hotel ranges in cost from $100 to $125.

Most vehicles fit six passengers comfortably. Your driver will meet you outside the baggage-claim area.

BY PUBLIC CAR Public cars, called *públicos,* are either vans or large sedans that are shared by passengers. The ride can sometimes be crowded, and it can take longer the more passengers there are. They are a bargain for budget travelers who have to travel a distance from the airport and do not want to rent a car. It will cost you $20 to get to Ponce and $10 to Caguas, plus baggage fee.

BY CAR All the major car-rental companies have kiosks at the airport. It's possible to rent a car once you arrive, but your best bet is to reserve one before you leave home.

To drive into the city, head west along Route 26 or the Baldorioty de Castro Expressway, which cuts just south of San Juan's Atlantic coastline. You will pass the towering oceanfront condominiums and hotels of Isla Verde on your right, then go through the Santurce section at the heart of San Juan, and then you will see exits for Condado, the city's other major beachfront tourism zone. The road then passes by the Condado Lagoon and crosses into Puerta de Tierra near the Caribe Hilton, merging into Avenida Muñoz Rivera, as it passes beautifully landscaped parks and El Escambrón public beach. The road climbs a bluff overlooking the Atlantic coastline, then passes the capitol building on your left, and then the historic Spanish fortress Fort San Cristóbal at the entrance of Old San Juan. Most major hotels have parking garages. In Old San Juan, parking options include the centrally located **La Cochera** near Plaza de Armas (no phone). The other parking options lie on or near Calle Recinto Sur and the San Juan Bay at the southern end of the city: **Paseo Portuario** parking garage (© 787/722-2233), the city-run **Doña Fela** parking garage (no phone), and the city-run **Covadonga Parking Garage** (© 787/721-6911). Operating hours vary, but they are open at least until midnight during weekdays and 3am weekends. Prices vary, with municipal-run lots cheaper than private lots, but figure on paying $1 per hour.

BY BUS Those with little luggage can take a bus at a cost of 75¢. You need to hop on the B-40 or the C-45, taking it one stop to Isla Verde. From there, you can take the A-5, which runs through Isla Verde, swings to Condado near Avenida de Diego, and then heads into Old San Juan.

VISITOR INFORMATION

Tourist information is available at the **Luis Muñoz Marín Airport** (© 787/791-1014) daily from 9am to 10pm. Another office is at **La Casita,** Pier 1, Old San Juan (© 787/722-1709), open Saturday to Wednesday 9am to 8pm, Thursday and Friday 8:30am to 6:30pm.

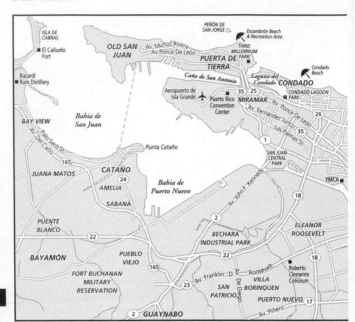

CITY LAYOUT

FINDING AN ADDRESS   Finding an address in San Juan isn't always easy. You'll have to contend not only with missing street signs and numbers but also with street addresses that appear sometimes in English and at other times in Spanish. The most common Spanish terms for thoroughfares are *calle* (street) and *avenida* (avenue). When it is used, the street number follows the street name; for example, the El Convento hotel is located at Calle del Cristo 100, in Old San Juan. Locating a building in Old San Juan is relatively easy. The area is only 7 square blocks, so by walking around, it's possible to locate most addresses. Also, sanjuaneros, for some unknown reason, still use the stop numbers, or *paradas,* from a trolley that stopped running back in the 1950s as a reference point for directions. For example, *parada* 18 is at the heart of Santurce. In general, the higher the stop number, the farther its distance from Old San Juan.

STREET MAPS   *¡Qué Pasa!,* the monthly tourist magazine distributed free by the tourist office, contains accurate, easy-to-read maps of San Juan and the Condado that pinpoint the major attractions.

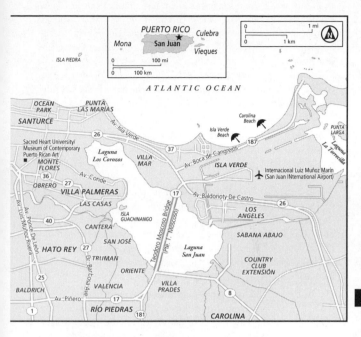

NEIGHBORHOODS IN BRIEF

Old San Juan One of the most historic areas in the Caribbean, the Spanish colonial city lies on the western end of an islet, with the Atlantic Ocean to the north and the tranquil San Juan Bay to the south. The historic Spanish wall built to hold off attacks still circles the city, which is filled with beautiful churches, shady plazas, majestic promenades, and wonderful residences and gardens. It's a robust cultural and commercial district with theaters, galleries, clubs, bars and restaurants, and some of the most interesting shops in the region.

Puerta de Tierra Puerta de Tierra lies just east of the old city walls of San Juan. It is dominated by the green **Luis Muñoz Rivera Park** and the oceanfront **Third Millennium Park** and adjacent **El Escambrón public beach.** It also hosts Puerto Rico's Capitol, Supreme Court, and the Caribe Hilton.

Miramar   Miramar is an upscale residential neighborhood with a small business district that has excellent restaurants. Near San Juan Bay, it has two marinas where fishing boats and yachts lie at anchor. The whole harborside area is being redeveloped, spearheaded by the state-of-the-art **Puerto Rico Convention Center.** A new hotel is under construction, and luxury retail, office, and residential units are being planned, as is a huge bayside promenade to connect the area to Old San Juan. It's also the site of **Isla Grande Airport,** where you can board flights to the islands of Vieques and Culebra.

Condado   This beach-bordering district wedged between the Atlantic Ocean and the Condado Lagoon has been undergoing a frenzy of redevelopment. It is one of the most coveted neighborhoods in Puerto Rico.

The beautiful oceanfront **Window of the Sea Park** is at the center of the area, which is now surrounded by designer fashion stores and chic restaurants. The former La Concha has opened next door after a 10-year renovation, and luxury condos are being built in the former Vanderbilt hotel nearby. Luxury hotels and more modest guesthouses fill the sector, as do wonderful restaurants of all types.

Ocean Park   This is a beachfront residential neighborhood with probably the prettiest and most low-key beach in San Juan. The beaches are wide, and the sun beats down on the beach longer because there are few large condominiums. The tree-covered streets are filled with beautiful suburban homes, a charming mix of Malibu, Spanish, and Caribbean influences. On its eastern end is the **Ultimate Trolley Beach and Barbosa Park,** which has a soccer field, running track, basketball courts, baseball fields, and tennis courts.

Isla Verde   Isla Verde is lined with luxury condos and hotels along a main oceanfront boulevard. But where Condado may score higher with its restaurants and shops, and its older and more artful architecture, Isla Verde wins hands down in the beach department—you'll find a wide, clean, white-sand beach running the full length of the neighborhood just off its main strip. The area has some of San Juan's best beaches and its most deluxe hotels.

Hato Rey   The city's financial district is the Wall Street of the West Indies, filled with many high-rises, a large federal complex, and many business and banking offices. The sector has been transformed by the **Puerto Rico Coliseum** and the **Tren Urbano,** which snakes through the towers of capitalism on elevated tracks. The new arena draws top acts (like the Rolling Stones). There's also the **Fine Arts Cinema,** with art and foreign films, luxury seats, gourmet food, and yes, beer and wine. The sector also contains the huge **Luis Muñoz Marín Park,** with miles of bicycle and jogging paths, picnic areas and fields, small ponds, and tropical vegetation. The park also features a top-notch amphitheater and a cable car ride.

Río Piedras This is the home to the **University of Puerto Rico,** which looks like an Ivy League school except for the tropical vegetation. It's dominated by the landmark **Roosevelt Bell Tower,** named for Theodore Roosevelt, who donated the money for its construction.

There's also a large shopping area surrounding the **Río Piedras Marketplace** (selling fresh fruit and vegetables) and the pedestrian walkway Paseo de Diego with bargains galore. The shops attract travelers from across the Caribbean.

The **UPR Botanical Gardens** are located here as well, with a beautifully arranged array of tropical trees and plants.

2 GETTING AROUND

BY TAXI The island's **Puerto Rico Tourism Company (Transportation Division; © 787/999-2100** or 253-0418) establishes flat rates between well-traveled areas within San Juan. (See above for fees to and from the Luis Muñoz Marín International Airport.) There are also set fees from the cruise-ship piers outside of Old San Juan to set destinations: Isla Verde, $19; Condado, $12; and Old San Juan, $7. You will also be charged 50¢ per bag for your first three bags and $1 per bag thereafter. Metered fares start off with an initial charge of $1.75, plus $1.90 per mile, and a 10¢ charge for each 25 seconds of waiting time. Tolls are not included in either fare. Normal tipping supplements of between 10% and 15% of these fares are appreciated. While meters are supposed to be used, on most trips outside the zoned rates drivers will probably offer you a flat rate of their own devising. San Juan cabbies are loath to use the meter, but usually quote a fair price. You can catch a cab outside any main hotel. Some large companies are **Metro Taxis (© 787/725-2870),** the **Rochdale Cab Company (© 787/721-1900),** and the **Major Cab Company (© 787/723-2460).**

BY BUS The **Metropolitan Bus Authority (© 787/767-7979** for route information) operates buses in the greater San Juan area. Bus stops are marked by upright metal signs or yellow posts that say

PARADA. The bus terminal is the dock area in the same building as the Covadonga parking lot next to the Treasury Department. Fares are 75¢.

This section of Old San Juan is the starting point for many of the city's metropolitan bus routes. One useful route is the A-5, which hits downtown Santurce, Avenida de Diego near Condado, then goes along Loíza Street and down Isla Verde's oceanfront drive where all the hotels are located. Another is C-53, which hits the Convention Center in Miramar, then heads down Condado's main strip, Avenida Ashford, continues along Loíza Street near Ocean Park, and then goes on into Isla Verde, along its oceanfront road.

Any bus marked ATI hooks up with the Tren Urbano, probably at its Sagrado Corazón Station, which is its last stop into the city. The ticket costs $1.50 but includes a transfer to take a trip on the train.

BY TROLLEY   When you tire of walking around Old San Juan, you can board one of the free trolleys that run through the historic area. Departure points include the Covadonga, La Puntilla, Plaza de Armas, and the two forts. The city has also begun operating a trolley along Loiza Street near Ocean Park.

BY LIMOUSINE   San Juan has nearly two dozen limousine rental companies offering a wide range of luxury vehicle rentals, called *limosinas* (their Spanish name), from Lincoln Town Car limousines to deluxe stretch Hummers. A simple pickup from the airport to your hotel ranges in cost from $100 to $125. Rentals for other standard trips range from about $70 to $125 per hour, with most cars seating six passengers comfortably. Many firms use drivers who hold tour-guide permits, and limousine operators often give tours of Old San Juan, El Yunque, or other sites to small groups or families. If the driver or another guide leaves the vehicle to tour a specific place by foot, it will cost another $15 to $25 hourly.

BY RENTAL CAR   See "Getting Around" in chapter 2 for details.

BY FERRY   The **Acua Expreso** (© 787/729-8714) connects Old San Juan with the industrial and residential community of Cataño, across the bay. Ferries depart daily every 30 minutes from 6am to 9pm. The one-way fare to Cataño is 50¢. Departures are from the San Juan Terminal at pier number 2 in Old San Juan. However, it's best to avoid rush hours because hundreds of locals who work in town use this ferry. The ride lasts 6 minutes.

BY PUBLIC CAR   Public cars, called *públicos,* are either vans or large sedans that are shared by passengers. Though they can be crowded and uncomfortable, more often than not they are quite comfortable and spacious. And they are a bargain for budget travelers

San Juan Mass-Transit: Tren Urbano

Tren Urbano links San Juan to its suburbs, such as Santurce, Bayamón, and Guaynabo. Costing about $2 billion, the system opened in 2005 to provide an easy mode of transportation to the most congested areas of metropolitan San Juan. During rush hour (5:30–9am and 3–6pm), the train operates every 8 minutes; otherwise, it runs every 12 minutes. There is no service daily from 11:20pm to 5:30am. The fare is $1.50 one-way and includes a transfer to buses. It's a beautiful ride and gives tourists a different experience of the city; the train passes on an elevated track through the modern Hato Rey financial district, plunges way underground in Río Piedras, and then snakes through upscale suburban neighborhoods, with tropical foliage and pools in many backyards. The fare includes a transfer because a special class of buses has been created to link up with particular Tren Urbano routes. The train and accompanying buses keep special expanded schedules during big events, like a festival in Old San Juan, and also for when big acts play at the Puerto Rico Coliseum, or the Tourism Company throws a New Year's Eve party at the Convention Center. For more information, call ℂ **866/900-1284** or log onto www.ati.gobierno.pr.

who have to travel a distance and do not want to rent a car. Most public cars travel set routes at prices far below what taxis would charge. You should consider taking one from the airport if traveling on a budget to areas outside of San Juan. In San Juan, *público* departure and arrival points include the airport, right outside Old San Juan near Plaza Colón, and by the Río Piedras public marketplace. Every town on the island has at least one area where *públicos* congregate.

Look in Yellow Pages under *la linea de carros* to hire a public car that will pick you up where you are staying and bring you to a specific destination at an agreed-upon price. A 2-hour drive from San Juan to Guánica costs $25 one-way. Since you travel with other passengers, you may have to wait until the driver takes them to their destinations first. He will pick up and drop off passengers according to what is best for his route and schedule.

Where to Stay in San Juan

Whatever your preferences in accommodations—a beachfront resort or a place in historic Old San Juan, sumptuous luxury or an inexpensive base from which to see the sights—you can find a perfect fit in San Juan.

Not all hotels here have air-conditioned rooms. We've pointed them out in the recommendations below. If air-conditioning is important to you, make sure "A/C" appears after *"In room"* at the end of the listing.

If you prefer shopping and historic sights to the beach, then Old San Juan might be your preferred nest. The high-rise resort hotels lie primarily along the Condado beach strip and the equally good sands of Isla Verde. The hotels along Condado and Isla Verde attract the cruise-ship and casino crowds. The hotels away from the beach in San Juan, in such sections as Santurce, are primarily for business clients.

The guesthouses of Ocean Park, free from the high-rises elsewhere but with an equally beautiful beach, attract a young urban crowd and those looking for a more low-key ambience.

TAXES & SERVICE CHARGES

All hotel rooms in Puerto Rico are subject to a tax that is not included in the rates given in this book. At casino hotels, the tax is 12%; at non-casino hotels, it's 9%. At government-sponsored country inns called *paradores puertorriqueños,* you pay a 7% tax. San Juan also began charging a head tax on hotel guests ranging from $3 to $5 nightly. Some hotels add a 10% service charge; if not, you're expected to tip for services rendered. Many large hotels also charge resort fees, ostensibly to offset the costs of facilities like a pool or health club, which can add substantially to your bill. Fees range from 12% to 22% of the cost of your room per night. When you're booking a room, it's a good idea to ask about these charges.

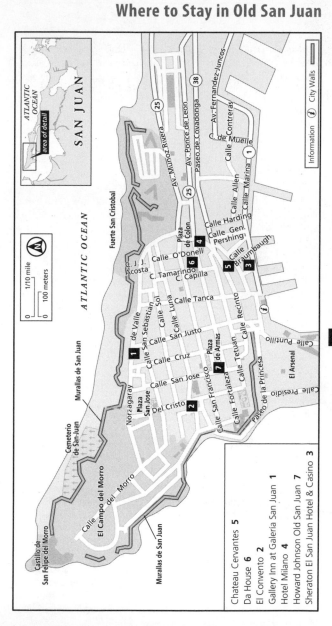

WHERE TO STAY IN SAN JUAN

WHERE TO STAY IN SAN JUAN

4

WHERE TO STAY IN SAN JUAN

Chateau Cervantes 5
Da House 6
El Convento 2
Gallery Inn at Galería San Juan 1
Hotel Milano 4
Howard Johnson Old San Juan 7
Sheraton El San Juan Hotel & Casino 3

Information ⓘ   City Walls

1 OLD SAN JUAN

Old San Juan is 1¹/₂ miles (2.4km) from the beach. Stay here if you're more interested in shopping and attractions than you are in watersports. For the locations of hotels in Old San Juan, see the map on p. 43.

EXPENSIVE

Chateau Cervantes ★★ This 12-unit boutique hotel blends 16th-century Spanish colonial charm with ultramodern interiors by local designer Nono Maldonado. The hotel's high ceilings, arched doorways, windows, and wrought-iron balcony railings are quintessential Old San Juan, but Maldonado, working from a gold and muted gemstone palette, has remade guest rooms into a plush world of velvet and silk, with marble bathrooms and paintings by island artist Carlos Dávila.

Calle Recinto Sur 307, Old San Juan, PR 00901. € **787/724-7722.** Fax 787/289-8909. www.cervantespr.com. 12 units. $225 double; $285 junior suites; $425 Cervantes suites; $925 penthouse for 4. Rates include continental breakfast. AE, MC, V. Bus: A5 or C53. **Amenities:** Restaurant; nonsmoking rooms. In room: A/C, TV/CD/DVD, dataport (in some), Wi-Fi, hair dryer, ironing board, safe.

Hotel El Convento ★★ This is one of the most charming historic hotels in the Caribbean and a quintessential Old San Juan experience. The core of the building was constructed in 1651 as the New World's first Carmelite convent, but over the years it played many roles, from a dance hall to a flophouse to a parking lot for garbage trucks. It was not until 1962 that it began life as a hotel. A restoration a decade ago brought the property back to its past glory, while injecting it with an urban, up-to-date feel, very much like Old San Juan itself. Its fourth-floor rooftop has a small pool, adjacent Jacuzzi, and a big sun terrace with views of the nearby Catedral de San Juan, as well as the bay and the Atlantic. The lower two floors feature a collection of fine restaurants and a few boutiques. A late-afternoon wine-and-cheese offering is served on a beautiful mid-floor dining area spilling onto an outdoor terrace overlooking Calle Cristo. The midsize accommodations include Spanish-style furnishings, throw rugs, beamed ceilings, paneling, and Andalusian terra-cotta floor tiles. Each unit contains king-size, queen-size, or two double or twin beds, fitted with fine linens.

Calle del Cristo 100, San Juan, PR 00901. € **800/468-2779** or 787/723-9020. Fax 787/721-2877. www.elconvento.com. 68 units. Winter $355–$410 double, from $650 suite; off season $225–$285 double. Rates include afternoon wine-and-cheese reception and free Wi-Fi. AE, DC, DISC, MC, V. Parking $20. Bus: Old Town

Trolley. **Amenities:** 4 restaurants; 3 bars; small rooftop plunge pool; fitness center; Jacuzzi; massage; laundry service; dry cleaning; rooms for those w/limited mobility. *In room:* A/C, TV, dataport, Wi-Fi, coffeemaker, hair dryer, iron, safe.

Sheraton Old San Juan Hotel & Casino ★ This may be convenient for cruise-ship passengers wanting to spend a few nights in San Juan before or after a cruise, but don't expect Old City charm. Opened in 1997, this nine-story, waterfront hotel was part of a $100-million renovation of San Juan's cruise-port facilities. The city lies across the street from major cruise-ship docks, on the outskirts of the Old City. When cruise ships pull into port, the hotel's lobby and bars are likely to be jammed with passengers stretching their legs after a few days at sea.

Calle Brumbaugh 100, San Juan, PR 00902. © **800/325-3535** or 787/721-5100. Fax 787/721-1111. www.sheraton.com. 240 units. Winter $255–$345 double, $395–$595 suite; off season $209–$345 double, $339–$475 suite. AE, DC, DISC, MC, V. Valet parking $21. Bus: A5 or C53. **Amenities:** 2 restaurants; 3 bars; outdoor pool; fitness center; Jacuzzi; car-rental desk; business center; room service (6:30am–11:30pm); nonsmoking rooms; casino; rooms for those w/limited mobility. *In room:* A/C, TV, dataport, minibar, coffeemaker, hair dryer, iron, safe.

MODERATE

Gallery Inn at Galería San Juan ★ (Finds) The location and ambience of this unique inn, which rambles through a 300-year-old building overlooking Old San Juan's northern sea wall, is perfect, with sweeping sea views and vistas stretching across colonial city rooftops down to San Juan Bay. Verdant courtyards, interior gardens, and patios and terraces appear around every bend one takes in the inn, and the chatter of tropical birds and the murmur of fountains are everywhere. Built in the 1700s by an aristocratic Spanish family, today the inn is owned by Jan D'Esopo and Manuco Gandia, a married couple who created it out of their home. It also houses Jan's art studio. The entire inn is covered with clay and bronze figures as well as other original art by Jan, and each guest room also functions as gallery space, with Jan's original silk screens, paintings, and prints on display. We suggest booking one of the least expensive doubles; even the cheapest units are fairly roomy and attractively furnished, with good beds. The rooftop Wine Deck has the best view in Old San Juan. Classical music concerts are often held in the Music Room and are free for guests. A small pool has also been added to the property.

Calle Norzagaray 204–206, San Juan, PR 00901. © **866/572-ARTE** (2783) or 787/722-1808. Fax 787/977-3929. www.thegalleryinn.com. 22 units (some with shower only). Year-round $225–$325 double; $410 suite. Off-season specials available. Rates include continental breakfast and 6pm wine-and-cheese reception. AE, DC, MC, V. 6 free parking spaces, plus parking on the street. Bus: Old Town trolley. **Amenities:** Breakfast room; pool. *In room:* A/C, dataport, hair dryer.

Room with a Local's View: Apartment Rentals

Despite the explosion of Old City hotel and guesthouse rooms over the past few years, one of the best ways to experience the city remains getting a furnished apartment for a short-term rental. Many are restored, historic quarters with beautiful roof-top terraces or verdant interior courtyards, or both. All have high ceilings, with large windows and the classic double wooden doors, and many open up onto balconies. The interiors often boast original artwork and beautiful furnishings. In short, you'll get a great sense during your vacation of what it feels like to live in this enchanted city, and you'll normally save money (especially if you're a large group). Many of the rentals cater to discriminating travelers, offering first-rate creature comforts like Swedish mattresses and plush bathrobes, as well as upscale kitchens and bathrooms.

Prices range from $500 weekly for a basic studio to $2,500 weekly for a three-bedroom, restored colonial beauty with rooftop terrace and ocean views. Short-term rentals are assessed a 7% tax, and many require a minimum 3-day or 4-day stay. Cleaning fees are also assessed, which can range from $50 to $75.

The expert in Old City short-term rentals is **Vida Urbana**, Calle Cruz 255, Old San Juan, PR 00901 (© **787/587-3031;** www.vidaurbanapr.com), a spinoff of Caleta Realty, a veteran in this field. Years ago, we found a three-bedroom apartment through Caleta, a place near Catedral de San Juan with huge adjoining living and dining rooms and a rooftop terrace running the length of the apartment. We loved it. We had a reception there, and a group of about eight friends stayed there for the week. A comparable apartment would cost

Hotel Milano There's not much remarkable about this hotel built from a 1920s warehouse, except clean, modern facilities at a good price in a great location, right near all the restaurants and bars along South Fortaleza Street. You enter a wood-sheathed lobby at end of Calle Fortaleza before ascending to one of the clean, well-lit bedrooms. The simple, modern rooms have cruise-ship-style decor and unremarkable views. The rooftop terrace has outstanding views and is a great spot to relax or enjoy the continental breakfast. The best around $1,500 for the week today. There are two lovely apartments for rent above the gallery and gift shop **Bóveda,** Calle Cristo 209, Old San Juan, PR 00901 (© **787/725-0263;** www. boveda.info), with artful, bright decor in a restored colonial building, complete with interior garden courtyard and balconies with double-door entrances. A cool tropical vibe flows through the duplex ($950 weekly) and studio suite ($500 weekly). The **Caleta Guesthouse,** Caleta de las Monjas 11, Old San Juan, PR 00901 (© **787/725-5347;** www.thecaleta. com), has affordable studios and one-bedroom furnished apartments. It's located on one of Old San Juan's most charming streets, across from a lookout over San Juan Bay, but the accommodations are fairly basic.

Likewise, **Condado** and **Isla Verde** also have an ample supply of short-term rentals for visitors wanting to spend the bulk of their time at the beach. Most of the beachfront condos in both areas have some apartments up for short-term lease. In addition to their prime location, many of the condos have first-class pools and other facilities like tennis courts, health clubs, and beautiful common areas for picnics or gatherings. And at rates ranging from $525 a week for a studio to $2,250 a week for a deluxe, modern, three-bedroom condo, it's a great deal for groups. **San Juan Vacations,** Cond. Marbella del Caribe, Ste. S-5, Isla Verde 00979 (© **800/266-3639** or 787/727-1591; www.sanjuanvacations.com), is the biggest name in the business. We've also worked through **Ronnie's Properties,** Calle Marseilles 14, Ritz Condominium, Ste. 11-F, San Juan, PR 00907 (www.ronniesproperties.com), which has an extensive and growing list of properties in Condado and Isla Verde.

rooms are on the upper floors overlooking the street. You're in SoFo, home to some of Puerto Rico's best restaurants.

Calle Fortaleza 307, San Juan, PR 00901. © **877/729-9050** or 787/729-9050. Fax 787/722-3379. www.hotelmilanopr.com. 30 units. Winter $95–$185 double; off season $85–$145 double. $5 continental breakfast. AE, MC, V. Bus: A5 or C53. **Amenities:** Rooftop terrace cafe; Wi-Fi; nonsmoking rooms; rooms for those w/ limited mobility. *In room:* A/C, TV, fridge, hair dryer.

INEXPENSIVE

Da House   This has the feel of a European hostel, with bright, sunny, affordable rooms and a young and creative clientele, all on top of the legendary Nuyorican Café. The rooftop sun deck is a great place to chill out with lounge chairs, a Tiki bar, great views, a hot tub, and showers. The downstairs cafe is a great venue for theater and music (it can be quite loud, so if you don't want to be in the middle of a nightlife scene, this is not your place). The Wi-Fi Internet cafe in the lobby is a good spot to pick up insider tourist tips. Great art adorns the guesthouse, and the staff is friendly and helpful. Rooms are clean and comfortable.

Calle San Francisco 312, entrance down Callejon de la Capilla, San Juan, PR 00901. ✆ 787/366-5074 or 977-1180. Fax 787/722-3379. www.dahousehotelpr.com. 30 units. Winter $80–$120 double. Off-season specials available. AE, MC, V. Bus: A5 or C53. **Amenities:** Pizza restaurant; bar; music and theater nightclub. *In room:* A/C, high-speed Internet.

Howard Johnson Old San Juan Hotel Plaza de Armas   This renovated apartment building at the center of Old San Juan gives you a sense of how sanjuaneros live in the historic quarter, with rooms wrapped around a prominent interior courtyard. It's right on Old San Juan's central Plaza de Armas, also home to San Juan City Hall and the Puerto Rico State Department. Like those at Hotel Milano (above), these are clean, comfortable rooms in the heart of the city. Visitors here know what to expect, and they leave satisfied. There are several spots for a meal, including an open-air cafe on the plaza serving tasty local coffee, as well as two drugstores, a supermarket, and Marshalls Department store—plus this is conveniently near all Old San Juan attractions. The entire plaza has Wi-Fi. Continental breakfast is served in the lobby.

Calle San José 202, San Juan, PR 00901. ✆ **877/722-9191.** Fax 787/725-3091. www.hojo.com. 30 units. Winter $179–$199 double, $109 single; off season $115–$175 double, $95 single. Rates include continental breakfast. AE, MC, V. Bus: A5 or C53. **Amenities:** Nonsmoking rooms; rooms for those w/limited mobility. *In room:* A/C, TV, high-speed Internet, hair dryer.

2 PUERTA DE TIERRA

Caribe Hilton ★★★   A pioneering hotel (it was considered Puerto Rico's first big luxury hotel and was the first Hilton built outside the continental U.S.), this has been an integral part of Puerto Rico's tourism industry since 1949 and remains one of the most up-to-date luxury properties in San Juan. Because of an unusual configuration of natural barriers and legal precedents, the hotel has the only

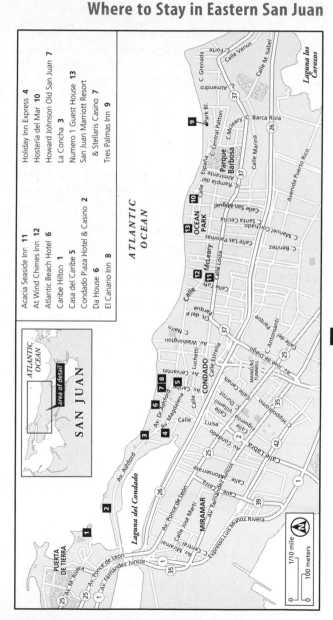

Acacia Seaside Inn **11**
At Wind Chimes Inn **12**
Atlantic Beach Hotel **6**
Caribe Hilton **1**
Casa del Caribe **5**
Condado Plaza Hotel & Casino **2**
Da House **6**
El Canario Inn **8**

Holiday Inn Express **4**
Hostería del Mar **10**
Howard Johnson Old San Juan **7**
La Concha **3**
Numero 1 Guest House **13**
San Juan Marriott Resort
& Stellaris Casino **7**
Tres Palmas Inn **9**

private beach on the island. The property abuts the historic Fort San Gerónimo, and a residential and commercial development is taking place on a portion of the Caribe's plot (which totaled 17 acres/6.9 hectares before the sale). Nonetheless, its sprawling facilities, with parks, gardens, and an exhibition center, are still a hit with conventions and tour groups. Only the Condado Plaza and the El San Juan rival it for nonstop activity.

Rooms have larger-than-expected bathrooms with tub/shower combos as well as comfortable, tropical-inspired furniture. In the Caribe Terrace Bar, you can order the bartender's celebrated piña colada, which was once enjoyed by movie legends Joan Crawford and Errol Flynn. Caribe lore has it that a bartender here invented the drink, but other places take credit as well. Overlooking the infinity pool area and the palm-fringed beach beyond it, the bar is one of the best places anywhere to enjoy a piña colada. An oceanfront spa and fitness center features such tantalizing delights as couples massages, body wraps, hydrotherapy tub treatments, and soothing cucumber sun therapies. The casino is closed, but there are great restaurants here.

The best place to stay here is in one of the 158 luxury villas with more than 1,500 square feet (139 sq. m) of space, all part of the Condado Lagoon Villas. Up for grabs are studios or one- or two-bedroom luxury accommodations, each with spectacular views of the Condado Lagoon and the Atlantic Ocean. Each comes with a kitchen, private balcony, and a marble bathroom with Jacuzzi. All the services of the Caribe Hilton's main hotel are provided to guests of the villas. This is a great spot for families, with one of the most extensive children's programs.

Calle Los Rosales, San Juan, PR 00901. ✆ **800/HILTONS** (445-8667) or 787/721-0303. Fax 787/725-8849. www.caribe.hilton.com. 646 units. Winter $320–$640 double; off season $159–$325 double; year-round $750–$1,600 villas and suites. Children 16 and under stay free in parent's room (maximum 4 people per room). AE, DC, DISC, MC, V. Valet parking $25; self-parking $15. Bus: B21. **Amenities:** 5 restaurants; 2 bars; Starbucks; outdoor pool; health club; spa; children's activities and playground; business center (7am–7pm weekdays, 8am–5pm weekends); limited room service; babysitting; laundry service; dry cleaning; nonsmoking rooms; rooms for those w/limited mobility. *In room:* A/C, TV, Wi-Fi, minibar, hair dryer, iron, safe.

3 CONDADO

The Condado has undergone a revitalization in recent years, with designer boutiques and trendy restaurants replacing tacky souvenir shops, and the beach is great.

Condado Plaza Hotel & Casino ★   This is one of the busiest hotels on Puerto Rico, with plenty of facilities and restaurants. A $65-million renovation spiffed up guest rooms and the multiple lobby areas. The pool area, with salt- and freshwater pools, overlooks a pretty beach at the entrance to Condado Lagoon, but there are both nicer beaches and hotels elsewhere in Condado and Isla Verde. The rooms, however, all have private terraces and are spacious, bright, and airy. They are fitted with deluxe beds and mattresses, either king-size or doubles, but most often twins. The good-size bathrooms contain tub/shower combinations. Only Hotel El San Juan has a larger choice of dining options. Its restaurants include Gusta de Italia, a casual delicious classic Italian eatery and the Strip House, which serves up delectable steaks in a boudoir-red interior with art that pays erotic homage to female beauty. The Eight Noodle Bar, outside its 24-hour casino, has become one of the favorite late-night snacking spots for San Juan's party set, with its kitchen open from noon to 4am daily. The casino remains one of the island's best.

Av. Ashford 999, San Juan, PR 00907. © **800/468-8588** or 787/721-1000. Fax 787/721-1968. www.luxuryresorts.com. 570 units. Winter $259–$499 double, $585–$1,500 suite; off season $150–$400 double, $450–$1,400 suite. AE, DC, DISC, MC, V. Valet parking $15; self-parking $10. Bus: C53 or B21. **Amenities:** 5 restaurants; 3 bars; 3 outdoor pools; 2 tennis courts; health club; spa; 3 Jacuzzis; watersports equipment; children's activities; car-rental desk; business center; salon; 24-hr. room service; laundry service; dry cleaning; nonsmoking rooms; casino; rooms for those w/limited mobility. *In room:* A/C, TV, minibar, coffeemaker, hair dryer, iron, safe.

La Concha: A Renaissance Resort ★★   The reopening of this hotel—50 years to the day from when it first opened to rave reviews in December 1958—took 7 years and carried a $220-million price tag, but it was well worth it. Thank former San Juan mayor and governor, Sila Calderón, and the Puerto Rico Architects Association for stopping the wrecking ball on this one. This renovation completes the comeback of Condado, with oceanfront rooms that feel as if they are part of the horizon and a multilevel infinity pool area and adjoining beaches that form a dreamscape in which guests willfully lose themselves. The water motif extends to the cascading fountain at its entrance, the fountains surrounding an open-air deck, and views of the sea from every vantage point. The lobby's Italian marble, white furniture, and huge window to sea also pull the resort's exteriors and interiors together. The signature shell structure, which sits on the beach surrounded by water, is home to Perla restaurant, a seafood restaurant run by prominent local chef Dayn Smith. The hotel's lobby bar is a great spot for tapas and wine, and the casino sits just off it.

Surrounded by designer boutiques and trendy restaurants, La Concha has been a local hot spot since it reopened, and its lobby area always has the sound of Latin rhythms.

Guest rooms have the latest high-tech gadgets; understated natural wood and beige interiors form a canvas for the beautiful views and tropical prints on the walls.

Av. Ashford 1077, San Juan, PR 00907. (C) **877/524-7778** or 787/721-7500. Fax 787/724-7929. www.laconcharesort.com. 248 units. Winter $369–$439 double, $522–$549 suite; off season $199–$258 double, $438–$459 suite. AE, DC, DISC, MC, V. Valet parking $25; self-parking $18. Bus: C53 or B21. **Amenities:** 6 restaurants; 2 bars; pools; full-service business center; high-speed Wi-Fi; room service; rooms for those w/limited mobility. *In room:* A/C, flatscreen TV, music players for any format, hair dryer, iron, coffeemaker, tea service, safe, full desk.

San Juan Marriott Resort & Stellaris Casino ★

This centrally located hotel is on one of the Condado's nicest beaches and is within walking distance of two parks and the best restaurants in the sector. The tallest building on the Condado, this 21-story landmark packs lots of postmodern style and has an open, comfortable lobby area. A hit with families and kids, it has extensive children's activities and a pool with two water slides. It also has a jumping casino and lobby area, the scene of big band and Latin jazz performances. Even the sports bar by the pool is active with sports fans from up and down the East Coast. The guest rooms are generally spacious, with good views of the water, and each comes with a tiled bathroom with a tub/shower combination. The pastel tones of the comfortable bedrooms are a bit too washed out for our taste, but that's the only legitimate gripe about this property. Junior suites have a living area with a sofa bed. We can't say enough about its great location in the best part of Condado, which is not immediately apparent to visitors. It's an easy walk to anywhere you want to go. And the staff is among the friendliest in town.

Av. Ashford 1309, San Juan, PR 00907. (C) **800/228-9290** or 787/722-7000. Fax 787/722-6800. www.marriottpr.com. 525 units. Winter $295–$410 double, $510 junior suite; summer $219–$309 double, $410 junior suite, $1,500 vice-presidential suite, $2,000 presidential suite. Suite rate includes breakfast. AE, DC, DISC, MC, V. Valet parking $20; self-parking $16. Bus: C53 or B21. **Amenities:** 3 restaurants; 3 bars; 2 pools; 2 tennis courts; health club; Jacuzzi; sauna; tour desk; car-rental desk; business center w/computers; 24-hr. room service; babysitting; laundry service; dry cleaning; casino; rooms for those w/limited mobility. *In room:* A/C, TV, Wi-Fi, minibar, coffeemaker, hair dryer, iron, safe.

MODERATE

Acacia Seaside Inn (Value) This inn, originally built as a private home in 1943 and transformed into a simple hotel in 1948, didn't become well known until the late 1960s, when its reasonable rates began to attract families with children and college students traveling in groups. It's a stucco-covered building with vaguely Spanish-colonial detailing on a residential street lined with similar structures. For the past 4 years, it has been a sister property of the At Wind Chimes Inn, and the inn has been steadily being made over since then. The lobby and the fabulous restaurant Niché have granite walls and tiled floors with mood lighting, and they are connected by an interior tropical garden. The guest rooms are bright and cheery, and there are great areas to hang out, including a rooftop terrace. The beach, among the city's finest, is at the end of the block, and guests can hang out at the Wind Chimes pool and cafe bar. Each unit has simple furniture and a small shower-only bathroom. There's a whirlpool and sun deck. You are literally steps from the beach here.

Calle Taft 8, Condado, San Juan, PR 00911. ℂ **787/725-0668.** Fax 787/728-0671. www.acaciaseasideinn.com. 15 units (shower only). Winter $120–$210 double; summer $105–$185 double. AE, DISC, MC, V. Bus: A5, C53, or B21. *In room:* A/C, TV, fridge (in some).

Atlantic Beach Hotel   This is the most famous gay hotel in Puerto Rico. Housed in a five-story building with vaguely Art Deco styling, the hotel is best known for its ground-floor indoor/outdoor bar—the most visibly gay bar in Puerto Rico. It extends from the hotel lobby onto a wooden deck about 15 feet (4.6m) above the sands of Condado Beach. The units are simple cubicles, all nonsmoking, with stripped-down but serviceable and clean decor. Some of the rooms are smaller than others, but few of the short-term guests seem to mind—maybe because the place can have the spirit of a house party. Each unit has a small, shower-only bathroom with plumbing that might not always be in prime condition.

Management insists it does not have a restrictive policy of not allowing a guest to take a visitor back to the room. But the front desk acknowledges that "hustlers" are not allowed on the property or in the guest rooms.

Calle Vendig 1, Condado, San Juan, PR 00907. ℂ **787/721-6900.** Fax 787/721-6917. www.atlanticbeachhotel.net. 36 units (shower only). Winter $130–$170 double; off season $89–$115 double. AE, DISC, MC, V. Bus: C53 or B21. **Amenities:** Restaurant; bar; laundry service; dry cleaning; rooms for those w/limited mobility. *In room:* A/C, TV, safe.

At Wind Chimes Inn ★ (Kids)   This restored and renovated Spanish manor, 1 short block from the beach and 3½ miles (5.6km) from the airport, is one of the best guesthouses on the Condado. Upon entering a tropical patio, you'll find tiled tables surrounded by palm trees and bougainvillea. There's plenty of space on the deck and a covered lounge for relaxing, socializing, and eating breakfast. Dozens of decorative wind chimes add melody to the daily breezes. The good-size rooms offer a choice of size, beds, and kitchens; all contain ceiling fans and air-conditioning. Beds are comfortable and come in four sizes, ranging from twin to king-size. The shower-only bathrooms, though small, are efficiently laid out. Families like this place not only because of the accommodations and the affordable prices but because they can also prepare light meals here, cutting down on food costs.

Av. McLeary 1750, Condado, San Juan, PR 00911. *C* **800/946-3244** or 787/727-4153. Fax 787/728-0671. www.atwindchimesinn.com. 22 units (shower only). Winter $80–$155 double; off season $65–$125 double. AE, DISC, MC, V. Parking $10. Bus: B21, C53, or A5. **Amenities:** Bar; outdoor pool; limited room service; rooms for those w/limited mobility. *In room:* A/C, TV, Wi-Fi, kitchen (in some).

Casa del Caribe (Value) Don't expect the Ritz, but if you're looking for a bargain on the Condado, this is it. This renovated guesthouse was built in the 1940s, later expanded, and then totally refurbished with tropical decor. A very Puerto Rican ambience has been created, with emphasis on Latin hospitality and comfort. On a shady side street just off Ashford Avenue, behind a wall and garden, you'll discover Casa del Caribe's wraparound veranda. The small but cozy guest rooms have ceiling fans and air conditioners, and most feature original Puerto Rican art. The bedrooms are inviting, with comfortable furnishings and efficiently organized bathrooms. The front porch is a social center for guests, and you can also cook out at a barbecue area. The beach is a 2-minute walk away, and the hotel is also within walking distance of some megaresorts, with their glittering casinos.

Calle Caribe 57, El Condado, San Juan, PR 00907. *C* **787/722-7139.** Fax 787/723-2575. www.casadelcaribe.net. 13 units. Winter $85–$125 double; off season $65–$99 double. Rates include continental breakfast. AE, DISC, MC, V. Parking $5. Bus: C53 or B21. **Amenities:** Nonsmoking rooms; 1 room for those w/limited mobility. *In room:* A/C, TV, kitchen (in some).

El Canario Inn (Value) This little bed-and-breakfast, originally built as a private home, is one of the best values along the high-priced Condado strip. The location is just 1 block from the beach (you can walk there in your bathing suit). This well-established hotel lies directly on the landmark Ashford Avenue, center of Condado action, and is close to casinos, nightclubs, and many restaurants in all price ranges. Although surrounded by megaresorts, it is a simple inn, with rather small but comfortable rooms and good maintenance by a helpful staff. All units are nonsmoking and have small, tiled, shower-only bathrooms. You can relax on the hotel's patios or in the whirlpool area, which is surrounded by tropical foliage. There is no elevator. This is the most charming of the three El Canario properties. El Canario by the Sea is right around the block, and El Canario by the Lagoon is a bit farther east.

Av. Ashford 1317, Condado, San Juan, PR 00907. © **800/533-2649** or 787/722-3861. Fax 787/722-0391. www.canariohotels.com. 25 units (shower only). Winter $119–$134 double; off season $90–$100 double. $3 energy fee. Rates include a continental breakfast. AE, DC, MC, V. Bus: B21, C53, or C10. *In room:* A/C, TV, safe.

Holiday Inn Express This seven-story, white-painted structure, expanded in 2003, offers a desirable Condado location but without the towering prices of the grand resorts along the beach. The hotel is about a 2-minute walk from Condado Beach and is convenient to Old San Juan (a 15-min. drive) and the airport (a 20-min. drive). Most accommodations have two double beds (ideal for families) and ceiling fans, and each has a small bathroom with tub and shower. Many open onto balconies with water views. There's a small pool with a nice shaded area as well. It's close to the renovated La Concha and the Window of the Sea Park beside it.

Calle Marinao Ramirez Bages 1, Condado, San Juan, PR 00907. © **888/465-4329** or 787/724-4160. Fax 787/721-2436. www.ichotels.com. 115 units. Winter $149 (daily), $189 (weekend) double; off season $119 (daily), $139 (weekend) double. Children 18 and under stay free in parent's room. Rates include continental breakfast. AE, DC, DISC, MC, V. Parking $10. Bus: C53 or B21. **Amenities:** Pool; whirlpool; health club; business center w/computers; laundry service; dry cleaning. *In room:* A/C, TV, dataport, hair dryer, iron, safe.

4 OCEAN PARK

Ocean Park is a beautiful residential neighborhood fronting a wide, white, palm-fringed beach. A clutch of guesthouses and inns provide San Juan's most low-key vacation experience.

MODERATE

Hosteria del Mar ★ The hotel on the beach boasts medium-size, oceanview rooms, with either balconies or patios, and basic tropical decor, lots of wicker and pastels. On a beachfront street completely enveloped by a canopy of trees, this is one of San Juan's most charming spots. Its restaurant, Uvva, is excellent.

Calle Tapía 1, Ocean Park, San Juan, PR 00911. © **877/727-3302** or 787/727-3302. Fax 787/268-3302. hosteria@caribe.net. 27 units. High season $89–$239 double, $244–$264 apt; off season $69–$179 double, $199–$209 apt. Children 11 and under stay free in parent's room. AE, DC, DISC, MC, V. Bus: A5 or C53. **Amenities:** Restaurant; limited room service. *In room:* A/C, TV, dataport, Wi-Fi, kitchenette (in 3 units), coffeemaker (in some).

Número Uno Guest House ★★ (Finds This is a charming, stylish guesthouse in front of one of the area's most popular beaches, with an excellent restaurant, outdoor cafe, and cheerful bar. There's a verdant garden within this walled compound replete with splashing fountains, a small swimming pool, and manicured shrubbery and palms. Stylish-looking bedrooms contain tile floors, wicker or rattan furniture, comfortable beds, and tiled, shower-only bathrooms. There's a beautiful sun deck and other common areas.

Calle Santa Ana 1, Ocean Park, San Juan, PR 00911. ℂ 866/726-5010 or 787/726-5010. Fax 787/727-5482. www.numero1guesthouse.com. 13 units (shower only). High season (Dec 15–Apr 30) $139–$279 double, $269–$279 apt, $249 suite; low season (Aug 1–Oct 31) $89–$179 double, $169–$179 apt, $159 suite; mid-season (May 1–July 31 and Nov) $75–$115 double, $165 apt, $145 junior suite. $20 each additional occupant of a double room. Rates include continental breakfast. AE, MC, V. Bus: A5 or C53. **Amenities:** Restaurant; bar; outdoor pool; limited room service; rooms for those w/limited mobility. *In room:* A/C, TV, dataport, Wi-Fi, mini-bar, hair dryer, iron, safe, ceiling fan.

INEXPENSIVE

Tres Palmas Inn (Value) Across the street from the ocean, this apartment-style guesthouse overlooks a windswept stretch of beach at the eastern end of Ocean Park, right before it disappears into the rocky coastline along Punta Las Marías. The beautiful beach at Ultimo Trolley is a block west, and the hotel's pool is located in a secluded courtyard. You can also relax on the rooftop sun deck while soaking in the whirlpool. The medium-size bedrooms are simply but comfortably furnished, with rather standard motel items. Each guest room has a private entrance and a ceiling fan, and most have small refrigerators. Larger rooms also have small kitchens, and each unit has a small, tiled bathroom with either a tub or a shower. We have friends who love this place and stay here for annual visits to the island.

Ocean Park Blvd. 2212, San Juan, PR 00913. ℂ 888/290-2076 or 787/727-4617. Fax 787/727-5434. www.trespalmasinn.com. 18 units (some with shower only, some with tub only). Winter $87–$175 double; off season $81–$146 double. Rates include continental breakfast. AE, MC, V. Bus: A5 or A7. **Amenities:** Pool; 2 whirlpools; sun deck; Internet; 1 room for those w/limited mobility. *In room:* A/C, TV, dataport, kitchen, fridge (in some), hair dryer, safe.

5 ISLA VERDE

Isla Verde has the largest beach and the largest number of hotels in the same area. It is closer to the airport than the Condado and Old San Juan. The hotels here are farther from Old San Juan than those in Miramar, Condado, and Ocean Park. It's a good choice if you don't mind the isolation and want to be near fairly good beaches. For the location of hotels in Isla Verde, see the map "Where to Stay in Isla Verde" on p. 57.

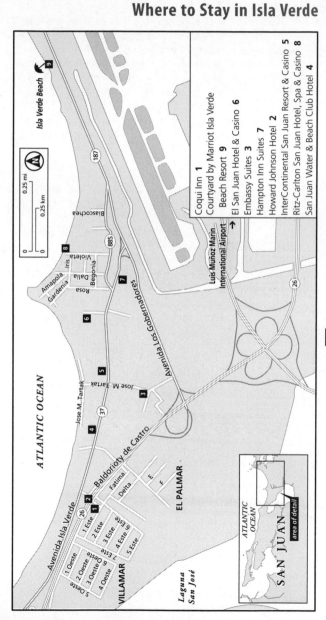

WHERE TO STAY IN SAN JUAN

4

ISLA VERDE

Coqui Inn **1**
Courtyard by Marriot Isla Verde
  Beach Resort **9**
El San Juan Hotel & Casino **6**
Embassy Suites **3**
Hampton Inn Suites **7**
Howard Johnson Hotel **2**
InterContinental San Juan Resort & Casino **5**
Ritz-Carlton San Juan Hotel, Spa & Casino **8**
San Juan Water & Beach Club Hotel **4**

VERY EXPENSIVE

El San Juan Hotel & Casino ★ (Kids)   Despite formidable competition by new properties like the Ritz-Carlton and the Water Club for elite and sophisticated travelers, this posh resort still has the power to dazzle. It's set amid 350 palms, century-old banyans, and tropical gardens, all lying along a 2-mile-long (3.2km) golden beach with aquamarine water. Lined with luxury hotels and condominiums, the beach is always full of activity and has great watersports available.

The lobby is the most opulent and memorable in the Caribbean. Entirely sheathed in red marble and hand-carved mahogany paneling, the public rooms stretch on almost endlessly. The hotel rivals any in the Caribbean for the rich diversity and high quality of its dining options. Oriental, Italian, Caribbean, and the world-famous Palm Restaurant steakhouse are just a few of the options. With live music and DJs playing at nightclubs nearly every night and a beautiful casino, El San Juan is still the place to be seen in the city.

The large, well-decorated rooms are outfitted with the latest in high tech, with Wi-Fi Internet access, flatscreen TVs with movie service, and iPod docking stations. The Vista guest rooms are bright and tropical, while the Lanai rooms are imbued with honey-hued woods and rattans, with darker wooden doors, windows, and other furnishings. Bathrooms have all the amenities and tub/shower combos; a few feature Jacuzzis. The oceanfront Lanai rooms overlook the fern-lined paths of the resort's tropical garden. There are also suites and one- and two-bedroom accommodations. While the larger units make sense for families, the hotel has cut down recently on organized activities for children, although there are still board games, pool toys, and a summer camp for children. It's still a great place for families, however.

Av. Isla Verde 6063, San Juan, PR 00979. ⓒ **787/791-1000.** Fax 787/791-0390. www.luxuryresorts.com. 382 units. Winter $279–$1,150 double, from $1,700–$2,200 suite; off season $192–$509 double, from $599–$799 suite. AE, DC, DISC, MC, V. Valet parking $15; self-parking $10. Bus: A5 or C53. **Amenities:** 7 restaurants; 4 bars; 2 outdoor pools; tennis courts; health club; spa; sauna and steam room; watersports equipment/rentals; children's programs; business center; 24-hr. room service; massage; babysitting; laundry service; dry cleaning; casino; rooms for those w/limited mobility. *In room:* A/C, TV w/in-house movies, Wi-Fi, iPod docking station, minibar, coffeemaker, hair dryer, iron, safe.

Ritz-Carlton San Juan Spa & Casino ★★★

The Ritz-Carlton is one of the most spectacular deluxe hotels in the Caribbean, set on 8 acres (3.2 hectares) of prime beachfront, within a 5-minute drive from the airport. The hotel's Continental elegance is infused with a Hispanic Caribbean flavor, bolstered by the works by prominent local artists. The most opulent public areas feature wrought-iron balustrades and crystal chandeliers.

Beautifully furnished, very large guest rooms open onto ocean views or the gardens of nearby condos. All have excellent furnishings, fine linens, and are high-tech ready. The marble bathrooms are exceptionally plush, with tub/shower combinations, scales, bathrobes, and deluxe toiletries. Preferred accommodations are in the ninth-floor Ritz-Carlton Club, which has a private lounge and personal concierge staff.

Renowned gourmet chains BLT Steak and Il Mulino of New York are both located here. The hotel also houses Puerto Rico's most stylishly elegant casinos, and one of its largest. A full range of children's activities and a great beach with lots of watersports options make this a great place for families.

Av. de los Gobernadores (State Rd.) 6961, no. 187, Isla Verde, PR 00979. ℂ 800/241-3333 or 787/253-1700. Fax 787/253-1777. www.ritzcarlton.com. 416 units. Winter $399–$769 double; off season $285–$599 double; year-round from $1,109–$1,529 suite. AE, DC, DISC, MC, V. Valet parking $22; self-parking $17. Bus: A5, B40, or C53. **Amenities:** 5 restaurants; 3 bars; nightclub; large pool; 2 tennis courts; health club; spa; children's program; salon; 24-hr. room service; babysitting; laundry service; dry cleaning; Caribbean's largest casino; rooms for those w/limited mobility. In room: A/C, TV, dataport, minibar, hair dryer, safe.

The Water Club ★★ A refreshing change from the megachain resorts of San Juan, this ultrachic boutique hotel is urbane and contemporary. This small and exclusive hotel has highly personalized and well-trained staff. Although avant-garde, the design is never off-putting. The illuminated lobby might recall *2001: A Space Odyssey,* but it's still warm and friendly. Behind glass are "waterfalls," even on the elevators, and inventive theatrical-style lighting is used to bring the outdoors inside. The one-of-a-kind glass-art doors are from Murano, the famed center of glassmaking outside Venice. Overlooking Isla Verde's best beach area, all the bedrooms are spacious and contain custom-designed beds positioned to face the ocean. Bathrooms are tiled and elegant, with tub/shower combinations. Unique features are the open-air 11th-floor exotic bar with the Caribbean's only rooftop fireplace. The pool is a level above; it's like swimming in an ocean in the sky. This hotel is super pet friendly; it offers four-legged friends complimentary doggie bags and their owners welcome drinks. Grooming, walking, and massage services are available.

Calle José M. Tartak 2, Isla Verde, Puerto Rico 00979. ℂ 888/265-6699 or 787/253-3666. Fax 787/728-3610. www.waterclubsanjuan.com. 84 units. Winter $275–$450 double; off season $209–$399 double. AE, DC, DISC, MC, V. Bus: A5 or C53. **Amenities:** Restaurant; 2 bars; outdoor rooftop pool; fitness center; Jacuzzi; limited room service; dry cleaning; nonsmoking rooms; rooms for those w/limited mobility. In room: A/C, TV, dataport, high-speed Internet, minibar, hair dryer, safe.

EXPENSIVE

Embassy Suites Hotel & Casino ★   The location is 2 blocks from the beach, and the hotel has its own water world, with waterfalls and reflecting ponds set against a backdrop of palms. As you enter, you're greeted with an aquarium, giving a tropical-resort aura to the place. The excellent accommodations are all suites, and they're comfortably furnished and roomy, with bedrooms separated from the living rooms. Each has a wet bar, a tub/shower combination bathroom, two phones, a safe, and a dining table. The most spacious suites are those with two double beds; each of the smaller suites is furnished with a king-size bed. The best view of the water is from units above the third floor. Two restaurants are on the premises, the Embassy Grill, a low-key indoor/outdoor affair, and an independently managed Outback Steakhouse branch. There's also a small-scale casino on the property.

Calle José M. Tartak 8000, Isla Verde, San Juan, PR 00979. ⓒ **800/362-2779** or 787/791-0505. Fax 787/991-7776. www.embassysuites.com. 299 suites. Winter $200–$420 1-bedroom suite, $400–$520 2-bedroom suite; off season $179–$215 1-bedroom suite, $350 2-bedroom suite. Rates include breakfast and free drinks 5:30–7:30pm. AE, DC, DISC, MC, V. Valet parking $16; self-parking $10. Bus: A5, C53, or B21. **Amenities:** 2 restaurants; 3 bars; pool; health club; car-rental desk; business center; limited room service; laundry service; coin-operated laundry; dry cleaning; small casino; rooms for those w/limited mobility. *In room:* A/C, TV, wet bar (in suites), fridge, coffeemaker, hair dryer, iron, safe, microwave.

MODERATE

Courtyard by Marriott Isla Verde Beach Resort ★ Kids   This is affordable Caribbean at its best. It's on a beautiful beach at the end of Isla Verde, with the public beach just to the east and Pine Grove beach, popular with surfers and sailors, just to the west. Close to the airport, the refurbished hotel serves meals on a wraparound veranda, and there are comfortable hammocks and beach chairs beside the pool and the beach in front. Updated comfort makes it su ..ble for business travelers, families, or the random vacationer. The 12-floor hotel rises on the site of the old Crowne Plaza. It's a big, bustling place with many amenities and midsize, well-furnished bedrooms. Art Deco furnishings dominate, and there is plenty of comfort. The casino and lobby restaurants are filled with the sounds of Latin rhythms at night. The pool and beach are great for kids. They can get surf lessons down the beach on foam boards designed for beginners.

Boca de Cangrejos Av. 7012, Isla Verde, PR 00979. ⓒ **800/791-2553** or 787/791-0404. Fax 787/791-1460. www.sjcourtyard.com. 293 units. Winter $189–$385 double, $485 suite; off season $160–$320 double, $395 suite. AE, DC, DISC, MC, V. Bus: M7. **Amenities:** 3 restaurants; ice-cream parlor; bar; pool; fitness center; kids' club; business center; high-speed Internet; limited room service; laundry service; dry cleaning; casino. *In room:* A/C, TV, dataport, minibar, hair dryer, iron, safe.

Hampton Inn (Kids) Opened in 1997, this chain hotel is set across the busy avenue from Isla Verde's sandy beachfront, far enough away to keep costs down but within a leisurely 10-minute walk of the casinos and nightlife. Two towers, with four and five floors, hold the well-maintained, well-furnished, and comfortable bedrooms. There's no restaurant on the premises and no real garden; other than a whirlpool and a swimming pool with a swim-up bar, there are very few facilities or amenities. Because of its reasonable prices and location, however, this Isla Verde newcomer could be a good choice. Families are especially fond of staying here despite the fact that there are no special children's programs; many of the rooms have two double beds, and suites have microwaves and refrigerators.

Av. Isla Verde 6530, Isla Verde, PR 00979. (C) **800/HAMPTON** (426-7866) or 787/791-8777. Fax 787/791-8757. 201 units. Winter $199–$219 double, $229 suite; off season $169–$199 double, $209 suite. Rates include breakfast bar. AE, DC, DISC, MC, V. Parking $5. Bus: A5 or C53. **Amenities:** Bar; pool; health club; whirlpool; high-speed Internet; babysitting; laundry service; dry cleaning; rooms for those w/ limited mobility. *In room:* A/C, TV, fridge (in suites), coffeemaker, hair dryer, iron, microwave (in suites).

Howard Johnson Hotel Rising eight stories above the busy traffic of Isla Verde, this chain hotel offers comfortable but small bedrooms, furnished simply with bland, modern furniture. They're done in typical motel style, with small but serviceable tub-and-shower bathrooms. Many guests carry a tote bag to the beach across the street, and then hit the bars and restaurants of the expensive hotels nearby. There's a restaurant and a pool. Though it's simple and not very personal, this is a good choice for the money. The Fontana di Roma Italian restaurant is excellent.

Av. Isla Verde 4820, Isla Verde, PR 00979. (C) **787/728-1300.** Fax 787/727-7150. www.hojo.com. 115 units. $150 double; $185 suite. AE, MC, V. Parking $6.50. Bus: A5 or C53. **Amenities:** 2 restaurants; pool; health club; laundry service; dry cleaning; rooms for those w/limited mobility. *In room:* A/C, TV, fridge, coffeemaker, hair dryer, iron.

INEXPENSIVE

The Coquí Inn (Value) This property incorporates three former guesthouses in the area (the Mango Inn, Green Isle Inn, and Casa Mathiesen). The beach is about a 10-minute walk, and you have to cross Baldorioty de Castro Expressway to get to Isla Verde's main drag and the beach (via pedestrian bridge)—but it's a real deal, and it's the nicest part of Isla Verde. Guests get access to three pools, each with terraces with lounge chairs and umbrellas. The three connected properties also offer an Asian restaurant and American–Puerto Rico cafe. You'll find free Wi-Fi, public computers, and movie rentals. Management is moving toward a green approach. Bedroom furnishings are summery, simple, and comfortable. Each has a tiled tub-and-shower bathroom.

Calle Uno 36, Villamar, Isla Verde, PR 00979. ⓒ **800/677-8860** or 787/726-8662. Fax 787/268-2415. www.coqui-inn.com. 54 units. Weekdays $89–$109 double; weekends $99–$119 double. AE, DISC, MC, V. Free parking. Bus: A5 or C53. **Amenities:** Restaurant; bar; 2 small pools; laundry service; shared areas w/microwaves and fridges; rooms for those w/limited mobility. *In room:* A/C, TV, kitchenette (in some), safe.

Where to Dine in San Juan

San Juan's fine-dining scene is the most varied and developed in the Caribbean, with excellent European, American, Italian, and Asian cuisines. Tasty Puerto Rican food has always been widely available, but now many of the island's best chefs take their hometown cuisine to new heights at some of its trendier eating establishments.

The restaurants listed in this chapter are classified first by area and then by price, using the following categories: **Very Expensive,** dinner from $50 per person; **Expensive,** dinner from $35 per person; **Moderate,** dinner from $25 per person; and **Inexpensive,** dinner under $25 per person. These categories reflect prices for an appetizer, a main course, a dessert, and a glass of wine.

1 BEST BETS

- **Best Steakhouse:** In the swanky Ritz-Carlton San Juan Hotel, **BLT Steak,** Av. de los Gobernadores 6961 (© **787/253-1700**), serves the most succulent steaks in Puerto Rico. French chef Laurent Tourondel reinvents the American steakhouse with the classic cooking techniques of his homeland, serving up aged beefs, other meats, and fresh seafood. Sauces, sides, and desserts are all heavenly remakes of your father's favorite food, and it still tastes good today.
- **Best Food Value: Bebo's Cafe,** Calle Loiza 1600 (© **787/726-1008**), has good *comida criolla,* plus steaks, sandwiches, and fruit frappes at incredibly low prices. That's why it draws crowds despite its rather slow, if well-intentioned, service. It's open all the time, nearly.
- **Best Italian Restaurant:** Across the street from Hotel El Covento, **Il Perugino,** Cristo St. 105 (© **787/722-5481**), takes you on a culinary tour of sunny Italy. Plate after plate of delectable northern Italian food is presented nightly—everything from grilled filets of fresh fish to succulent pastas. Service is first-rate, and the welcome warm.

- **Best French Restaurant:** Housed in a beautifully renovated building across the street from the Museo de Arte de Puerto Rico, **Bistro de Paris,** Plaza de Diego, Av. José de Diego 310 (© **787/998-8929**), takes elements of a classic Parisian bistro and kicks up the comfort level several notches. This is classic French cuisine with innovative flourishes, prepared and served with love and precision by talented chefs and a near-perfect waitstaff.

- **Best for a Romantic Dinner:** It's erotic meeting your lover outside the bathroom in the dimly lit, breathtaking lobby of the Museum of Art of Puerto Rico when it is closed. And you'll still have opportunities for appreciation of the arts at **Pikayo,** Av. José de Diego 299 (© **787/721-6194**), where the walls of the dining room serve as a rotating gallery, and chef Wilo Benet delivers food every bit as artful as the surroundings. Taste the masterpiece of reinvented *comida criolla* together.

- **Best Nuevo Latino Cuisine: Parrot Club,** Calle Fortaleza 363 (© **787/725-7370**), wows taste buds with its modern interpretation of Puerto Rican specialties. Even San Juan's mayor and the governor have made it their favorite. Husband-and-wife team Emilio Figueroa and Gigi Zafero borrow from a repertoire of Puerto Rican and Spanish recipes, and they also use Taíno and African influences in their cuisine. The seared tuna is the best in town, and their Creole-style flank steak is worth the trek from Condado Beach.

- **Best Burgers:** Patrons freely admit that **El Patio de Sam,** Calle San Sebastián 102 (© **787/723-1149**), is not always on target with its main dishes. But they agree on one thing: The hamburgers are the juiciest and most delectable in San Juan. The Old City atmosphere is also intriguing—with an airy courtyard and lots of local artwork.

- **Best Local Cuisine:** Devoted to *comida criolla,* **Ajili Mójili,** Av. Ashford 1006 (© **787/725-9195**), features food that islanders might have enjoyed in their mamas' kitchens. Try such specialties as *mofongos* (green plantains stuffed with veal, chicken, shrimp, or pork) or the most classic *arroz con pollo* (juicy chicken baked right in the middle of the pot of saffron rice).

- **Best Late-Night Dining:** This is where your waitress and bartender go when they get off of work. With an after-hours menu that's available until dawn, **Tantra,** Calle Fortaleza 356 in Old San Juan (© **787/977-8141**), is the place to go when midnight munchies strike. Try some tandoori chicken kabobs, coconut sesame shrimp in a mango peach salsa, or fried calamari in tomato masala sauce. There are plenty of tasty choices from the Indian-Latin fusion menu. Although the kitchen officially closes at 2am, it stays open until the crowd stops asking for more. It's a good place to find out what's going on around town as well.

- **Best Pizza:** For pizza pies like the ones from the boardwalk stands on the Jersey shore, try **Mike & Charlie's,** Av. Ashford 1024 (📞 787/723-0242). As much about the tomato as the cheese, the slices are huge, but the crust is so light, they are never overfilling. We can't say the same about the huge and delicious submarines, calzones, and pasta dishes also served here.

- **Best Ice Cream:** On a cobble-covered street in Old San Juan, **Ben & Jerry's,** Calle del Cristo 61 (📞 787/977-6882), is a block from the landmark cathedral, Catedral de San Juan, across from the entrance to Hotel El Convento. This North American chain offers the best ice cream in San Juan. Any of the 32 flavors—10 of them low-fat—tastes particularly good on hot, steamy days, when their names, such as Chubby Hubby and Phish Food, seem ironic and flavorful, depending on your point of view.

- **Best Drinks:** We get thirsty just thinking about the **San Juan Water & Beach Club,** Tartek St. 2 (📞 787/728-3666), the ultra-chic Isla Verde boutique hotel, where water gushes through the translucent walls of the lobby and elevator, which you take to **Wet.** You can have sushi and any drink you want under the stars at this rooftop bar. The elegant African, world-beat decor, which matches the music, is perfect with the ocean breeze and the view that goes all the way down the coast. Grab a seat at the long bar or one of the comfortable lounge seats.

2 OLD SAN JUAN

For the locations of Old San Juan restaurants, see the map "Where to Dine in Old San Juan" on p. 67.

VERY EXPENSIVE

Aquaviva ★★ LATINO/SEAFOOD   Located on Calle Fortaleza near Plaza Colón at the entrance of Old San Juan, this aquamarine seafood emporium has bioluminescent cocktails; a hip raw bar here features sushi and a host of ceviches. The hot and cold appetizer towers are great for small groups (fried oysters, coco-flavored shrimp, fried octopus, and calamari). How about grilled mahimahi with smoky shrimp, salsa, and coconut-poached yuca or seared medallions of halibut with a fondue of spinach and crabmeat or a succulent version of paella garnished with seafood and pork sausage?

Calle Fortaleza 364. ℂ **787/722-0665.** Reservations not accepted. Main courses $16–$45. AE, MC, V. Lunch daily 11am–4pm; dinner Mon–Wed 6–11pm, Thurs–Sat 6pm–midnight, Sun 4–11pm. Bus: A5 or C53.

Il Perugino ★★ ITALIAN   Across from Hotel El Convento, this is Puerto Rico's finest Italian restaurant, serving inspired cuisine from chef and owner Franco Seccarelli's homeland in Umbria. Homemade pastas include black fettuccine with a shellfish ragout or ricotta and spinach gnocchetti with fresh tomatoes. The shrimp salad with grilled zucchini is a sublime dish, as is the scallop and porcini mushroom salad. Seccarelli shines with his pheasant breast alla Cacciatora and his rack of lamb with fresh herbs and a rich red-wine sauce. Great desserts, a wine cellar in a converted dry well, and impeccable and friendly service round out the experience.

Cristo St. 105. ℂ **787/722-5481.** Reservations recommended. Main courses $29–$41. AE, DISC, MC, V. Thurs–Sat 11:30am–2:30pm; Tues–Sun 6:30–11pm. Bus: Old San Juan Trolley.

EXPENSIVE

Barú ★ CARIBBEAN/MEDITERRANEAN   Among the most fashionable and popular of the wave of imaginative new restaurants in Old San Juan, it has an attractive and hard-playing clientele, many of whom look like television stars. It occupies a stately looking, high-ceilinged space capped with massive timbers, fronted with a hyper-convivial mahogany bar, and decorated with paintings by such Colombia-born artistic luminaries as Botéro.

Many dishes are in the gray area between an appetizer and a main-course platter, but we started with the almond-encrusted goat cheese with Jamaican jerk mango dip and yuca chips, and sliced filet mignon. Menu items include an unusual choice of five different kinds of carpaccio (tuna, halibut, salmon, beef, or Serrano ham), citrus mahimahi ceviche, and marinated lamb chops in a paprika-and-pineapple mojo sauce.

Calle San Sebastián 150. ℂ **787/977-7107.** Reservations recommended. Main courses $15–$28. AE, MC, V. Mon–Sat 6pm–3am; Sun 6pm–midnight. Bus: Old Town Trolley.

Carli Café Concierto ★ INTERNATIONAL   The gold disk hanging on the wall of this stylish restaurant stems from its owner Carli Muñoz's previous role as a pianist for the Beach Boys. Now, guests are entertained nightly with a combination of standards, romantic jazz, and original material on his grand piano. The chef tempts visitors with an imaginative international menu, including such delights as plantain-crusted sea scallops with a coconut curry

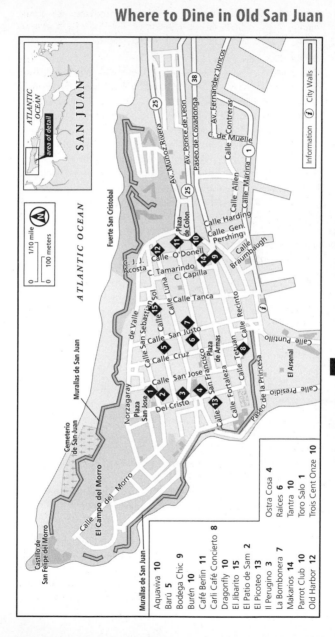

ATLANTIC
OCEAN

SAN JUAN

SAN JUAN

area of detail

ATLANTIC OCEAN

0   1/10 mile
0   100 meters

Castillo de
San Felipe del Morro

Cementerio
de San Juan

Murallas de San Juan

Calle del Campo del Morro

El Campo del Morro

Fuerte San Cristobal

Murallas de San Juan

Av. Muñoz Rivera

Av. Ponce de León

Paseo de Covadonga

Av. Fernández Juncos

C. de Muelle

Calle Marina

Calle Allen

Calle Harding

Calle Gen.
Pershing

Calle
Braumbaugh

Plaza
de Colon

Calle O'Donell

C. J. J.
Acosta

C. Tamarindo

C. Capilla

Calle Luna

Calle Tanca

Calle Recinto

Calle San Sebastián

de Valle

Calle
Sol

Calle San Justo

Calle Cruz

Calle San Jose

Calle Cristo

Plaza
San Jose

Nozagaray
Del Cristo

San Francisco

Calle San Jose

Calle Fortaleza

Plaza
de Armas

Calle Tetuan

El Arsenal

Calle Presidio

Paseo de la Princesa

El Presidio

Calle Puntilla

Calle Marina

Av. Contreras

1
2
3
4
5
6
7
8
9
10
11
12
13
14
15

Information ⓘ   City Walls

Murallas de San Juan

Aquaviva **10**
Barú **5**
Bodega Chic **9**
Burén **10**
Café Berlin **11**
Carli Café Concierto **8**
Dragonfly **10**
El Jibarito **15**
El Patio de Sam **2**
El Picoteo **13**
Il Perugino **3**
La Bombonera **7**
Makarios **14**
Parrot Club **10**
Old Harbor **12**

Ostra Cosa **4**
Raíces **6**
Tantra **10**
Toro Salo **1**
Trois Cent Onze **10**

sauce. The filet of salmon and a mouthwatering rack of lamb are among the finest main dishes. The bar, with its mahogany and brass fittings, is an ideal spot to chill out. The concert starts every night at 8pm.

Edificio Banco Popular, Calle Tetuàn 206, off Plazoleta Rafael Carrión. ℂ 787/725-4927. Reservations recommended. Main courses $16–$36. AE, V. Mon–Fri 3:30–11pm; Sat 4–11:30pm. Bus: A5 or C53.

Parrot Club ★★ NUEVO LATINO/CARIBBEAN This Nuevo Latino bistro and bar, owned by husband-and-wife team Emilio Figueroa and Gigi Zafero, kicked off a culinary revival in Old San Juan and remains one of its most sought-after restaurants. A modern blend of the Spanish, Taíno, and African influences behind traditional Puerto Rican cookery, Parrot Club is housed in a stately 1902 building transformed by bright tropical colors and spirited artwork. The delectable dishes are as good as anything at more renowned Nuevo Latino restaurants in New York and Miami, and the atmosphere is kept upbeat with friendly, efficient service and good music (with live Latin jazz and salsa a few nights a week and something fine on the sound system all the time). The updated *churrasco* (grilled beef), Latino crab cakes, and tuna in dark rum sauce are just a few of the standouts; the drink special is a "Parrot Passion," made from lemon-flavored rum, triple sec, oranges, and passion fruit.

Calle Fortaleza 363. ℂ 787/725-7370. Reservations not accepted. Main courses $18–$36 at dinner, $12–$20 at lunch. AE, DC, MC, V. Daily 11am–4pm and 6–11pm. Closed 2 weeks in Sept. Bus: A5 or C53.

Toro Salao ★★ SPANISH TAPAS With dark wood and Spanish colonial architecture, bullfighting posters and splashes of red, this is the kind of place Ernest Hemingway would have written home about. Toro Salao, "the salty bull" in Spanish, is another restaurant by Emilio Figueroa and Gigi Zaferos (owners of the Parrot Club and Aguaviva, among others) that seamlessly matches the cuisine with the restaurant ambience. We gorged on a Spanish flatbread pizza with artichokes and Mediterranean olives; a *papas bravas* (spicy potatoes) redux; and seared octopus with sun-dried tomato vinaigrette and mussels in a chunky green salsa that were crisp and clean. Also recommended are the sweet veal meatballs with romesco sauce, plantains, and *churrasco*. Full meals (like paella seafood with chicken and sausage) can also be had. Try the sangria—there's an entire menu that has several inventive offerings, including a tropical fruit version, which adds flavor without ever losing the essence of this Spanish tavern standard.

Calle Tetuàn 367. ℂ 787/722-3330. Reservations not accepted. Tapas $12–$25; main courses $22–$35. AE, MC, V. Mon–Sat 6pm–midnight. Bus: A5 or C53.

Bodega Chic ★ ⟨Finds⟩ FRENCH BISTRO This small French/ Algerian bistro blends Mediterranean and Caribbean flavors with reasonable prices and unpretentious, friendly service. Chef and partner Christophe Gourdain trained with chef Jean-Georges Vonegerichten and learned well, crafting such appetizers as the baked goat cheese croustillant with eggplant caviar and the grilled calamari. The hangar steak with sautéed potatoes and string beans is as close to perfection as the fresh mussels Provençal. The braised lamb shank is also worthy, and the roasted chicken breast in curry banana sauce is much better than it sounds. The high-ceilinged dining room and small adjacent barroom open out onto Calle Cristo just around the corner from the popular Calle San Sebastián. Desserts include a fantastic crème brûlée and warm chocolate cake.

Calle Cristo 51. ⟨✆⟩ **787/722-0124.** Reservations recommended. Main courses $15–$26. AE, MC, V. Tues–Fri 6pm–midnight; Sun 11:30am–4pm. Bus: Old Town Trolley.

Burén ★ ⟨Value⟩ INTERNATIONAL This friendly, funky little place serves up unique, flavorful pizza, plus pastas and Latino grilled steaks—and inventive entrees are surprisingly sophisticated as well. The main bar and adjoining lounge area are brightly colored, while the back courtyard is all about earth tones. The *plátano* soup and *tostones* stuffed with shrimp in tomato sauce are excellent starters, as are the classic Greek salad and the spinach salad served with mozzarella cheese and passion-fruit dressing. Pizza lovers will be happy with the usual ingredients, or some creative combinations: The Tamarindo combines prosciutto, sun-dried tomatoes, and manchego cheese, while the Las Monjas has feta cheese, black olives, tomatoes, and peppers. If you can resist the pizza, try the veal *osso buco* in a basil-rosemary emulsion served with fettuccini. Juicy pork medallions are served in a peppercorn-pineapple sauce.

Calle Cristo 103. ⟨✆⟩ **787/977-5023.** Reservations recommended Sat–Sun. Main courses $16–$26. AE, DC, DISC, MC, V. Daily 6–11pm. Bus: Old Town Trolley.

Café Berlin INTERNATIONAL Other than the hardworking staff, there's very little about this place that's particularly Hispanic. What you'll get is a corner of central Europe, identified by a *Jugendstil*-inspired sign, serving coffee, pastries, and a limited array of light platters such as pasta, on tiny marble-top tables like what you'd expect in Vienna. Paintings, all of them for sale, are displayed on scarlet-colored walls, and lavishly caloric pastries are arranged behind glass display cases. More substantial, rib-sticking fare includes salmon in

An Authentic *Criollo* Restaurant

When you've had too many hotel meals or patronized too many first-class restaurants and want something authentic, head for **El Jibarito,** Calle del Sol 280 (© **787/725-8375**), where locals flock for food like their mamas used to make.

Set within a residential section of Old San Juan that's a few blocks removed from the showcase-style tourist haunts, this is a bustling local restaurant that's known to virtually everyone in the Old City for its avid loyalty to the kind of cuisine that many sanjuaneros remember from their child-hoods. Established as a testimonial to their rustic (*jíbaro*) backgrounds by Pedro and Aida Ruiz, it's a high-ceilinged, decent, and very clean enclave of brightly painted walls (mostly pinks and tones of green), paper napkins, solid por-celain, and completely unpretentious *criolla* cuisine. Menu items focus on rich, sometimes starchy, food that kept Puerto Rico alive throughout the early 20th century. Exam-ples include fritters studded with pieces of seasoned pork, cube steak with onions, conch salad, oven-baked grouper, fried red snapper, chicken filets with garlic, and shrimp in garlic. A whopping portion of *mofongo* (chopped plantains with butter and seasonings) can be ordered as a folkloric side dish, and salad comes with every main course. Dessert might include a genuinely excellent wedge of coconut flan. Service is attentive, unpretentious, and extremely polite. Main courses cost $8 to $18 and are served daily from 10am to 9pm. American Express, Diners Club, MasterCard, and Visa are accepted.

orange- and garlic-flavored herb broth, scallops in pesto sauce, and turkey breast Stroganoff.

Plaza de Colón 407. © **787/722-5205.** Main courses $8–$19. AE, MC, V. Mon–Fri 10am–10pm; Sat–Sun 8am–10pm. Bus: Old Town Trolley.

Dragonfly ★★ LATIN/ASIAN FUSION   One of San Juan's hot-test restaurants, the place has been compared to both an Old San Francisco bordello and a Shanghai opium den—descriptions that evoke as much the lusty appeal and addictive power of its cuisine as the red-walled interior, a world of fringed lamps and gilded mirrors behind beaded curtains. It's good for a late meal, as the portion sizes, called *platos* or plates, are somewhere between appetizers and entrees.

We always order the marinated churrasco and the pork and plantain dumplings with orange dipping sauce. Other standouts: seared tuna in green peppercorn sauce, tempura rock shrimp tacos with chunky salsa, and the Chino Latino lo mein. This is the island's first Latin-Asian menu, and it remains one of the best anywhere. There's also a lounge and full sushi bar, but as one of the city's trendiest eateries, crowds keep filling the place.

Calle Fortaleza 364. © **787/977-3886.** Reservations not accepted. Main courses $8–$30. AE, MC, V. Mon–Wed 6–11pm; Thurs–Sat 6pm–midnight. Bus: A5 or C53.

El Patio de Sam AMERICAN/PUERTO RICAN   Established in 1953, this joint has survived several generations of clients, who came here for booze, fantastic juicy burgers, Puerto Rican food, and dialogue. Dining usually occurs in a skylit garden-style courtyard in back where there is no view but a welcome sense of calm, with tropical plants and beautiful local artwork. In addition to those burgers, you can also order more sophisticated dishes such as Puerto Rican–style fried pork, ceviche, shellfish paella, chicken and rice, and *churrasco* (Argentine-style grilled meats).

Calle San Sebastián 102 (across from the Iglesia de San José). © **787/723-1149.** Sandwiches, burgers, and salads $9–$11; platters $13–$35. AE, DISC, MC, V. Daily noon–1am. Bus: Old Town Trolley.

El Picoteo ★★ (Moments) SPANISH   Spilling across a front and interior terrace overlooking the courtyard of the historic El Convento Hotel, this is the best place in the Old City to savor some drinks and tapas, while watching the action near Calle San Sebastián. On most nights, there's a parade of people walking up and down Calle Cristo in front of the restaurant, as they go back and forth to the bars and restaurants just up the hill. We love the spicy potatoes *(papas bravas),* shrimp in garlic sauce, and the brick-oven pizza, but there are also full meals like seafood paella. With 80 tapas to choose from, there's also real Spanish flavor here, in such dishes as garbanzo salad, sausages, various ceviches, fresh octopus, and the best selection of cheese in the city. The setting amid Spanish colonial facades and wildly blooming bougainvillea is one of the Old City's most charmed. It's equally inviting for a weekend lunch. Try the champagne-laced sangria. Dinner is festive, accompanied by salsa and lights in the courtyard.

In El Convento hotel, Calle del Cristo 100. © **787/723-9202.** Reservations recommended. Main courses $6–$17; paella $20–$35. AE, MC, V. Tues–Sun noon–midnight. Bus: Old Town Trolley.

Makarios GREEK/LEBANESE   Set above a sometimes raucous cafe-bar, a few steps from piers 1, 2, and 3 in Old San Juan, this is the only restaurant in Old San Juan that serves Lebanese and, to a lesser degree, Greek food. To reach it, you'll climb a flight of stairs immediately adjacent to the entrance to reach the second-floor dining room. Here, beneath a gracefully arched ceiling of a dining room trimmed in varnished wood, you can order good-tasting dishes that include baba ghanouj, hummus, falafel, baked halibut, salmon with honey-mustard dressing, grilled shrimp, grilled snapper, shish kabob, and cous-cous. On Friday and Saturday there is belly dancing from 9 to 11pm. The high-energy cafe is on the establishment's street level, where blaring music combines traditional Greek and Arabic rhythms with a danceable house and garage beat. It also serves from a menu that includes simple selections from the dinner menu (kabobs, hummus, falafel, and so forth) as well as tasty brick-oven pizza.

Calle Tetuàn 361. (C) **787/723-8653.** Reservations not necessary. Main courses $15–$24. AE, DISC, MC, V. Daily noon–midnight (until 3am Fri–Sat). Bus: A5 or C53.

Old Harbor Brewery Steak and Lobster House ★ AMERI-CAN

San Juan's only microbrewery also has top-drawer tavern fare in an upscale mariner setting. Brewmaster Brad Mortensen handcrafts five distinct house beers, as well as seven seasonal beers, on the premises in state-of-the-art brewing facilities. The restaurant specializes in top-quality steaks and fresh Puerto Rican spiny lobster. The cuts are served steakhouse-style with a choice of sauces (we recommend the mushroom and chimichurri) and a la carte sides (our favorites are the lyonnaise potatoes and asparagus with béarnaise). The restaurant dates to the 1920s, when it housed the New York Federal Bank, and it was beautifully restored before opening in 2005. A classic tavern setup surrounds the elegant brew vats, but the place is formal, with fully dressed tables, classic black-and-white tiles, and metal and wooden finishings.

Calle Tizol 202 (near Recinto Sur). (C) **787/721-2100.** Reservations recommended. Platters and main courses $13–$38. AE, MC, V. Daily 8am–7pm. Bus: A5 or C53.

Ostra Cosa ★ (Finds) ECLECTIC/SEAFOOD

This artfully sensual restaurant is one of Old San Juan's most romantic, set in a colonial courtyard surrounded by a 16th-century building that was once the home of the colony's governor. With domesticated quail, chirping tree frogs, and a massive quenepe tree, it's far removed from the cares of the city. Former advertising executive Alberto Nazario, a lifestyle guru who mingles New Age thinking with culinary techniques to promote love, devotion, and a heightened sexuality, created Ostra Cosa. The ceviche is superb; the small grilled (still-shelled) prawns were tasty but difficult (and a bit messy). But it is the conch, known as Caribbean Viagra, that rates "Wow!" or "Ay Ay Ay!"

Calle del Cristo 154. ✆ **787/722-2672.** Reservations recommended. Main courses $18–$29. AE, MC, V. Sun–Wed noon–10pm; Fri–Sat noon–11pm. Bus: Old Town Trolley.

Tantra ★ Ⓥⓐⓛⓤⓔ INDO-LATINO   Set in the heart of "restaurant row" on Calle Fortaleza, it has become famous for a sophisticated fusion of Latino with South Indian cuisine. Its chef and owner, Indian-born Ramesh Pillai, oversees a blend of slow-cooked tandoori cuisine from South India with Puerto Rico–derived spices, flavors, and ingredients. All of this occurs within a warm, candlelit environment that focuses on Indian handicrafts and Hindu and Buddhist symbols. Menu highlights include sesame masala-crusted sushi tuna with peanut sauce, fried coconut sesame jumbo shrimp with Indian noodles, chicken tikka masala with nan (flatbread), and rice and chicken rolls with passion-fruit sauce. The late kitchen and inviting ambience draws a crowd; the bar is always lively.

Calle Fortaleza 356. ✆ **787/977-8141.** Reservations only for groups. Main courses $13–$19. AE, MC, V. Mon 3pm–3am; Tues–Sat noon–3pm; Sun noon–midnight. Bus: A5 or C53.

INEXPENSIVE

La Bombonera ★ Ⓥⓐⓛⓤⓔ PUERTO RICAN   This place offers exceptional value in its homemade pastries, well-stuffed sandwiches, and endless cups of coffee—and it has done so since 1902. Its atmosphere evokes turn-of-the-20th-century Castille transplanted to the New World. The food is authentically Puerto Rican, homemade, and inexpensive, with regional dishes such as rice with squid, roast leg of pork, and seafood *asopao* (a thick rice soup). For dessert, you might select an apple, pineapple, or prune pie, or one of many types of flan. Service is polite, if a bit rushed, and the place fills up quickly at lunchtime.

Calle San Francisco 259. ✆ **787/722-0658.** Reservations recommended. American breakfast $4.50–$6.45; main courses $6–$18. AE, MC, V. Daily 7:30am–8pm. Bus: Old Town Trolley.

Raíces ★ PUERTO RICAN   Don't let the apparent touristy trappings fool you; it's not the cheapest meal in town, but it's among the tastiest and most authentic, and we recommend it for a big taste of Puerto Rican cuisine. The kitchen knows its stuff, so enjoy the rustic Puerto Rican setting—beautifully outfitted with local arts and crafts—and the waitresses and waiters decked out in the beautiful folkloric dress. The "typical festival" combines a number of classic island treats, like meat turnovers, stuffed fried plantain fritters, codfish fritters, and mashed cassava, but you'll also want to try the rich plantain soup. The *mofongo* comes stuffed with the typical chicken or shrimp, but the options here range to breaded pork, skirt steak, and Creole-style mahimahi. Coconut flan and guava cheesecake are other hits. Traditional Puerto Rican music, with occasional live entertainment, further complements the experience.

Calle Recinto Sur 315. (℃ **787/289-2121.** Reservations not necessary. Main courses $10–$26. AE, MC, V. Mon–Fri 11am–4pm and 6–10pm; Sat 11am–11pm; Sun noon–11pm. Bus: A5 or C53.

3 PUERTA DE TIERRA

EXPENSIVE

Morton's of Chicago ★★ STEAKHOUSE   Beef lovers, from Al Gore to Liza Minnelli, have known since 1978 they'll get quality meats perfectly cooked at Morton's. Carts laden with everything from prime Midwestern beefsteaks to succulent lamb or veal chops are wheeled around for your selection. And Morton's has the island's best prime rib. The bartenders make stiff drinks, and the waiters tempt you with their fresh fish, lobster, and chicken dishes. The vegetables here are among the freshest in the area. The house specialty is a 24-ounce porterhouse. Appetizers include perfectly cooked jumbo shrimp with cocktail sauce and smoked Pacific salmon. For dessert, gravitate to one of the soufflés, like raspberry or Grand Marnier. Other fine restaurants at the Caribe Hilton include **Palmeras** and **Madrid-San Juan.**

In the Caribe Hilton, Calle Los Rosales. (℃ **787/977-6262.** Reservations required. Main courses $20–$40. AE, DC, DISC, MC, V. Daily 5–11pm. Bus: B21.

INEXPENSIVE

El Hamburger ★ BURGERS   This no-frills burger stand offers tasty grilled burgers and hot dogs, cold beer, and perfectly golden french fries and onion rings. From its perch overlooking the Atlantic on the oceanfront drive into San Juan, the grill has become a late-night local favorite for those leaving the bars of Old San Juan and is also popular for a bite during work or after the beach. A really good, cheap opportunity to soak up some real local atmosphere, the ramshackle wooden establishment is the kind of burger joint that has disappeared throughout much of the United States with the advent of the modern fast-food restaurant. One of its joys lives on here with a selection of condiments, from onions to relish to thick tomatoes to pickles, which is brought to your table with your burger. There's a patch of palm trees on the undeveloped coastal bluff across the street,

and the ocean breeze flows all through the white wooden building. It's
always packed, but service is still super fast and the conversation
animated.

Muñoz Rivera 402. ℭ **787/721-4269.** Reservations not accepted. Burgers from
$3.50. No credit cards. Sun–Thurs 11am–11pm; Fri–Sat 11am–1am. Bus: A-5 or
M-1.

4 CONDADO

VERY EXPENSIVE

Budatai ★★★ LATIN/ASIAN   The new home of Puerto Rico's
"Iron Chef" mixes local flavors with Asian ingredients to deliver one
of San Juan's finest dining experiences. Scrumptiously situated in an
Art Deco town house overlooking an oceanfront park at the heart of
Condado's redevelopment revival, Budatai's muted brown interior is
as stylish as the designer boutiques surrounding it. With wall-size
windows inside and a rooftop terrace, diners have great views and are
pampered with oversize tables and leather chairs. Chef Roberto
Trevino, who fell just short against Mario Batali on the Food Network's Iron Chef America (the secret ingredient was catfish), reworks
the Nuevo Latino and Asian fusion concepts he developed at Old San
Juan's Parrot Club, Dragonfly, and Aguaviva restaurants and kicks up
the portion sizes. Get started with the sesame-crusted, pork-wrapped
asparagus with a soy mayonnaise, an explosion of flavor and texture;
or if sushi's your thing, the geisha roll—lobster, cream cheese, jicama,
and meringue kisses. The soy-glazed salmon with coconut hash main
course artfully balances the salty and sweet, while the veal sirloin with
lobster-mashed Asian potatoes is as rich as it sounds. The second-
floor bar and lounge is a hot spot for the city's young and beautiful,
especially on weekends.

Av. Ashford 1056, Condado. ℭ **787/725-6919.** Main courses $24–$35. AE, MC, V.
Daily 11am–midnight. Bus: A5 or C53.

EXPENSIVE

Ajili Mójili ★ PUERTO RICAN/CREOLE   This restaurant serves
comida criolla, the starchy, down-home cuisine that developed on the
island a century ago. It's housed in a huge two-story building on the
Condado Lagoon. Locals come here for a taste of the food they
enjoyed at their mother's knee, like *mofongo* (green plantain casserole
stuffed with veal, chicken, shrimp, or pork), *arroz con pollo* (chicken
and rice), *medallones de cerdo encebollado* (pork loin sautéed with
onions), *carne mechada* (beef rib-eye stuffed with ham), and *lechon*

asado con maposteado (roast pork with rice and beans). Wash it all down with an ice-cold bottle of local beer. The staff will eagerly describe menu items in colloquial English.

Av. Ashford 1006. ✆ **787/725-9195.** Reservations recommended. Main courses $18–$39; lunch $13–$26. AE, DISC, MC, V. Mon–Thurs 11:45am–3pm and 6–10pm; Fri noon–3pm and 6–11pm; Sat 11:45am–3:30pm and 6–11pm; Sun 12:30–4pm and 6–10pm. Bus: A5 or C53.

Bodega Compostela ★★ TAPAS/WINE CELLAR   This established Galician restaurant, which for years has served the finest Spanish food in the capital, was reborn this year as a chic wine and tapas bar without losing anything in the transition. Diners walk through an accompanying wine cellar, with a translucent floor over corks, to a long bar area, or retreat back to the dining room. There are over 50 tapas, or appetizers, served here, ranging from crispy goat cheese–mesclun salad to lentil stew with chorizo and pancetta to octopus carpaccio with sun-dried tomatoes. Seafood selections are plentiful, but we also gorged on the red pepper stuffed with barbecued Spanish sausage and potato stuffed with lamb shank confit. For those wanting more traditional meals, Compostela still offers the outstanding dishes grounded in Spanish traditions that garnered it such a strong reputation over the years, like seared tuna with apple julienne and couscous, or a large platter of rice with veal, pork, sausage, rabbit, and chicken for two. There's a daily dessert special. The wine cellar, comprising some 10,000 bottles, is one of the most impressive in San Juan.

Av. Condado 106. ✆ **787/724-6099.** Reservations required. Tapas $3–$26; main courses $34–$45. AE, DC, MC, V. Mon–Fri noon–3pm; Mon–Sat 6:30–10:30pm. Bus: M2.

Niché ★★ (Finds) LATIN FUSION   Just inside an Asian garden, this small restaurant makes a big impression, wowing guests with its boldly modern, yet natural design, and a menu as awesome in taste as audacity. The single-room restaurant is outfitted with a small bar and tables with seating for 20 or so diners. Its spare design, employing natural wood, glass, and metal, makes it feel much bigger than it is. Strolling through the lobby of the quiet guesthouse on a residential block to get here, we at first felt as if we stumbled onto a fabulous party just steps from the choicest beach in Condado. Chef Juan Camacho delivers dishes as awe-inspiring as the surroundings, preparing world cuisine heavy on rare meats and seafood with down-home Puerto Rican flavor.

At the Acacia Boutique Hotel, Calle Taft 8. ✆ **787/725-0669.** Reservations recommended. Main courses $20–$40. AE, MC, V. Daily 6–11pm. Bus: A5 or C53.

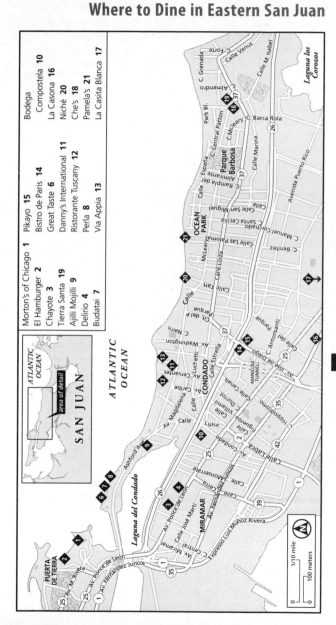

Morton's of Chicago **1**
El Hamburger **2**
Chayote **3**
Tierra Santa **19**
Ajilli Mojilli **9**
Delirio **4**
Budatai **7**

Pikayo **15**
Bistro de Paris **14**
Great Taste **6**
Danny's International **11**
Ristorante Tuscany **12**
Perla **8**
Via Appia **13**

Bodega
Compostela **10**
La Casona **16**
Niché **20**
Che's **18**
Pamela's **21**
La Casita Blanca **17**

ATLANTIC
OCEAN

SAN JUAN

area of detail

ATLANTIC
OCEAN

Ristorante Tuscany ★★ NORTHERN ITALIAN The Marriott's showcase restaurant continues to rack up culinary awards, with entrees like grilled veal chops with shallots and glaze of Madeira, and grilled chicken breast in cream sauce with chestnuts, asparagus, and brandy, surrounded with fried artichokes. The seafood selections are excellent, especially the fresh red snapper sautéed in olive oil, garlic, parsley, and lemon juice. The risottos prepared al dente in the traditional northern Italian style are the finest on the island, especially the one made with seafood and herbs. The cold and hot appetizers are virtual meals unto themselves, with such favorites as grilled polenta with sausages or fresh clams and mussels simmered in herb-flavored tomato broth.

In the San Juan Marriott Resort, Av. Ashford 1309. ⓒ **787/722-7000.** Reservations recommended. Main courses $20–$34. AE, DC, DISC, MC, V. Daily 6–11pm. Bus: A5 or C53.

MODERATE

Most main courses in the restaurants below are at the low end of the price scale. These restaurants each have only two or three dishes that are expensive, almost invariably involving shellfish.

Great Taste ★★ CHINESE This is the place where the island's Chinese community goes to eat dim sum, and with good reason, as this restaurant has been serving up some of the best Chinese food on the island for decades. About 5 years ago, it also installed a sushi bar and added a few menu items. Set in a 1970s condominium with a tattered facade, the dining room is spacious, comfortable, and bright, with Japanese prints, huge lobster tanks, and an enviable view over the Condado lagoon. We come here for the Chinese, and everything we've tried from the cashew chicken to the Peking duck to the shrimp in lobster sauce is excellent, but we really come for the dim sum: the sticky rice in lotus leaf, skewered beef, and steamed vegetable dumplings. Sunday specials attract droves of diners from the local Chinese community and elsewhere with a refined sense of what good dim sum is all about.

Av. Ashford 1018. ⓒ **787/721-8111.** Reservations recommended. Main courses $10–$45. AE, MC, V. Daily 11am–midnight. Bus: A5 or C53.

INEXPENSIVE

Cielito Lindo Ⓥalue MEXICAN This restaurant retains moderate prices and an utter lack of pretension, despite the expensive Condado real estate that surrounds it. Something about it might remind you of a low-slung house in Puebla, Mexico, home of owner Jaime Pandal, who maintains a vigilant position from a perch at the cash register. Walls are outfitted with an intriguing mix of Mexican arts and crafts and ads for popular tequilas and beer. None of the selections has changed since the restaurant was founded, a policy that long-term clients find reassuring. The place is mobbed, especially on weekends, with those looking for heaping portions of well-prepared, standardized Mexican food. Examples include fajitas of steak or chicken; strips of filet steak sautéed with green peppers and onions, covered with tomatoes and spicy gravy; enchiladas of chicken or cheese, covered with cheese and served with sour cream; and several kinds of tacos.

Av. Magdalena 1108. ✆ **787/723-5597.** Reservations recommended for dinner. Main courses $5–$20. AE, MC, V. Mon–Fri 11am–11pm; Sat–Sun 5–11pm. Bus: A5 or C53.

Danny's International Restaurant PIZZA CAFE   Don't expect atmosphere, but you can sit at the tables out on the front terrace and watch the street parade down Condado's main drag. The pizzas are thick and tasty, and there's an extensive selection, including the *mariscos,* which has mussels, calamari, shrimp, octopus, and a special sauce, and the *bomba,* with local sausage, olives, hot peppers, and blue cheese. There's also a complete menu of hot Italian subs and cold subs, a variety of cheese steaks, and burgers and club sandwiches. Skip the few Italian entree selections, which compare to the offerings right across the street. The pizza is excellent, however. The place is also one of the better restaurants serving American-style breakfasts near major area lodgings like the Marriott and the Ambassador and guesthouses like El Canario. Tables are spread throughout a single dining room, and there's a round bar filled with newspapers and outfitted with televisions you can eat at from morning to night.

Av. Ashford 1351. ✆ **787/724-0501** or 724-2734. Reservations not accepted. Main courses $7–$15. AE, MC, V. Daily 7am–1am. Bus: A5 or C53.

Via Appia ★ PIZZA/ITALIAN   A favorite of sanjuaneros with a craving for Italian, Via Appia offers praiseworthy food at affordable prices. Its pizzas are among the best on the island, and basic pasta dishes like baked ziti, lasagna, and spaghetti taste like somebody's Italian grandmother prepared them. However, the restaurant really shows its stuff with dishes like clams posillipo, veal and peppers, broiled sirloin with red-wine mushroom sauce, and the delectable chicken française. The house sangria is tasty and packs a punch, and the house wine is tasty and helps keep a meal here in the budget category. A wine bar and more formal dining room have been added to the original deli-like main building, but the place to sit is on one of the two terraces fronting the establishment.

Av. Ashford 1350. ✆ **787/725-8711.** Pizza and main courses $9–$16. AE, MC, V. Mon–Fri 11am–11pm; Sat–Sun 11am–midnight. Bus: A5 or C53.

EXPENSIVE

Chayote ★ PUERTO RICAN/INTERNATIONAL   The cuisine of this restaurant is among the most innovative in San Juan. It draws local business leaders, government officials, and visiting celebs like Sylvester Stallone and Melanie Griffith. It's an artsy, modern, base-ment-level bistro in a surprisingly obscure hotel (the Olimpo). The restaurant changes its menu every 3 months, but you might find appetizers like a yuca turnover stuffed with crabmeat and served with mango and papaya chutney, or ripe plantain stuffed with chicken and served with fresh tomato sauce. For a main dish, you might try red-snapper filet with citrus vinaigrette made of passion fruit, orange, and lemon. An exotic touch appears in the pork filet seasoned with dried fruits and spices in tamarind sauce and served with green banana and taro-root timbale. To finish off your meal, there's nothing better than the mango flan served with macerated strawberries.

In the Olimpo Hotel, Av. Miramar 603. (✆) **787/722-9385.** Reservations recom-mended. Main courses $21–$28. AE, MC, V. Tues–Fri noon–2:30pm; Tues–Sat 7–10:30pm. Bus: A5.

Deliro ★★★ (Finds) NUEVO LATINO   The latest venture by the godfather of Nuevo Latino cuisine is his boldest and tastiest yet—and one of the prettiest restaurants in San Juan. The restaurant rambles through three rooms of a wooden, century-old manor house made modern with boudoir red and flat gray interiors, steel bead curtains, and other metallic decor—yet, like Ayala's cuisine, the design man-ages to remain true to the building's traditional, classic roots. Ayala calls his food Puerto Rican cuisine influenced by flavors of the world and inspired by his life experiences in South America, Africa, Asia, and Europe. The menu changes seasonally to enable the use of the freshest ingredients. We started with grouper ceviche salad with New World sweet potatoes and corn and avocado in a pomegranate honey dressing, plus duck meatballs in a Moroccan sauce with balsamic and passion-fruit extract with Spanish almonds. The roasted cod filet was served in a Puerto Rican celeriac purée, with leeks and sweet pea cream, while the beef tenderloin was bathed in a mushroom Proven-çal sauce. The signature dish is probably the pan-seared tuna with bacon crust, served with lime risotto in a Parmesan broth. Ayala is a serious mixologist as well; two recent creations are the Delirium Tre-mens (beet-infused white rum, yuzu lime, and rosemary) and the Caribbean Breeze (white rum, ginger juice, cream of tartar, and lime juice). We can't wait to return. Deliro occasionally hosts cooking workshops and other special events.

Av. Ponce de León 762. 📞 **787/722-0444** or 722-6042. Reservations recommended. Main courses $20–$40. AE, MC, V. Tues–Thurs noon–3:30pm and 6–10:30pm; Fri noon–3:30pm and 6–11:30pm; Sat 6–11:30pm. Bus: M1 or A5.

6 SANTURCE & OCEAN PARK

VERY EXPENSIVE

Bistro de Paris ★★ FRENCH   This elegant version of a classic Paris bistro has moved to freshly restored quarters across from Puerto Rico's beautiful art museum, but the growing legend of its classic French cuisine continues to attract a huge local following. The restrained beige-and-green bistro has a front terrace under shaded awnings and a dining room with huge glass windows and doors all around. Roomy and comfortable chairs and tables are the only things not authentic about the place. Basic genre dishes like French onion soup, niçoise salad, and mussels Provençal are executed with perfection. The boneless whole trout in meunière sauce was the best fish one member of our party ever tried, and the shrimp blazed with pastis, ratatouille, and sun-dried tomatoes also knocked some socks off. A big question each night is whether to go for the strip loin with tomatoes Provençal or the steak au poivre. The crème brûlée is fantastic, but the warm apple tart also reins supreme.

Plaza de Diego, Av. José de Diego 310. 📞 **787/998-8929.** Reservations recommended. Main courses $25–$37; weekend brunch $17. AE, MC, V. Sun and Tues–Thurs noon–10pm; Fri–Sat noon–midnight. Bus: A5.

La Casona ★ SPANISH/INTERNATIONAL   In a turn-of-the-20th-century mansion surrounded by gardens, La Casona offers the kind of dining usually found in Madrid, complete with a strolling guitarist. The much-renovated but still charming place draws some of the most fashionable diners in Puerto Rico. Paella marinara, prepared for two or more, is a specialty, as is *zarzuela de mariscos* (seafood medley). Or you might select filet of grouper in Basque sauce, octopus vinaigrette, *osso buco,* or rack of lamb. Grilled red snapper is a specialty, and you can order it with almost any sauce you want, although the chef recommends one made from olive oil, herbs, lemon, and toasted garlic. The cuisine here has both flair and flavor.

Calle San Jorge 609 (at the corner of Av. Fernández Juncos). 📞 **787/727-2717.** Reservations required. Main courses $25–$35. AE, DC, MC, V. Mon–Fri noon–3pm; Mon–Sat 6–11:30pm. Bus: M1 or A5.

Pikayo ★★★ (**Moments**) PUERTO RICAN FUSION   This is an ideal place to go for the next generation of Puerto Rican fusion cuisine. Pikayo not only keeps up with the latest culinary trends, but it also often sets them, thanks to the inspired guidance of owner and celebrity chef Wilo Benet. Formal but not stuffy, and winner of more culinary awards than virtually any other restaurant in Puerto Rico, Pikayo is a specialist in the *criolla* cuisine of the colonial age, emphasizing the Spanish, Indian, and African elements in its unusual recipes. Appetizers include a dazzling array of taste explosions: Try shrimp spring rolls with peanut *sofrito* sauce; crab cake with aioli; or perhaps a ripe plantain, goat-cheese, and onion tart. Main-course delights feature charred rare yellowfin tuna with onion *escabeche* and red-snapper filet with sweet-potato purée served with foie gras butter. Our favorite remains the grilled shrimp with polenta and barbecue sauce made with guava.

In the Museum of Art of Puerto Rico, Av. José de Diego 299. (**€**) **787/721-6194.** Reservations recommended. Main courses $28–$40; fixed-price menus $65. AE, DC, MC, V. Tues–Fri noon–3pm; Mon–Sat 6–11pm. Bus: A5.

EXPENSIVE

Pamela's ★ (**Finds**) CARIBBEAN FUSION   One of San Juan's new oceanfront restaurants, the food here matches its impressive setting on a white-sand beach free of the high-rises that dominate much of the city's coast. The menu takes flavors from distinct Caribbean cuisines and wraps them around classic Continental fare. The result is appetizers like green lip mussels served in *sofrito* (a Puerto Rican blend of onion, garlic, sweet peppers, and herbs) and spicy tomato sauce and plantain-crusted calamari with toasted African peanut and chili vinaigrette. Main courses include roasted chicken over caramelized ripe plantain in a coriander au jus and grilled lamb chops with dark rum and star anise sauce. Diners can eat in a courtyard, marked by hand-painted tiles and stone fountains, or take a table under a palm tree outside and listen to the rumble of the ocean. Tasty snacks—like club sandwiches stuffed with barbecued shrimp and cilantro-flavored mayonnaise or Jamaican jerk chicken—and a full-service bar make this a great spot for a beach break, too.

In the Número 1 Guest House, Calle Santa Ana 1, Ocean Park. (**€**) **787/726-5010.** Reservations recommended. Lunch $8–$24; main courses $15–$35. AE, MC, V. Daily noon–3pm and 7–10:30pm. Tapas daily 3–7pm. Bus: A5 or C53.

INEXPENSIVE

Repostería Kasalta (**Value**) SPANISH/PUERTO RICAN   This is the most widely known of San Juan's cafeterias/bakeries/delicatessens. You'll enter a cavernous room flanked with sun-flooded windows and a long row of display cases filled with meats, sausages, and pastries appropriate to the season. Patrons line up to place their orders at a cash register, then carry their selections to one of the many tables. Knowledge of Spanish is helpful but not essential. Among the selections are steaming bowls of Puerto Rico's best *caldo gallego*, a hearty soup laden with collard greens, potatoes, and sausage slices, served in thick earthenware bowls with hunks of bread. Also popular are Cuban sandwiches (sliced pork, cheese, and fried bread); steak sandwiches; a savory octopus salad; and an assortment of perfectly cooked omelets. Paella Valenciano is a Sunday favorite.

Av. McLeary 1966. © **787/727-7340.** Reservations not accepted. Full American breakfast $3.50–$5; soups $3–$6; sandwiches $4.50–$6; platters $4–$22. AE, DC, MC, V. Daily 6am–10pm. Bus: A5 or C53.

7 NEAR OCEAN PARK

EXPENSIVE

Che's ARGENTINE This established Argentine steakhouse re-creates some of the color and drama of the Argentine pampas in a relaxed, informal atmosphere. You'll get one of the best *churassacos*, grilled flank steak, in the city. If you're not in the mood for beef, your options run toward pasta, seafood, and chicken dishes. These, along with the standard sides and desserts, are perfectly prepared. There's nothing fancy here, but the quality is top drawer and its unpretentiousness is refreshing. The meats here are very tender and well flavored, and the chimichurri sauce is the city's best.

Calle Caoba 35. © **787/726-7202.** Reservations recommended for dinner. Main courses $15–$30. AE, DC, DISC, MC, V. Sun–Thurs 11:30am–10:45pm; Fri–Sat noon–midnight. Bus: A5 or C53.

Tierra Santa Restaurant (Finds MIDDLE EASTERN Housed in fanciful quarters, with glass mosaics etched into the facade and the main dining room adorned with Arabian fabric and scenic oil paintings, this is one of the better of the city's many fine Middle Eastern restaurants. We always start out with the hummus and falafel, and get the baba ghanouj if there are more than two of us. The succulent, perfectly seasoned grilled chicken, beef, and shrimp kabobs are what draw us here, but we have also enjoyed the grilled lamb shank, curry chicken, and the stuffed grape leaves. The entrees are served with a tasty cucumber and tomato salad and Arabian rice pilaf with almonds. Don't leave without trying the baklava; there's a reason it's the oldest dessert in the world. On Thursday, Friday, and Saturday nights, a belly-dancing show starts at 9pm. It's a great show.

Calle Loíza 2440. © **787/726-6491.** Reservations not necessary. Main courses $11–$30. AE, MC, V. Daily 11am–midnight. Bus: A5.

MODERATE

La Casita Blanca ★ (Finds) CREOLE/PUERTO RICAN   Island politicians are said to have the best noses for good home cooking. We don't know if that is true or not, but one of their favorite places is this eatery. Governor wannabes (what politician doesn't want to be?) come here to order excellent regional fare and enjoy an ambience that oozes the culture of the Puerto Rican countryside. This is a converted family home that opened its door to diners in the mid-1980s, and it's been a favorite of locals from all walks of Puerto Rican society ever since. Off the tourist trail and best reached by taxi, the restaurant does down-home island fare like *guisado y arroz con gandule* (beef stew with rice and small beans), or *bacalao* (salt codfish with yuca). Guaranteed to put hair on your chest is *patita* (pigs' trotters in a Creole sauce). Veal with sautéed onions is popular, as is grilled red snapper or chicken fricassee. A typical chicken *asopao*, a soupy rice stew, is also served. If you ever wanted to try stewed rabbit or goat, this is the place.

Calle Tapía 351. (✆ **787/726-5501.** Main courses $8–$16; Sun buffet $12–$13. MC, V. Mon–Thurs 11:30am–6:45pm; Fri–Sat 11:30am–9:30pm; Sun noon–4:30pm. Bus: C10 or C11.

8 ISLA VERDE

VERY EXPENSIVE

BLT Steak ★★ STEAKHOUSE   French chef Laurent Tourondel takes the American steakhouse to new highs with an awesome selection of Black Angus, prime, and Kobe beef, as well as chicken, lamb, veal, and fresh fish. There's nothing fancy here—just the best steakhouse fare you can imagine prepared by a chef with the talent to match the quality of the ingredients. We started with some littleneck clams from the raw bar and the crab cakes. The signature steak is a bone-in sirloin for two, which was among the finest cuts we've had on the island. The sautéed Dover sole is an old-school classic that hits its mark. We loved the potato gratin and Parmesan gnocchi, as well as the roasted tomatoes and poached green beans. Steaks are served with a selection of sauces including chimichurri, béarnaise, peppercorn, and horseradish. The blueberry lemon pie makes for a refreshing finale. There's also peanut butter chocolate mousse with banana ice cream and warm coconut bread pudding with rum ice cream if you dare.

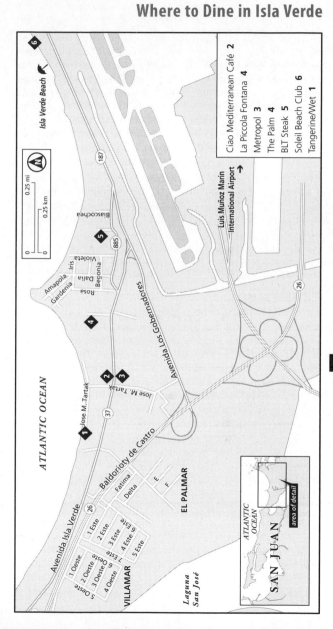

Ciao Mediterranean Café 2
La Piccola Fontana 4
Metropol 3
The Palm 4
BLT Steak 5
Soleil Beach Club 6
Tangerine/Wet 1

Isla Verde Beach

ATLANTIC OCEAN

Avenida Isla Verde

Baldorioty de Castro

José M. Tartak

Avenida Los Gobernadores

Luis Muñoz Marín
International Airport

187

885

Biascochea

Violeta
Iris
Begonia
Amapola
Gardenia
Dalia
Rosa

37

26

Fatima
Delta
E
F

EL PALMAR

VILLAMAR

5 Oeste
4 Oeste
3 Oeste
2 Oeste
1 Oeste

1 Este
2 Este
3 Este
4 Este
5 Este
6 Este
7 Este

Laguna
San José

0   0.25 mi
0   0.25 km

ATLANTIC
OCEAN

SAN JUAN

area of detail

In the Ritz-Carlton San Juan Hotel, Spa & Casino, Av. de los Gobernadores (State Rd.) 6961, no. 187, Isla Verde. ☎ **787/253-1700.** Reservations required. Main courses $22–$88; fixed-price menus $45–$75. AE, DC, DISC, MC, V. Sun–Thurs 6–10:30pm; Fri–Sat 6–11pm. Bus: A5.

The Palm ★★ STEAK/SEAFOOD The management of San Juan's most elegant hotel invited the Palm, a legendary New York steakhouse, to open a branch on the premises. The setting includes a stylish, masculine-looking saloon, where drinks are stiff, and a dining room with artfully simple linen-covered tables and caricatures of local personalities. If you've hit it big at the nearby casino, maybe you'll want to celebrate with the Palm's famous and famously pricey lobster. Otherwise, there's a tempting number of options, all served in gargantuan portions: jumbo lump crabmeat cocktail; Caesar salad; lamb chops with mint sauce; grilled halibut steak; prime porterhouse steak; and steak "a la stone," which finishes cooking on a sizzling platter directly atop your table. One thing is certain—you'll never go hungry here.

In El San Juan Hotel & Casino, Av. Isla Verde 6063. ☎ **787/791-1000.** Reservations recommended. Main courses $18–$40, except lobster, which is priced by the pound and can easily cost $22 per pound or more. AE, DC, MC, V. Daily 5–11pm.

EXPENSIVE

La Piccola Fontana ★ NORTHERN ITALIAN Just off a luxurious wing of El San Juan Hotel, this restaurant delivers plate after plate of delectable food nightly. From its white linens to its classically formal service, it enjoys a fine reputation. The food is straightforward, generous, and extremely well prepared. You'll dine in one of two neo-Palladian rooms whose wall frescoes depict Italy's ruins and landscapes. Menu items range from the appealingly simple (grilled filets of fish or grilled veal chops) to more elaborate dishes such as *tortellini San Daniele,* made with veal, prosciutto, cream, and sage; or *linguine scogliere,* with shrimp, clams, and seafood. Grilled medallions of filet mignon are served with braised arugula, Parmesan cheese, and balsamic vinegar.

In El San Juan Hotel & Casino, Av. Isla Verde 6063. ☎ **787/791-0966.** Reservations required. Main courses $18–$30. AE, MC, V. Daily 6–11pm. Bus: A5 or C53.

MODERATE

Ciao Mediterranean Café ★★ (Kids) MEDITERRANEAN This is the most charming restaurant in Isla Verde, and it is one of our enduring favorites. It's draped with bougainvillea and set across a boardwalk running along the front of the hotel property overlooking the public beach. It's a hit with hotel guests and locals wandering in barefoot from the beach for delicious tropical drinks. Pizzas and pastas are popular here, and there's delicious seafood salad, deep-fried squid with ratatouille and spicy marinara sauce, and rack of lamb with Provençal herbs.

Compared to most of the restaurants around here, this cafe serves lighter fare that kids go for, especially in its selection of pizzas and pastas. The desserts are also some of the most luscious at Isla Verde, especially the ice cream.

In the Inter-Continental San Juan Resort & Casino, Av. Isla Verde 5961. ℂ **787/ 791-6100.** Reservations recommended for dinner. Pizzas and salads $8–$20; main courses $14–$30. AE, MC, V. Daily 11:30am–11pm. Bus: A5.

Metropol CUBAN/PUERTO RICAN/INTERNATIONAL   This is part of a restaurant chain known for serving the island's best Cuban food, although the chefs prepare a much wider range of dishes. Metropol is the happiest blend of Cuban and Puerto Rican cuisine we've ever had. The black-bean soup is among the island's finest, served in the classic Havana style with a side dish of rice and chopped onions. Endless garlic bread accompanies most dinners, including Cornish game hen stuffed with Cuban rice and beans or perhaps marinated steak topped with a fried egg (reportedly Castro's favorite). Smoked chicken and chicken-fried steak are also heartily recommended; portions are huge. Plantains, yuca, and all that good stuff accompany most dishes. Finish with a choice of thin or firm custard. Most dishes are at the low end of the price scale.

Club Gallistico, Av. Isla Verde. ℂ **787/791-4046.** Main courses $10–$30. AE, MC, V. Daily 11:30am–11:30pm. Bus: A5.

9 NEAR ISLA VERDE

Soleil Beach Club Piñones ★★ (Finds) CARIBBEAN   When it opened in 1997, Soleil was a pioneer in operating a fine-dining establishment among the barbecues, wooden shacks, and open-air bars of the Piñones dining scene. More than a decade later, Soleil still rules from its roost amid the sand dunes and palm trees of the undeveloped beach it fronts. Soak in that breeze and listen to those waves from a table or the bar on the oceanfront terrace and have a drink as the sun goes down before dinner. The food here's as good as its rustic beachfront surroundings. For starters, we like the fish skewers with mango sauce and the coconut breaded shrimp in aioli sauce. The surf and turf pairs Argentine-style skirt steak with shrimp, baby octopus, mahimahi, and scallops. The halibut is served in an oriental beurre blanc sauce and cassava *mofongo;* the tuna is grilled, topped with a tropical fruit salsa, and served with cilantro jasmine rice. This is one of the best places for oceanfront dining in San Juan and one of the best in Puerto Rico. Today, the restaurant hosts corporate dinners and special events, with facilities for concerts and live shows, a dance floor, and DJ area. There's also Wi-Fi.

Soleil Beach Club, Carretera 187 Km 4.6, Piñones. (C) **787/253-1033.** Reservations recommended. Lunch and dinner main courses $13–$39; lunch specials $7–$10. AE, DISC, MC, V. Sun–Thurs 11am–11pm; Fri–Sat 11am–2am. Call ahead to arrange free transportation to and from your hotel in the Soleil Beach Club van.

6

Exploring San Juan

The Spanish began to settle in the area now known as Old San Juan around 1521. At the outset, the city was called Puerto Rico ("Rich Port"), and the whole island was known as San Juan.

The streets are narrow and teeming with traffic, but a walk through Old San Juan—in Spanish, *El Viejo San Juan*—makes for a good stroll. Some visitors have likened it to a "Disney park with an Old World theme." Even fast-food restaurants and junk stores are housed in historic buildings. It's the biggest and best collection of historic buildings, stretching back 5 centuries, in all the Caribbean. You can do it in less than a day. In this historic 7-square-block area of the western side of the city, you can see many of Puerto Rico's chief sightseeing attractions and do some shopping along the way.

On the other hand, you might want to plop down on the sand with a drink or get outside and play.

1 SEEING THE SIGHTS

FORTS

San Juan National Historic Site Castillo de San Felipe del Morro ★ **Kids** This site is composed of the Old City's two major fortifications, **Castillo de San Felipe del Morro,** called "El Morro," and **Fort San Cristóbal.** The U.S. National Park Service protects the fortifications of Old San Juan, which have been declared a World Heritage Site by the United Nations. The forts are connected by ancient underground tunnels, but today two modern trolleys ferry visitors back and forth. The walk, however, is beautiful along the oceanfront Calle Norzagary. Historical and background information is provided in English and Spanish at both forts. Park rangers lead hour-long tours for free, but there's enough information provided to go on your own.

With some of the most dramatic views in the Caribbean, you'll find El Morro, standing over a rocky promontory dominating the entrance to San Juan Bay, an intriguing labyrinth of dungeons, barracks, vaults, lookouts, and ramps. Constructed in 1540, the original fort was a round tower, which can still be seen deep inside the lower levels of the castle. More walls and cannon-firing positions were added, and by 1787, the fortification attained the complex design you see today. This fortress was attacked repeatedly by both the English and the Dutch.

A museum at El Morro provides a history of the fort through exhibits of historic photographs and artifacts, written orientations, and a video presentation. A guided tour is offered hourly, but informational brochures allow you to walk around on your own while learning the story. There's also a gift shop. Make sure to walk out on the northernmost point, a narrow wedge overlooking the waves crashing into the rocky coast. The promenade circling the base of the fort is also worth exploring. The grounds of El Morro are a great spot to fly a kite, and families and children are out every weekend doing so. An annual festival is in March. You can buy a kite at stands right in front of the fort, or at Puerto Rico Drug or Walgreens on Plaza Colón.

San Cristóbal, begun in 1634 and reengineered in the 1770s, is one of the largest forts ever built in the Americas by Spain. Its walls rise more than 150 feet (46m) above the sea—a marvel of military engineering. San Cristóbal protected San Juan against attackers coming by land as a partner to El Morro, to which it is linked by a half-mile (.8km) of monumental walls and bastions filled with cannon-firing positions. A complex system of tunnels and dry moats connects the center of San Cristóbal to its "outworks," defensive elements arranged layer after layer over a 27-acre (11-hectare) site. Be sure to see the Garita del Diablo (the Devil's Sentry Tower), one of the oldest parts of San Cristóbal's defenses and famous in Puerto Rican legend.

Calle Norzagaray, Old San Juan. ✆ **787/729-6960.** http://www.nps.gov/archive/ saju/morro.html. Admission $3 adults (16 and older) 1 fort, $5 both forts, free for children 15 and under. Daily 9am–5pm. Bus: A5 or C53; then the free trolley from Covadonga station to the top of the hill.

CHURCHES

Capilla de Cristo   Cristo Chapel was built to commemorate what legend says was a miracle. In 1753 a young rider lost control of his horse in a race down this very street during the fiesta of St. John's Day and plunged over the precipice. Moved by the accident, the secretary of the city, Don Mateo Pratts, invoked Christ to save the youth, and he had the chapel built when his prayers were answered. Today it's a landmark in the old city and one of its best-known historical monuments. The chapel's gold and silver altar can be seen through its glass doors. Because the chapel is open only 1 day a week, most visitors have to settle for a view of its exterior.

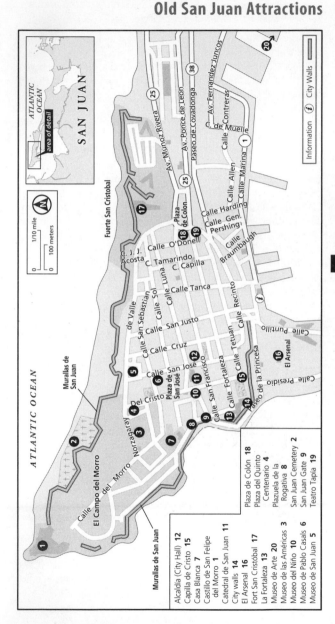

ATLANTIC OCEAN

SAN JUAN

ATLANTIC OCEAN

area of detail

Murallas de San Juan

Fuerte San Cristobal

El Campo del Morro

Calle del Morro

Murallas de San Juan

0   1/10 mile
0   100 meters

Av. Muñoz Rivera
Av. Ponce de Leon
Paseo de Covadonga
Av. Fernandez Juncos
Calle Contreras
Calle Marina
C. de Muelle
Calle Allen
Calle Harding
Calle Gen. Pershing
Calle Braumbaugh
Plaza de Colón
Calle O'Donell
C. J. J. Acosta
C. Tamarindo
C. Capilla
Calle Luna
Calle Tanca
Calle Sol
de Valle
Calle San Sebastián
Calle San Justo
Calle Cruz
Calle San José
Plaza de San José
Del Cristo
Calle San Francisco
Calle Fortaleza
Calle Tetuan
Calle Recinto
Calle Puntillo
Paseo de la Princesa
El Arsenal
Calle Presidio
Norzagaray

Information   (i)   City Walls

Alcaldía (City Hall) **12**
Capilla de Cristo **15**
Casa Blanca **7**
Castillo de San Felipe
  del Morro **1**
Catedral de San Juan **11**
City walls **14**
El Arsenal **16**
Fort San Cristóbal **17**
La Fortaleza **13**
Museo de Arte **20**
Museo de las Américas **3**
Museo del Niño **10**
Museo de Pablo Casals **6**
Museo de San Juan **5**

Plaza de Colón **18**
Plaza del Quinto
  Centenario **4**
Plazuela de la
  Rogativa **8**
San Juan Cemetery **2**
San Juan Gate **9**
Teatro Tapia **19**

Calle del Cristo (directly west of Paseo de la Princesa). ☏ **787/722-0861.** Free admission. Tues 8am–5pm. Bus: Old Town Trolley.

Catedral de San Juan This, the spiritual and architectural centerpiece of Old San Juan, as you see it in its present form, was begun in 1540 as a replacement for a thatch-roofed chapel that was blown apart by a hurricane in 1529. Chronically hampered by a lack of funds and a recurring series of military and weather-derived disasters, it slowly evolved into the gracefully vaulted, Gothic-inspired structure you see today. Among the many disasters to hit this cathedral are the following: In 1598 the Earl of Cumberland led the British navy in a looting spree, and in 1615 a hurricane blew away its roof. In 1908 the body of Ponce de León was disinterred from the nearby Iglesia de San José and placed in a marble tomb near the transept, where it remains today. The cathedral also contains the wax-covered mummy of St. Pio, a Roman martyr persecuted and killed for his Christian faith. The mummy has been encased in a glass box ever since it was placed here in 1862. To the right of the mummy is a bizarre wooden replica of Mary with four swords stuck in her bosom. After all the looting and destruction over the centuries, the cathedral's great treasures, including gold and silver, are long gone, although many beautiful stained-glass windows remain. The cathedral faces Plaza de las Monjas (the Nuns' Square), a shady spot where you can rest in front of Hotel El Convento and Museo del Niño.

Calle del Cristo 153 (at Caleta San Juan). ☏ **787/722-0861.** Free admission. Mon–Sat 8am–4pm; Sun 8am–2pm. Bus: Old Town Trolley.

MUSEUMS

Many of the museums in Old San Juan close for lunch between 11:45am and 2pm, so schedule your activities accordingly if you intend to museum-hop.

Caleta de San Juan 51, at Recinto Oeste. ☏ **787/723-1897.** Free admission. Mon–Fri 9am–4pm. Bus: Old Town Trolley.

Museo de Arte de Puerto Rico ★★ Puerto Rico's most important art museum since opening in 2000, it was constructed at a cost of $55 million and is a state-of-the-art showcase for the island nation's rich cultural heritage, as reflected mainly through its painters. Housed in a former city hospital in Santurce, the museum features both a permanent collection and temporary exhibitions. Prominent local artists are the stars—for example, Francisco Oller (1833–1917), who brought a touch of Cézanne or Camille Pissarro to Puerto Rico (Oller actually studied in France with both of these Impressionists). Another leading star of the permanent collection is José Campeche, a late-18th-century classical painter. The museum is like a living textbook of Puerto Rico, beginning with its early development and going on to showcase camp aspects, such as the poster art created here in the mid–20th century. All the important modern island artists are also presented, including the late Rafael Tufiño and Angel Botello, Arnaldo Roche Rabelle, and Antonio Martorell. The building itself is a gem, and you have to stroll through the relaxing botanical gardens behind.

Av. José de Diego 299, Santurce. ℂ 787/977-6277. www.mapr.org. Admission $6 adults; $3 students, seniors, and children; free for children 4 and under and seniors 76 and over. Tues and Thurs–Sat 10am–5pm; Wed 10am–8pm; Sun 11am–6pm. Bus: A5 or C23.

Museo de las Américas ★ This museum showcases the artisans of North, South, and Central America, featuring everything from carved figureheads from New England whaling ships to dugout canoes carved by Carib Indians in Dominica. It is unique in Puerto Rico and well worth a visit. Also on display is a changing collection of paintings by artists from throughout the Spanish-speaking world, some of which are for sale, and a permanent collection called "Puerto Rican *Santos*," donated by Dr. Ricardo Alegría.

Sala Cuartel de Ballajá, at Calle Norzagaray and Calle del Morro. ℂ 787/724-5052. www.museo.org. Free admission, except the Indigenous Peoples of the Americas exhibition is $2, which is a must-see. Tues–Sun 10am–4pm. Bus: Old Town Trolley.

HISTORIC SIGHTS

In addition to the forts and churches listed above, you might want to see the sites described below.

San Juan Gate, Calle San Francisco and Calle Recinto Oeste, built around 1635, just north of La Fortaleza, several blocks downhill from the cathedral, was the main point of entry into San Juan if you arrived by ship in the 17th and 18th centuries. The gate is the only one remaining of the several that once pierced the fortifications of the old walled city. Bus: Old Town Trolley.

Plazuela de la Rogativa, Caleta de las Monjas, is a little plaza with a statue of a bishop and three women, commemorating one of Puerto Rico's most famous legends. In 1797, from across San Juan Bay at Santurce, the British held Old Town under siege. That same year they mysteriously sailed away. Later, the commander claimed he feared that the enemy was well prepared behind those walls; he apparently saw many lights and believed them to be reinforcements. Those lights were torches carried by women in a *rogativa,* or religious procession, as they followed their bishop. Bus: T1.

The **city walls** around San Juan were built in 1630 to protect the town against both European invaders and Caribbean pirates. They are part of one of the most impregnable fortresses in the New World and even today are an engineering marvel. Their thickness averages 20 feet (6m) at the base and 12 feet (3.7m) at the top, with an average height of 40 feet (12m). At their top, notice the balconied buildings that served for centuries as hospitals and also residences of the island's various governors. Between Fort San Cristóbal and El Morro, bastions were erected at frequent intervals. The walls come into view as you approach from San Cristóbal on your way to El Morro. To get there, you can take the Old Town Trolley.

Alcaldía (City Hall) The City Hall, with its double arcade flanked by two towers resembling Madrid's City Hall, was constructed in stages from 1604 to 1789. Still in use, this building today contains a tourist-information center downstairs plus a small art gallery on the first floor.

Calle San Francisco. ℂ **787/724-7171.** Free admission. Mon–Fri 8am–5pm. Closed holidays. Bus: Old Town Trolley.

Casa Blanca Ponce de León never lived here, although construction of the house—built in 1521, 2 years after his death—is sometimes attributed to him. The work was ordered by his son-in-law, Juan García Troche. The parcel of land was given to Ponce de León as a reward for services rendered to the Crown. Descendants of the explorer lived in the house for about 2¹/₂ centuries, until the Spanish government took it over in 1779 for use as a residence for military commanders. The first-floor museum is furnished with antiques, paintings, and artifacts from the 16th through the 18th centuries. In back is a garden with spraying fountains, offering an intimate and verdant respite.

Calle San Sebastián 1. ℂ **787/725-1454.** Admission $3. Tues–Sat 9am–noon and 1–4:30pm. Bus: Old Town Trolley.

La Fortaleza The office and residence of the governor of Puerto Rico is the oldest executive mansion in continuous use in the Western Hemisphere, and it has served as the island's seat of government for more than 3 centuries. Its history goes back even further than that to 1533, when construction began on a fortress to protect San Juan's Spanish settlers during raids by Carib tribesmen and pirates. The original medieval towers remain, but as the edifice was subsequently enlarged into a palace, other modes of architecture and ornamentation were also incorporated, including baroque, Gothic, neoclassical, and Arabian. La Fortaleza has been designated a national historic site by the U.S. government. Proper attire is required (informal okay).

Calle Fortaleza, overlooking San Juan Harbor. ℂ **787/721-7000,** ext. 2211. Free admission. 30-min. tours of the gardens and building (conducted in English and Spanish) given every half-hour. Mon–Fri 9am–3:30pm. Bus: Old Town Trolley.

Museo Nuestras Raíces Africanas   Set within the Casa del Contrefueras, this museum documents the African contribution to the sociology of Puerto Rico. You'll find a series of tastefully arranged art objects, including musical instruments, intricately carved African masks, drums, graphics, and maps that show the migratory patterns, usually through the slave trade, from Africa into Puerto Rico. There are graphic depictions of the horrendous disruptions to families and individuals caused by the slave trade during the plantation era.

Plaza San José, Calle San Sebastián. ℂ **787/724-4294.** Admission $2 adults; $1 seniors, children, and students; free for ages 12 and under. Tues–Sat 8:30am–4:30pm. Bus: Old Town Trolley.

Teatro Tapía   Standing across from the Plaza de Colón, this is one of the oldest theaters in the Western Hemisphere, built about 1832. In 1976 a restoration returned the theater to its original appearance. Much of Puerto Rican theater history is connected with the Tapía, named after the island's first prominent playwright, Alejandro Tapía y Rivera (1826–82). Various productions—some musical—are staged here throughout the year, representing a repertoire of drama, dance, and cultural events.

Av. Ponce de León. ℂ **787/721-0180.** Prices vary. Access limited to ticket holders at performances. Bus: A5, C53, or any other to Old San Juan Station.

HISTORIC SQUARES

In Old San Juan, **Plaza del Quinto Centenario (Quincentennial Plaza)** overlooks the Atlantic from atop the highest point in the city. A striking and symbolic feature of the plaza, which was constructed as part of the 1992–93 celebration of the 500th anniversary of the discovery of the New World, is a sculpture that rises 40 feet (12m) from the plaza's top level. The black granite and ceramic monument symbolizes the earthen and clay roots of Puerto Rican history; two needle-shaped columns point skyward to the North Star, the guiding light of explorers, and it is surrounded by fountains, columns, and sculpted steps that represent various historical periods in Puerto Rico's 500-year history.

Sweeping views extend from the plaza to El Morro Fortress at the headland of San Juan Bay and to the Dominican Convent and San José Church, a rare New World example of Gothic architecture. Asilo de Beneficencia, a former indigents' hospital dating from 1832, occupies a corner of El Morro's entrance and is now the home of the Institute of Puerto Rican Culture. Adjacent to the plaza is the Cuartel de Ballajá, built in the mid–19th century as the Spanish army headquarters and still the largest edifice in the Americas constructed by Spanish engineers; it houses the Museum of the Americas.

Tips **The Best Places to See Puerto Rican Art**

With its dozen or so museums and even more art galleries, Old San Juan is the greatest repository of Puerto Rican arts and crafts. Galleries sell everything from pre-Columbian artifacts to paintings by well-known artists to contemporary traditional crafts, like *santos,* the hand-carved wooden saints the island is known for.

Noches de galleria, or Gallery Nights, take place the first Tuesday of each month—an excellent opportunity to view the island's vibrant art scene. Most galleries have openings or special exhibits, as well as wine-and-cheese receptions, and occasionally live music or theatrical performances. Bars and restaurants get into the act and hold art shows or performances. Around about midnight, it all mixes into a terrific party along Calle San Sebastián. If you'd rather visit during the day, a cluster of galleries is spread along Calle Cristo and Calle San José, which is 1 block east. The **Galería Nacional,** or National Gallery, located inside Old San Juan's Antiguo Convento de los Dominicos, a restored former convent, has exhibits from the Institute of Puerto Rican Culture's vast holdings. It displays many of the most important works by Puerto Rican painters, from José Campeche and Francisco Oller to Rafael Tufiño and the generation of painters from the 1950s (✆ **787/977-2700**). Santurce, however, is as important as the Old City now that it has some of the island's top museums. The grandest repository of art in San Juan is at the **Museo de Arte de Puerto Rico** (p. 92), which is a virtual textbook on all

Plaza de Colón at the main entrance to Old San Juan can bustle at times, but it has some deliciously shady spots, with benches under a canopy of trees. At its center is a huge monument to Columbus. Grab a spot to sit and grab something cool to drink from a corner store. **Plaza de Las Armas,** at the heart of Old San Juan, is home to San Juan City Hall, built in 1789 as a replica of the Madrid City Hall, and the Puerto Rico State Department, a beautiful 18th-century colonial building. The Cuatro Estaciones fountain represents the four seasons. The name also extends to the outdoor cafe, a nice spot for a strong cup of coffee or a cold drink.

the big names in the art world who rose from Puerto Rico, often to international acclaim. The gorgeously restored building is also part of the appeal, as are the adjoining botanical gardens. The **Museo de Arte Contemporáneo** (🕻 **787/977-4030;** avenidas Ponce de León and Robert H. Todd) is also an exceptional museum in a restored brick schoolhouse, showing contemporary art from Puerto Rico and throughout Latin America and the Caribbean.

Outside San Juan, the greatest art on the island can usually be seen at the **Museo de Arte de Ponce,** home to European masters like Reubens, Van Dyck, and Murillo, as well as Latin American artists like Mexico's Diego Rivera and Puerto Ricans José Campeche and Francisco Oller. Unfortunately, the museum is closed for major renovations until 2010—but it continues to be a force in the island's art scene through an exhibition space at the San Juan's **Plaza Las Américas,** the largest mall in the Caribbean, where it will hold shows until its south-coast home is renovated. **MAPR at Plaza** (Av. Roosevelt 525, 3rd floor, Plaza Las Américas; 🕻 **787/200-7090** or 848-0505).

CIRCO, an international art fair held at the new Puerto Rico Convention Center annually in April, is growing in stature and quality each year, and many local art venues plan special shows for the occasion.

The **Paseo de la Princesa** is a wide bayside promenade with outstanding views, running beneath the imposing Spanish colonial wall that surrounds the Old City. It's home to **La Princesa,** a former prison in the 1800s that has been blissfully restored and now houses the Puerto Rico Tourism Company Headquarters. The sexy fountain at its center, "Raíces," or "Races," shoots powerful streams of water over the bronze naked Adonises and Amazon warrior goddesses riding huge horses and fish, so you'll get wet if you get too close. Spanish artist Luis Sanguino undertook the work as part of the 500th anniversary of San Juan's founding. The statue is meant to show the Taíno,

African, and Spanish roots of Puerto Rico and its people. Farther along, the promenade bends around the bay and passes a shaded area before heading down to San Juan Gate. The new El Morro trail, which goes around the base of the fortress, is actually an extension of this promenade. There are food and drink vendors and often artisans selling their crafts, especially at the start of the route near the cruise ship docks. Enter near the cruise ship docks at the corner of Recinto Sur and Calle La Puntilla or via the San Juan Gate (Calle San Francisco and Calle Recinto Oeste).

PARKS & GARDENS

Jardín Botánico   Administered by the University of Puerto Rico, Jardín Botánico is a lush tropical garden with some 200 species of vegetation. You can pack a picnic lunch and bring it here if you choose. The orchid garden is exceptional, and the palm garden is said to contain some 125 species. Footpaths blaze a trail through heavy forests opening onto a lotus lagoon.

Barrio Venezuela (at the intersection of routes 1 and 847), Río Piedras. (C) 787/765-1845. Free admission. Daily 6am–6pm. Bus: C18 or C31.

Luis Muñoz Marín Park ★ (Kids)   This 140-acre (57-hectare) park is the best-known, most frequently visited children's playground in Puerto Rico—although it has equal appeal to adults. Conceived as a verdant oasis in an otherwise crowded urban neighborhood, it's a fenced-in repository of swings, jungle gyms, and slides set amid several small lakes and rolling green fields. Here you'll also find an incomparable view of San Juan. A small-scale cable car carries passengers aloft at 10-minute intervals for panoramic views of the surrounding landscape ($2 per person).

Av. Piñero, at Hato Rey. (C) 787/763-0787. Free admission for pedestrians; parking $2 or $3. Wed–Sun 8am–6pm. Bus: B17.

Luis Muñoz Rivera Park   This 27-acre (11-hectare) park is a green rectangle in the middle of Puerta de Tierra. You'll drive by the seaward-facing park on your way to San Juan. It's filled with picnic areas, wide walks, shady trees, landscaped grounds, and recreational areas. There's a new children's playground that's filled with fun on weekends. Its centerpiece, El Pabellon de la Paz, is sometimes used for cultural events and expositions of handicrafts. A new pedestrian and bicycle path connects the park with the oceanfront Tercer Milenio, or Third Millennium Park, across Avenida Muñoz Rivera. The Commonwealth Supreme Court is located at the eastern side of the park.

Btw. avenidas Muñoz Rivera and Ponce de León. (C) 787/721-6133. Free admission. Daily 24 hr. Bus: A5.

The Cathedral of Rum

Called "the Cathedral of Rum," the **Bacardi Distillery** at Rte. 888 Km 2.6 at Cataño (✆ **787/788-1500**), is the largest of its kind in the world. Reached by taking a 20-minute ferry ride across San Juan Bay (50¢ each way), the distillery produces 100,000 gallons of rum daily. At the site, you can go to the **Casa Bacardi Visitor Center,** Carretera 165, Cataño (✆ **787/ 788-8400**), for free 90-minute tours Monday to Saturday from 9am to 4:30pm, Sunday 10am to 3:30pm. You are taken on a visit of seven historical displays, including the Bat Theatre and the Golden Age of the Cocktail Art Deco bar, and there are free samples.

Parque Central Municipio de San Juan   This mangrove-bordered park was inaugurated in 1979 for the Pan-American Games. It covers 35 acres (14 hectares) and lies southeast of Miramar. Joggers appreciate its labyrinth of trails, and a long boardwalk runs along mangrove canals. Recently renovated, it boasts 20 tennis courts, 4 racquetball courts, a full track-and-field area with stadium bleachers, a cafe, and children's play area (just look for the huge jacks sculpture). A golf course is being developed on an adjacent former landfill, and a brand-new Olympic-standard diving-and-swimming arena was completed in 2006. Fat, huge iguanas slither from the mangrove-choked channels and into the park's pathways.

Calle Cerra. ✆ **787/722-1646.** Free admission for pedestrians; parking $1. Mon–Thurs 6am–10pm; Fri 6am–9pm; Sat–Sun 6am–7pm. Bus: B8.

ESPECIALLY FOR KIDS

Puerto Rico is one of the most family-friendly islands in the Caribbean, and many hotels offer family discounts. Programs for children are also offered at a number of hotels, including day and night camp activities and babysitting services.

Ben & Jerry's Café Galería Puerto Rico (Kids)   A visit here is the perfect ending to an afternoon of exploring the ancient oceanfront forts and flying kites, something a kid will always remember. There's plenty of their famous flavors—Cherry García, the Chocolate Fudge Brownie, and the Chunky Monkey, but the place also has homemade goodies, pita pizzas, sandwiches, burgers, salads, and snacks. They also have DJ music, art exhibits, Internet access, books, magazines, and more. A great place.

Calle del Cristo 61. (𝒞 **787/977-6882.** www.benjerry.com. Daily 11am–11pm. Bus: Old Town Trolley.

Museo del Niño (Children's Museum) (Kids) Housed in a 300-year-old villa directly across from the city's cathedral, the museum features playful, interactive exhibits, where children can learn the benefits of brushing teeth or recycling cans. Nothing here is terribly cerebral and won't compel you to return, but it's great for small children. There's a fun rooftop nature area.

Calle del Cristo 150. (𝒞 **787/722-3791.** Admission $5 adults, $4 children 14 and younger. Tues–Thurs 9am–3:30pm; Fri 9am–5pm; Sat–Sun 12:30–5pm. Bus: Old Town Trolley.

Time Out Family Amusement Center (Kids) Right at the main food court, all the latest electronic games are here.

Plaza de las Américas, Las Américas Expwy. at Av. Roosevelt, Hato Rey. (𝒞 **787/753-0606.** Free admission (prices of activities vary). Mon–Thurs 9:30am–10pm; Fri–Sun 9am–11pm. Bus: A3 or B22 from Old San Juan.

2 DIVING, FISHING, TENNIS & OTHER OUTDOOR PURSUITS

Active vacationers have a wide choice of things to do in San Juan, from beaching to windsurfing. The beachside hotels, of course, offer lots of watersports activities (see chapter 4).

THE BEACHES

All beaches on Puerto Rico, even those fronting the top hotels, are open to the public. Public bathing beaches are called *balnearios* and charge for parking and for use of facilities, such as lockers and showers. Beach hours in general are 9am to 5pm in winter, to 6pm off season. Most *balnearios* are operated by the Puerto Rico National Parks Company, with others operated by island municipalities. There are two public beaches in the San Juan area with lifeguards, bath and changing rooms, and showers. **El Escambrón public beach** (Av. Muñoz Rivera, Puerta de Tierra; (𝒞 **787/721-5185;** Wed–Sun and holidays 8:30am–5pm; parking $3) is right next to the Caribe Hilton and surrounded by two sprawling parks. The other is **Isla Verde public beach** (Av. Los Gobernadores, Carolina; (𝒞 **787/791-8084;** daily 8am–6pm; parking $2), a huge expanse of white sand and tranquil waters between Isla Verde and Piñones. There are lifeguards, changing rooms, bathrooms and showers, and picnic areas and barbecue grills.

Back in the 1920s, **Condado Beach ★★** put San Juan on the map as a tourist resort. Backed up against high-rise hotels, it seems more like Miami Beach than any other beach in the Caribbean. All sorts of watersports can be booked at the activities desk of the hotels. A small beach near the Condado Plaza hotel is the only one with lifeguards, which are on duty from 8:30am to 5pm. There are also outdoor showers. The beaches in the rest of the Condado are much nicer, but as there are no lifeguards and the surf can get rough, particularly by the San Juan Marriott, swimmers should exercise caution. People-watching is a favorite sport along these golden strands, which stretch from the Ventana del Mar park to beyond the Marriott. The best stretch of beach in the Condado runs from the Ashford Presbyterian hospital to Ocean Park. The area behind the Atlantic Beach Hotel is popular with the gay crowd.

One of the most attractive beaches in the Greater San Juan area is **Ocean Park Beach ★★**, a mile (1.6km) of fine gold sand in a neighborhood east of Condado. This beach attracts young people, travelers looking for a guesthouse rather than the large hotel experience, and those looking for a big gay crowd. The beach runs from Parque del Indio in Condado all the way to the Barbosa Park in the area known as El Ultimo Trolley and offers paddle tennis, kite-boarding, and beach volleyball. You can grab lunch and refreshments from several area guesthouses, and vendors walk up and down the beach, selling cold beer, water and soft drinks, and even such snacks as fried seafood turnovers. Farther east, there's no real beach at **Punta Las Marías,** but it's one of the favorite launch points for windsurfers.

Isla Verde Beach ★★ is the longest and widest in San Juan. It is ideal for swimming, and it, too, is lined with high-rise resorts a la Miami Beach. Isla Verde is good for watersports, including parasailing and snorkeling, because of its calm, clear waters, and many kiosks will rent you equipment, especially by the El San Juan. There are also cafes and restaurants at hotels and more reasonably priced individual restaurants nearby. Pine Grove beach, behind the Ritz-Carlton, is a great swimming beach and very popular as well, particularly with surfers and sailors.

SPORTS & OTHER OUTDOOR PURSUITS

BIKE RENTALS   The best places to bicycle are in city parks like Luis Muñoz Marín (Hato Rey) and Luis Muñoz Rivera (Puerta de Tierra). You can make it from Condado to Old San Juan driving mostly through the latter park. There are also bicycle trails; we recommend the coastal boardwalk running along Piñones, which is beautiful and safe, especially on the weekends. There are bike rentals available in the area during weekends, although most San Juan streets are too crowded for bicycle riding. **Hot Dog Cycling,** Av. Isla Verde 5916, La Plazoleta Shopping Center (✆ 787/721-0776), is open Monday to Saturday 9am to 6pm and charges $5 per hour for rentals, $25 for a full day.

CRUISES For the best cruises of San Juan Bay, go to **Caribe Aquatic Adventures** (see "Scuba Diving," below). Bay cruises start at $25 per person.

DEEP-SEA FISHING ★ The big game fishing grounds are very close offshore from San Juan, making the capital an excellent place to hire a charter. A half-day of deep-sea fishing (4 hr.) starts at around $550, while full-day charters begin at around $900. Most charters hold six passengers in addition to the crew.

There are three marinas with fishing charters and boat rentals available in the San Juan metropolitan area. The **Cangrejos Yacht Club** (Rte. 187, Piñones; ✆ 787/791-1015) is right near the airport on Route 187, the road from Isla Verde to Piñones, while the two other marinas are next to each other near the Condado bridge and the Convention Center in Miramar: **San Juan Bay Marina** (✆ 787/721-8062) and **Club Nautico de San Juan** (✆ 787/722-0177).

Capt. Mike Benítez, of **Benítez Fishing Charters** (✆ 787/723-2292), is the most experienced operator in San Juan sailing out of Club Nautico. His crew is knowledgeable and informative, and the 45-foot air-conditioned deluxe Hatteras called the *Sea Born* is plush and comfortable. We also recommend another veteran outfit, **Castillo Fishing Charters** (✆ 787/726-5752), that has been running charters out of the San Juan Bay Marina since 1975. Capt. Omar Orracar of **Caribbean Outfitters** (✆ 787/396-8346) runs deep-sea fishing charters but also runs fly-fishing trips in San Juan lagoons for snook and tarpon. The boat is docked at Cangrejos Yacht Club.

GOLF The island's best golf courses are within a short drive of San Juan. The legendary Dorado courses are 45 minutes west at the **Dorado Beach Resort & Club** (✆ 787/796-8961). Designed by Robert Trent Jones, Sr., these courses have hosted professional tournaments, including the World Cup of Golf (see the "World-Class Golf at the Former Hyatt Dorado" box on p. 127). Fees for guests are $160.

Driving east for 45 minutes will get you to the world-class golf courses of Río Grande and Fajardo. The **Wyndham Río Mar Beach Resort** golf offerings (✆ 787/888-7060) include two world-class courses, stretching out in the shadow of El Yunque rainforest along a dazzling stretch of coast. There is a 6,782-yard (6,201m) ocean course by Tom and George Fazio and a 6,945-yard (6,354m) course by Greg

Norman that cuts through jungle and mountain areas. Greens fees for guests are $175, for walk-ins $200. The **Trump International Golf Club** (© 787/657-2000), also in Río Grande, is actually four different 9-hole courses sprawled out across 1,200 acres (486 hectares) of coast. Each course is named after its surrounding environment: the Ocean, the Palms, the Mountains, and the Lakes. Fees range from $140 to $160 for visitors.

Berwind Country Club (© 787/876-5380) in **Loiza** is the nearest full-size course to the city. Built on a former coconut plantation, it's a beautiful place with ocean views, towering palms, and frenzied tropical foliage. Experts say the course is quite challenging, with plenty of water hazards and three of the toughest holes to finish on the island. And with greens fees of $65, it's a bargain. On weekend mornings, the course is reserved for members. The 9-hole **Río Bayamón Golf Course** (© 787/740-1419) is a municipal course in the San Juan suburb Bayamón. Greens fees are $30 and rentals just $15.

HORSE RACING Great thoroughbreds and outstanding jockeys compete year-round at **Camarero Racetrack,** Calle 65 de Infantería, Rte. 3 Km 15.3, at Canóvanas (© 787/641-6060), Puerto Rico's only racetrack, a 20-minute drive east of the center of San Juan. Races begin at 3pm Monday, Wednesday, Friday, Saturday, Sunday, and holidays. The clubhouse has a fine-dining restaurant, the Terrace Room, that serves good local food, and there's Winner's Sports Bar with pub fare. The grandstand has free admission.

SCUBA DIVING In San Juan, the best outfitter is **Caribe Aquatic Adventures,** Normandie Hotel San Juan, Calle 19 1062, Villa Nevarez (© 787/281-8858; www.diveguide.com/p2046.htm). Dives begin at $125 per person, and a resort course for first-time divers also costs $125. Escorted dive and snorkeling jaunts to the eastern shore are also offered. Snorkeling lessons or tours lasting 1 hour and including basic equipment go for $50. Another good outfitter is **Ocean Sports,** Av. Isla Verde 77 (© 787/268-2329), which offers diving courses.

SNORKELING If you don't have time to explore greater Puerto Rico, one of the best places to snorkel in San Juan is at Escambrón Beach, but you are better off taking a day trip to Fajardo, where you'll get a real Caribbean snorkeling experience, with tranquil, clear water and stunning reefs teaming with tropical fish. Several operators offer day trips (10am–3:30pm) leaving from Fajardo marinas, but transportation to and from your San Juan hotel can also be arranged. Prices start at around $69 per person or $99 including transportation

---

(Tips) **Swimmers, Beware**

You have to pick your spots carefully if you want to swim along Condado Beach. The waters at the beach beside the Condado Plaza Hotel are calmer than in other areas because of a coral breakwater. The beach near the Marriott is not good for swimming because of rocks, a strong undertow, and occasional riptides. There are no lifeguards except at public beaches. Ocean Park is better for swimming but can still be hazardous when the tides kick up. Isla Verde beach is generally much calmer, especially at its eastern end.

---

to and from San Juan. Even if you don't particularly want to snorkel, the trips are still worth it for a day of fun in the sun. The trips usually take place on large luxury catamarans, holding about 20 passengers or more. Most have a cash bar serving drinks and refreshments, a sound system, and other creature comforts. Typically, after a nice sail, the cat will weigh anchor at different snorkeling spots and then in sheltered waters near one of the scores of small islands lying off Fajardo's coast, the perfect spot for a swim or sunbathing. Most trips include lunch, which usually is served on a beach. There are many reputable companies, including **Traveler Sailing Catamaran** (© 787/853-2821), **East Island Excursions** (© 787/860-3434), and **Catamaran Spread Eagle** (© 787/887-8821). **Erin Go Bragh Charters** (© 787/860-4401) offers similar day trips aboard a 50-foot sailing ketch, which is an equally pleasurable experience.

SPAS & FITNESS CENTERS If a spa figures into your holiday plans, the grandest and largest such facility in San Juan is found at **Ritz-Carlton San Juan Hotel, Spa & Casino** ★, Av. de los Gobernadores 6961, no. 187, Isla Verde (© 787/253-1700). You get it all here: the luxury life, with state-of-the-art massages, body wraps and scrubs, facials, manicures, pedicures, and a salon guaranteed to make you look like a movie star. In an elegant marble-and-stone setting, there are 11 rooms for pampering, including hydrotherapy and treatments custom-tailored for individual needs. The spa also features a 7,200-square-foot outdoor swimming pool.

The Olas Spa at the **Carib Hilton,** Calle Los Rosales (© 787/721-0303), offers everything from traditional massages to more exotic body and water therapies, using such products as honey, cucumber, sea salts, seaweed, or mud baths. **El San Juan Hotel & Casino,** Av. Isla Verde 6063 (© 787/791-1000), offers a stunning panoramic view of San Juan that almost competes with the facilities, which offer full amenities. **Zen Spa,** Av. Ashford 1054, Condado (© 787/722-8433), has massages, facial treatments, body wraps, and therapeutic services. It's open 8am to 7pm weekdays, 9am to 6pm weekends.

TENNIS Most of the big resorts have their own tennis courts for their guests. There are 20 public courts, lit at night, at **San Juan Central Park,** at Calle Cerra (exit on Rte. 2; © 787/722-1646), open daily. Fees are $3 per hour from 6am to 5pm and $4 per hour from 6 to 10pm. There are also four racquetball courts here. The **Isla Verde Tennis Club** (© 787/727-6490) is open all week, weekdays from 8am to 10pm, Saturdays from 8am to 7pm, and Sundays from 8am to 6pm. Courts cost from $15 to $20 hourly.

WINDSURFING/KITE SURFING The most savvy windsurfing and kite-surfing advice and equipment sales and rental are available at **Velauno,** Calle Loíza 2430, Punta Las Marías in San Juan (© 787/982-0543). A beginner's class with equipment rental in either kite- or windsurfing is $150; private lessons with gear included are $50 hourly. One-day rental cost for windsurfing gear is $75, 3 days $150, and 1 week $225; for kite-surfing gear 1 day is $40, 3 days $90, and 1 week $130. The staff here will guide you to the best windsurfing, right near the store in Punta Las Marías and Ocean Park. Office hours are Monday to Friday 10am to 7pm, Saturday 11am to 7pm. There is a summer windsurfing camp for kids.

---

3 SHOPPING

Since November 2006, a local 7% sales and use tax has been instituted on most goods and services. Malls in San Juan are generally open Monday to Saturday 9am to 9pm, Sunday 11am to 5pm. Regular stores in town are **usually open Monday to Saturday 9am to 6pm.** In Old San Juan most stores are open on **Sunday, too, from about 11am to 5pm.**

Native handicrafts, paintings, and sculptures by Puerto Rican artists, the carved wooden religious idols known as *santos* (saints), handmade and boutique jewelry, coffee, rum, and clothing are among the good buys you'll find.

Plaza Las Américas, in the financial district of Hato Rey, is the largest mall in the Caribbean, with more than 200 mostly upscale shops, several top-notch restaurants, a full Cineplex, plus art galleries and food stores. If you want a break from the sun (or if it's raining), there are entertainment options here for all.

Unless otherwise specified, the following stores can be reached via the Old City Trolley.

El Alcazar (Finds)   This is the largest emporium of antique furniture, silver, and art objects in the Caribbean. The best way to sift through the massive inventory is to begin at the address listed below, but there are three other buildings that are literally stuffed with important art and antiques. There are antique silver, crystal, delicate porcelain, glittering chandeliers, Russian icons, and objects of religious devotion such as *santos*. The antiques are both from Puerto Rico and culled from estates and galleries throughout Europe. Calle San José 103. © 787/723-1229.

ART

Butterfly People   Butterfly People is a gallery in a handsomely restored building in Old San Juan. Butterflies, sold here in artfully arranged boxes, range from $35 for a single mounting to thousands of dollars for whole-wall murals. The butterflies are preserved and will last forever. The dimensional artwork is sold in limited editions and can be shipped worldwide. Most of these butterflies come from farms around the world, some of the most beautiful hailing from Indonesia, Malaysia, and New Guinea. It's open Saturday and Sunday from 10am to 6pm. Calle Cruz 257. © 787/723-2432. www.butterflypeople. com.

Galería Botello ★   A contemporary Latin American art gallery, Galería Botello is a living tribute to the late Angel Botello, one of Puerto Rico's most outstanding artists. Born after the Spanish Civil War in a small village in Galicia, Spain, he fled to the Caribbean and spent 12 years in Haiti. His paintings and bronze sculptures, evocative of his colorful background, are done in a style uniquely his own. This galería is his former colonial mansion home, which he restored himself. Today it displays his paintings and sculptures, showcases the works of many outstanding local artists, and offers a large collection of Puerto Rican antique *santos,* hand-carved wooden statues of the saints. Calle del Cristo 208. © 787/723-9987. www.botello.com.

Galería San Juan   This shop, located at the Gallery Inn, specializes in the sculpture and paintings of Jan D'Esopo, a Connecticut-born artist who has spent a great deal of time in Puerto Rico. Many of her fine pieces are in bronze. In the Gallery Inn, Calle Norzagaray 204. © 787/722-1808. www.thegalleryinn.com.

Haitian Gallery   This is the best store, now with two locations, in San Juan for Haitian art and artifacts. Its walls are covered with framed versions of primitive Haitian landscapes, portraits, crowd scenes, and whimsical visions of jungles where lions, tigers, parrots, and herons take on quasi-human personalities and forms. Most paintings range from $20 to $350, although you can usually bargain them down a bit. Look for the brightly painted wall hangings crafted from sheets of metal. Also look for satirical metal wall hangings, brightly painted, representing the *tap-taps* (battered public minivans and buses) of Port-au-Prince. They make amusing and whimsical souvenirs of a trip to the Caribbean. Open daily from 10am to 6pm. Calle Fortaleza 206. © 787/721-4362. The other location is at Calle Fortaleza 367. © 787/725-0986. www.haitiangallerypr.com.

Obra Galería Alegría   A bit off the well-worn gallery route along Calle Cristo and Calle San José, this gallery is worth searching out for its representation of such important masters as Lorenzo Homar; Domingo García; Julio Rosado del Valle; and younger, accomplished, contemporary artists like Nick Quijano, Jorge Zeno, and Magda Santiago. The gallery was started by José Alegría, with the assistance of his uncle Ricardo Alegría, the founder of the Institute of Puerto Rican Culture. It's open Tuesday through Saturday from 10am to 6pm. Calle Cruz 301 (corner Recinto Sur). © 787/723-3206. www.obra galeria.com.

BOOKS

La Tertulia   A bookstore with a wide selection of books and music in a large, beautiful setting, La Tertulia carries the latest hits in Spanish and English, plus nonfiction, fiction, and classics in both Spanish and English. It's open Monday through Saturday from 9am to 10pm and Sunday from 10am to 8pm. Recinto Sur 305, Old San Juan. © 787/724-8200.

Librería Cronopios   This is the leading choice in the Old Town, with the largest selection of titles. It sells a number of books on Puerto Rican culture as well as good maps of the island. Calle San José 255. © 787/724-1815.

CARNIVAL MASKS

La Calle   Every Puerto Rican knows that the best, and cheapest, place to buy brightly painted carnival masks *(caretas)* is in Ponce, where the tradition of making them from papier-mâché originated. But if you can't spare the time for a side excursion to Ponce, this store in Old San Juan stocks one of the most varied inventories of *vegigantes* in the Puerto Rican capital. Tangles of menacing horns, fang-toothed leers, and bulging eyes are common features of these masks, which at carnival time are worn by costumed revelers. Depending on their size and composition (some include coconut shells, gourds, and flashy metal trim), they range from $10 to $2,500 each. Side-by-side with the pagan-inspired masks, you'll find a well-chosen selection of paintings by talented local artists, priced from $25 to $2,800 each. Calle Fortaleza 105. (② 787/725-1306.

CIGARS

The Cigar House   This retail outlet has a great selection of cigars, including Puerto Rican–based *jibarito* cigars, but it sells quality Dominican brands as well. It's a no-frills cigar shop with a nice selection. At the Doll House (which sells souvenirs now, "no dolls," the owner will shriek at you). Calle Fortaleza 255. (② 787/723-7797 or 725-0652.

Don Collin's Cigars   This is the main store of this locally produced brand of cigars, hand rolled on the island from locally grown tobacco and wraps, and sometimes mixed with fine tobacco from the Dominican Republic and elsewhere. There are nine varieties, and five-count and nine-count variety packs are available. Open daily from 9am to 8pm. Calle Cristo 59. (② 787/977-2983.

CLOTHING & BEACHWEAR

Costazul   This surf shop stocks major brands of beachwear, surfwear, sunglasses, and bathing suits for men, women, and children. The prices are not bad, and the merchandise is top rate. Worth a stop if you really need something for the beach. Calle San Francisco 264. (② 787/722-0991.

Hecho a Mano   The ethnic clothing for women here is made locally, using island fabric but also those from Guatemala, Indonesia, India, and Africa. Styles range from willowy dresses and wraps in tribal patterns, to more modern, tropical-fashion party dresses. It has gorgeous clothes, plus handmade jewelry and other interesting finds. The ambience in the store is wonderful, complete with incense, world music, and the beautiful sales staff outfitted in the store's fashion. Founded in 1993, the company prides itself on its dealings with its artisans and its efforts to undertake practices and designs in harmony with nature. Now with 12 locations, including Condado and Plaza Las Américas. Main location open Monday through Saturday from 10am to 7pm, Sunday from 11am to 5pm. Calle San Francisco 260, Viejo San Juan. (② 787/722-5322.

Nono Maldonado   Named after its owner, a Puerto Rico–born designer who worked for many years as the fashion editor of *Esquire* magazine, this is one of the most fashionable and upscale haberdashers in the Caribbean. Selling both men's and women's clothing, it contains everything from socks to dinner jackets, as well as ready-to-wear versions of Maldonado's twice-a-year collections. Both ready-to-wear and couture are available here. Av. Ashford 1051. (② 787/721-0456. Bus: A7.

Wet Boutique The ever chic Erika has been selling the sexiest swimsuits in town for decades. There's a wide selection of the top-name bikini and one-piece designs, plus upscale beach accessories. Calle Cruz 150, Old San Juan. (✆ 787/722-2052.

COFFEE & SPICES

Casa Galesa With "style and harmony" as its motto, this shop has beautiful stuff for home and gourmet items. From soap and candles to kitchen utensils, there's some beautiful stuff here for homebodies, or those who want to get a gift for one. Calle Cristo. (✆ 787/977-0400.

Spicy Caribbee This shop has the best selection of Puerto Rican coffee, which is gaining an increasingly good reputation among afi-cionados. Alto Grande is the grandest brand, but other specialty brands, like Yauco Selecto, are also quite wonderful. Other favorite brands of Puerto Rican coffee are Café Crema, Café Rico, Rioja, and Yaucono—in that order. The shop also has Old City's best array of hot spicy and sweet sauces of the Caribbean. Calle Cristo 154. (✆ 787/725-4690.

DEPARTMENT STORES

Marshalls This store, part of the U.S. discount chain, is one of our favorite department stores in the whole Caribbean. There's an incredible amount of quality stuff at good prices for the traveler: from bathing suits to shorts to sandals to luggage to sunglasses. In fact, this is probably your best bet for an affordable bathing suit. Calle Rafael Cordero 154, Old San Juan. (✆ 787/722-3020.

GIFTS & HANDICRAFTS

Bared & Sons (Value) Now in its fourth decade, this is the main outlet of a chain of at least 20 upper-bracket jewelry stores on Puerto Rico. It has a worthy inventory of gemstones, gold, diamonds, and wristwatches on the street level, which does a thriving business with cruise-ship passengers. But the real value of this store lies one floor up, where a monumental collection of porcelain and crystal is on display in claustrophobic proximity. It's a great source for hard-to-get and discontinued patterns (priced at around 20% less than at equivalent stateside outlets) from Christofle, Royal Doulton, Wedgwood, Limoges, Royal Copenhagen, Lalique, Lladró, Herend, Baccarat, and Daum. San Justo 206 (at the corner of Calle Fortaleza). (✆ 787/724-4811.

Bóveda This long, narrow space is crammed with exotic jewelry, clothing, greeting cards with images of life in Puerto Rico, some 100 handmade lamps, antiques, Mexican punched tin and glass, and Art Nouveau reproductions, among other items. Calle del Cristo 209. (✆ 787/725-0263.

DMR Designs   Located at La Cochera parking garage in the heart of the historic zone, this gallery of fine-art furniture and furnishings is a cool respite and well worth a look. The designs by Diana M. Ramos are reproductions and originals of classic Caribbean plantation furniture, more traditional Spanish colonial work, and spare, modern pieces. Their common traits are the artistic standards brought to them through their organic form and creativity. Calle Luna 204, Old San Juan. ℂ 787/722-4181.

Puerto Rican Arts & Crafts   Set in a 200-year-old colonial building, this unique store is one of the premier outlets on the island for authentic artifacts. Of particular interest are papier-mâché carnival masks from Ponce, whose grotesque and colorful features were originally conceived to chase away evil spirits. Taíno designs inspired by ancient petroglyphs are incorporated into most of the sterling silver jewelry sold here. There's an art gallery in back, with silk-screened serigraphs by local artists. The outlet has a gourmet Puerto Rican food section with items like coffee, rum, and hot sauces for sale. A related specialty of this well-respected store involves the exhibition and sale of modern replicas of the Spanish colonial tradition of *santos,* which are carved and sometimes polychromed representations of the Catholic saints and the infant Jesus. Priced from $50 to $1,100 each, and laboriously carved by artisans in private studios around the island, they're easy to pack in a suitcase because the largest one measures only 12 inches (31cm) from halo to toe. Open Monday through Saturday 9:30am to 6pm and Sunday 11am to 5pm. Calle Fortaleza 204. ℂ 787/725-5596.

Tienda del Instituto de Cultura Puertorriqueño   The official store of the Institute of Puerto Rican Culture sells books and other publications, audio and video productions, arts and crafts, typical foods, and other items related to Puerto Rico culture. You'll find high-quality work by artisans who practice time-treasured crafts with considerable skill. Closed Sunday. Plaza San José, beside the San José Church. ℂ 787/721-6866.

Vaughn's Gifts & Crafts   This store offers crafts from Puerto Rico and elsewhere but specializes in straw and Panamanian hats. It's quite a large collection for the tropical hat collector, plus other colorful crafts from the island and elsewhere in the region. Calle Fortaleza 262. ℂ 787/721-8221.

JEWELRY

Barrachina   It offers one of the largest selections of jewelry, perfume, cigars, and gifts in San Juan. There's a patio for drinks where you can order a piña colada. There is also a Bacardi rum outlet (bottles cost less than stateside but cost the same as at the Bacardi distillery), a costume jewelry department, a gift shop, and a section for authentic silver jewelry, plus a restaurant. Calle Fortaleza 104 (btw. Calle del Cristo and Calle San José). ✆ 787/725-7912.

Eduardo Barquet Known as a leading cost-conscious place to buy fine jewelry in Old San Juan, this shop has 14-karat Italian gold chains and bracelets that are measured, fitted, and sold by weight. You can purchase watches or beautiful gems in modern settings in both 14- and 18-karat gold. The store's collection also includes emerald, ruby, diamond, and pearl jewelry, along with platinum bridal jewelry. Calle Fortaleza 200 (at the corner of Calle La Cruz). ✆ 787/723-1989.

Joyería Riviera This emporium of 18-karat gold and diamonds adjacent to Plaza de Armas has an impeccable reputation. Its owner, Julio Abislaiman, stocks his store from such diamond centers as Antwerp, Tel Aviv, and New York. This is the major distributor of Rolex watches on Puerto Rico. Prices in the store range from $250 into the tens of thousands of dollars—at these prices, it's a good thing you can get "whatever you want," according to the owner. Calle Fortaleza 257. ✆ 787/725-4000.

Reinhold Jewelers This is one of Puerto Rico's top shops featuring work by local and world-renowned jewelry designers. Its main location, and the adjacent David Yurman design boutique, spreads across two locations at the ground floor of Plaza Las América inside one of its main entrances, and it's beautiful gazing through the long windows at the dazzling creations inside. There's also a location at El San Juan Hotel Gallery. This store's presence makes it necessary for the serious jewelry connoisseur to travel outside Plaza Las Américas. Plaza Las Américas 24A, 24B, Hato Rey. ✆ 787/554-0528. Other location at El San Juan Hotel Gallery, Isla Verde. ✆ 787/796-2521.

LEATHER & ACCESSORIES

Coach Here you can find fine leather goods, from belts to bags to purses. This outlet sells discontinued products so you can find some real bargains. Calle Cristo 150. ✆ 787/722-6830.

Dooney & Bourke Factory Store Leather lovers will also want to pass through here, especially for the buttery smooth women's handbags. It's right nearby, and it too has factory outlet prices, which means occasional bargains. Calle Cristo 200, Old San Juan. ✆ 787/289-0075.

MALLS

Plaza Las Américas The island's first big mall and still the largest in the Caribbean, Plaza, as it is known by locals, is a world unto itself. Even by U.S. standards, it's a remarkable place with top-name retailers, full-service restaurants, a Cineplex, two food courts, plus spa and hair stylists. Retail outlets include Macy's, Armani Exchange, Banana Republic, and Guess, as well as high-quality designer boutiques, with over 300 stores in all. There is also a U.S. Post Office, branches of all major island banks, and a full medical and office center. There are often shows and special events—from boat and race-car exhibits to fashion shows and concerts—taking place along its hallways. There's action from morning to night, and it's a quick trip from any San Juan hotel. Av. FD Roosevelt 525, Hato Rey. ℰ 787/767-5202. www.plazalas americas.net. Bus: B21.

MARKETS

Plaza del Mercado de Santurce   Come here if you'd like to visit an old-fashioned Puerto Rican market, something likely to be found in a small South American country. The central market is filled with "botanicas" hawking everything from medicinal herbs to Puerto Rican bay rum. Here is your best chance to pick up some patchouli roots. What are they used for? In religious observances and to kill unruly cockroaches. Some little cantinas here offer very typical Puerto Rican dishes, including roast pork, and you can also order the best mango banana shakes on the island. The seafood and *criollo* restaurants are some of the best in the city, at affordable prices. Calle Dos Hermanos at Calle Capitol, Santurce. ℰ 787/723-8022. Bus: B5.

---

4 SAN JUAN AFTER DARK

From the vibrant performing-arts scene to street-level salsa and the casinos, discos, and bars, San Juan offers entertainment every evening. Nightlife begins very late, especially on Friday and Saturday nights.

THE PERFORMING ARTS

Centro de Bellas Artes   In the heart of Santurce, the Performing Arts Center is a 6-minute taxi ride from most of the Condado hotels. It contains the Festival Hall, Drama Hall, and the Experimental Theater. Some of the events here will be of interest only to Spanish speakers; others attract an international audience. Av. Ponce de León 22. ℰ 787/724-4747 or 725-7334 for the ticket agent. Tickets $40–$200; 50% discounts for seniors. Bus: 1.

THE CLUB & MUSIC SCENE

Club Brava   The young and privileged, local celebs, and urbane visitors mix it up to a mix of house, reggaeton, and Latin music styles. The nightclub is designed in the form of a circle, with a central dance floor and a wraparound balcony, where onlookers and voyeurs—a 25- to 45-year-old age group—can observe the activities on the floor below. As one patron put it, "Here's where gringos can shake their bon-bons with San Juan's old guard." There's also a stage for special shows and events. Its location within the most exciting hotel in San Juan allows guests the chance to visit the hotel's bars, its intricately decorated lobby, and its casino en route. Open Thursday through Saturday from 10pm until 3am. In El San Juan Hotel & Casino, Av. Isla Verde 6063, Isla Verde. ✆ **787/791-2781.** Cover $15, free for guests of El San Juan Hotel. Bus: A5.

Club Lazer This Old San Juan Club has been hopping for nearly 2 decades through various transformations. A huge, cavernous place in the middle of town, it has salsa and other tropical music Friday nights and reggaeton Saturdays. Sundays, ladies night, are particularly jamming. The club opens at 10pm Wednesday and Friday through Sunday and attracts a large local crowd as well as regular customers who work on the cruise ship lines and young people from throughout the world. Calle Cruz 251, Old San Juan. ✆ **787/722-7581.**

Lupi's Mexican Grill & Sports Cantina You can hear some of the best Spanish rock at this Mexican pub and restaurant. It is currently a hot spot with typical South of the Border decoration and such familiar dishes as fajitas, nachos, and burritos. A wide range of people of all ages are attracted to the place, although after 10pm patrons in their 20s and 30s predominate. Live rock groups perform after 11pm. In addition to the nightly rock bands, Caribbean music is also played on Friday and karaoke on Sunday. There are also plenty of televisions throughout for sporting events. The Mexican food and pub fare are pretty good, too. There are both Isla Verde and Old San Juan locations. Isla Verde: Av. Isla Verde, Km 187. ✆ **787/253-1664.** Old San Juan: Recinto Sur 313. ✆ **787/722-1874.**

Nuyorican Café When the Rolling Stones played the new Coliseum during their last world tour, Mick Jagger and Keith Richards came straight here to listen to the salsa. There's live music here every

---

Music While You Munch

Several restaurants in Old San Juan, and elsewhere throughout the city, have live music on certain days of the week, including many listed here: **Amadeus Bistro Bar,** the **Parrot Club, Carli Café Concierto, Barrachina Restaurant, La Playita** in Isla Verde, and **Yerba Buena** in Condado.

night, with Latin jazz and reggae also complementing the salsa and Cuban music played on stage. There are also theatrical performances, art exhibits, and a damn good kitchen (the pizza is one of the island's best). Recent performers have included the top names in Puerto Rican music, including Pedro Guerra, Roy Brown, Alfredo Naranjo, Cultura Profética, and salsa greats Bobbie Valentín, Ray Santiago, Polito Huerta, Luis Marín, Jerry Medina, and Tito Allen. The cafe also hosts special weeklong musical festivals and has put on long-running performance art and theatrical programs, usually earlier in the evening before the bands get going. The Polito Huerta house band on Saturday nights plays smoking salsa, and Tuesday nights are Latin jazz. Rock lovers should head here Monday nights for some very fine rock *en español*. Pizzas are served to 1am, at least; bar until at least 3am. Calle San Francisco 312 (entrance down the alley), Old San Juan. ✆ 787/977-1276 or 366-5074. www.nuyoricancafepr.com.

Rumba This club has a full bar up front, a huge back room with a stage for live bands, and a huge dance floor. It's so photogenically hip that it was selected as the site for the filming of many of the crowd scenes within *Dirty Dancing: Havana Nights*. Set immediately adjacent to the also-recommended restaurant, Barú, with which it's not associated, it's known as another great venue for live music, with excellent salsa, Latin jazz, and other tropical music. There's a great crowd here, of different styles ranging from college kids to well-dressed gray beards who remember the music back in its 1970s heyday. The common denominator is the love of the music and dance. Open Tuesday to Sunday 9pm to 4am. Calle San Sebastián 152, Old San Juan. ✆ 787/725-4407.

THE BAR SCENE

Unless otherwise stated, there is no cover charge at the following bars.

El Batey Graffiti and business cards cover the walls of this dive bar with a great jukebox and a view of the procession up and down Calle Cristo during weekend nights. Drawings of the legends of this storied watering hole are hung in its main room. There's always somebody to talk to at the bar, which draws an eccentric local crowd and independent-minded visitors. Patrons play chess and backgammon as well. The jukebox has great classic and psychedelic rock, some great Sinatra, and some priceless jazz standards by the likes of Duke Ellington and Charlie Parker. Calle Cristo 101. ✆ 787/725-1787. No bus.

Ficus Café This modern, open-air cafe has caught on fast as a favorite with sanjuaneros. It's a fabulous spot, with the illuminated Convention Center looming behind it and a huge fountain in front performing an unending dance of liquid and light as if this were the

The Birth of the Piña Colada

When actress Joan Crawford tasted the piña colada at what was then the Beachcombers Bar in the **Caribe Hilton,** Calle Los Rosales (© 787/721-0303), she claimed it was "better than slapping Bette Davis in the face."

This famous drink is the creation of bartender Ramon "Monchito" Marrero, now long gone, who was hired by the Hilton in 1954. He spent 3 months mixing, tasting, and discarding hundreds of combinations until he felt he had the right blend. Thus, the frothy piña colada was born. It's been estimated that some 100 million of them have been sipped around the world since that fateful time.

Monchito never patented his formula and didn't mind sharing it with the world. Still served at the Hilton, here is his not-so-secret recipe:

2 ounces light rum
1 ounce coconut cream
1 ounce heavy cream
6 ounces fresh pineapple
$1/2$ cup crushed ice
Pineapple wedge and maraschino cherry for garnish

Pour rum, coconut cream, cream, and pineapple juice in blender. Add ice. Blend for 15 seconds. Pour into a 12-ounce glass. Add garnishes.

better future to which Puerto Rico is headed. The haute tropical ambience is also at work in the tapas and entrees of chef Luis Alvarez Príncipe. The drinks taste great washing down grilled shark bites, Caribbean hummus, lobster dumplings, cinnamon chicken croquettes with mango coleslaw, and sausages in wine with focaccia toast. The cafe is open Thursday through Saturday 5 to 11pm. There are special activities: Saturday nights have been dedicated to jazz and tapas, while Thursdays local liquor companies hold happy hours and sponsor DJs or other special activities. At the Puerto Rico Convention Bureau, 100 Convention Blvd. © 787/641-7722.

La Sombrilla Rosa   It's a nice neighborhood bar with daily happy hours, a relaxed atmosphere with friendly staff and patrons, and good music. Weekdays, until 3pm, it serves great *comida criolla* at prices ranging from $5.50 to $8. You'll find basic stuff like steak and onions and grilled chicken, everything with rice and pink beans and *tostones*.

La Rumba Party Cruise

The trouble with most nightlife venues in San Juan is that the real parties in conventional nightclubs begin at hours so impossibly late that the average visitor will tend to be deep asleep by the time the first dancers begin to rock 'n' roll. So if you love to salsa and merengue, but if you maintain relatively conservative ideas about your bedtime, consider the *La Rumba Party Cruise* as a viable option. It all takes place aboard a neon-lit two-level minicruiser that's moored most of the time to a point near Old San Juan's cruise pier no. 1 (Plaza Darsenas). Schedules vary according to business, but cruises tend to last 120 minutes each, and depart every Friday and Saturday at 10:30pm, 12:30am, and 2:30am; and every Sunday at 7:30, 9:30, and 11:30pm. And if you show up about an hour prior to a scheduled departure, you can fit in up to an extra hour's worth of shaking your booty to Latino music as the boat sits in port, music blaring, waiting for other clients. Cruises cost $15 per person (tax included), with children's rates $7.50 and seniors $11. There's a cash bar on board selling beer for between $4 and $6 each, depending on the brand. There's a sightseeing benefit to the experience as well: En route, as it chugs out to sea, participants garner sea-fronting views of both of San Juan's 18th-century forts and the coastline of Isla Verde. For reservations and more information, call ☎ **787/375-5211.**

6

Open from 9:30am to 3pm for lunch, then from 7pm to at least 3am nightly. Calle San Sebastián 154. ☎ **787/725-5656.** Bus: Old Town Trolley.

Palm Court Lobby   This is the most beautiful bar on the island—perhaps in the entire Caribbean. Hotel guests are the main clientele, but well-heeled locals make up at least a quarter of the business at this fashionable rendezvous. Set in an oval wrapped around a sunken bar area, amid marble and burnished mahogany, it offers a view of one of the world's largest chandeliers. After 7pm on Monday through Saturday, live music, often salsa and merengue, emanates from an adjoining room (El Chico Bar). Watch the models strut by, the honeymoon couple, or the table of high rollers from New York having a drink before trying their luck again. This is still the place to be seen in the city. Open daily 6pm to 3am. In El San Juan Hotel & Casino, Av. Isla Verde 6063, Isla Verde. ☎ **787/791-1000.** Bus: A5.

Raven Room Set on the upper floor of an antique building near the cruise-ship docks, this trendy, appealing lounge is a labyrinth of artfully minimalist rooms with comfortable seating, a changing array of dramatic oil paintings, and a mixture of bright lights and shadow that makes anyone look years younger. Although the place opens, at least theoretically, at 10pm, it doesn't begin to jump 'til after midnight. Open nightly until at least 2am. Recinto Sur 305. © 787/977-1083. Bus: Old Town Trolley.

Wet Bar This chic drinking spot operates out of San Juan's finest boutique hotel, the Water Club. This is the best bar for watching the sun set over San Juan. Lying on the 11th floor, it features jazz music and the Caribbean's only rooftop fireplace for those nippy nights in winter when you want to drink outside. The sensuous decor here includes striped zebrawood stools, futons, pillowy sofas, and hand-carved side tables. The walls feature Indonesian carved teak panels. It overlooks the brilliant Isla Verde coastline and its palm-fringed beachfront below. Latin rhythms mix with R&B standards and world rhythms. You can order sushi under the stars or some other delicacies from a limited menu. It's a beautiful place, with trendy martinis and plush comforts. Thursday through Saturday the Wet Bar is open 7pm to 1am. In the San Juan Water & Beach Club, Calle José M. Tartak 2. © 787/728-3666. www.waterbeachclubhotel.com/wet.php. Bus: A5.

HOT NIGHTS IN GAY SAN JUAN

Straight folks are generally welcome at gay venues, and many local couples show up for the hot music and dancing.

Beach Bar This is the site of a hugely popular Sunday afternoon gathering, which gets really crowded beginning around 4pm and stretches into the wee hours. There's an open-air bar protected from rain by a sloping rooftop and a space atop the seawall with a panoramic view of the Condado beachfront. Open daily 11am to 1am or later. On the ground floor of the Atlantic Beach Hotel, Calle Vendig 1. © 787/721-6900. Bus: B21.

Krash Klub Formerly Eros, this two-level nightclub is still the city's biggest gay club. Patterned after the dance emporiums of New York, but on a smaller scale, the club has cutting-edge music and bathrooms with creative decor. Regrettably, only 1 night a week (Wed) is devoted to Latino music; on other nights, the music is equivalent to what you'd find in the gay discos of either Los Angeles or New York City. Open Wednesday to Sunday 10pm to 3am or 5am. Av. Ponce de León 1257, Santurce. © 787/722-1131. www.krashklubpr.com. Cover $5. Bus: 1.

Barhopping

More than any other place in the Caribbean, San Juan has a nightlife that successfully combines New York hip with Latino zest and the music of the Spanish Tropics.

A good place to start your night is the bright and enchanting **El Picoteo** in the El Convento Hotel, Calle del Cristo 100 (© **787/723-9020**). Get warmed up with some tapas and a fine sangria as you sit at one of the tables on a terrace overlooking Cristo Street and the hotel's interior courtyard. It's a good hangout for late-night dialogues. At the bar inside, you can often hear live jazz.

Afterward, head for a pair of holes in the wall across the street from the El Convento Hotel. **El Batey,** Calle del Cristo 101 (no phone), and **Don Pablo,** Calle del Cristo 103 (no phone), are battered, side-by-side hangouts with a clientele of locals, expatriates, and occasional visitors. Whereas El Batey's music remains firmly grounded in the rock-'n'-roll classics of the 1970s, with a scattering of Elvis Presley and Frank Sinatra hits, Don Pablo prides itself on cutting-edge music that's continually analyzed by the counterculture aficionados who hang out here. El Batey is open daily from 2pm to 6am; Don Pablo, daily from 8pm to 4am.

You'll next want to head up the hill to **San Sebastián Street,** a place where Puerto Ricans have been partying for years. There is a line of restaurants and bars, running from Calle Cristo along this street down to Calle Cruz. On weekend evenings, the area is packed with fashionable crowds out for

CASINOS

Nearly all the large hotels in San Juan/Condado/Isla Verde offer casinos. The atmosphere in the casinos is casual, but still you shouldn't show up in bathing suits or shorts. Most casinos open around noon and close after 2am. Guest patrons must be at least 18 years old to enter.

The 18,500-square-foot (1,719-sq.-m) **Ritz-Carlton Casino,** Avenue of Governors, Isla Verde (© **787/253-1700**), is Puerto Rico's largest. With elegant 1940s decor and tropical fabrics, this is one of fun. **Nono's,** San Sebastion 100 at the corner of Cristo (© **787/579-5851**), is a great spot to watch the action out on Plaza San José. **El Patio de Sam** has been a favorite watering hole for locals and tourists since the 1950s. **Candela,** Calle San Sebastián 100 (© **787/977-4305**), is a late night avant-garde club that plays eclectic lounge music until the earlier morning hours. There are often festivals of experimental music and art held here. Any of the bars along this strip is worth a look; many have pool tables and jukeboxes with great selections of classic salsa. A must-stop, however, is **Rumba,** San Sebastián 152 (© **787/977-4305**), where you will find live salsa and other tropical music. Your final stop will likely be **Aqui Se Puede,** corner of San Justo, Calle San Justo 50 (© **787/579-5851**), which has great music, either live or on the jukebox, plus frequent special events like performances and art shows.

If you need sustenance after all that drinking, head to **Tantra,** Calle Fortaleza 356 (© **787/977-8141**), which has the best late-night menu in town, as well as a creative martini menu, including versions with mango, passion fruit, and a personal favorite, a version with cinnamon and clove. Live belly dancers amuse the crowd on Friday and Saturday nights, and any night of the week you can rent, for $20, a Mogul-style hookah pipe for every member of your dining table If the idea of playing pasha for a night appeals to you.

the plushest and most exclusive gaming houses in the Caribbean. One of the splashiest of San Juan's casinos is at the **Old San Juan Hotel & Casino,** Calle Brumbaugh 100 (© 787/721-5100), where five-card stud competes with some 240 slot machines and roulette tables. You can also try your luck at the **El San Juan Hotel & Casino** (one of the most grand), Av. Isla Verde 6063 (© 787/791-1000), or the **Condado Plaza Hotel & Casino,** Av. Ashford 999 (© 787/721-1000). You do not have to flash passports or pay any admission fees.

7

Near San Juan

Within easy reach of San Juan's cosmopolitan bustle are superb attractions and natural wonders. With San Juan as your base, you can explore the island by day and return in time for dinner and an evening on the town.

1 EL YUNQUE ★★★

25 miles (40km) E of San Juan

The El Yunque rainforest, a 45-minute drive east of San Juan, is a major attraction in Puerto Rico. The El Yunque National Forest is the only tropical forest in the U.S. National Forest Service system. The 28,000-acre (11,331-hectare) preserve was given its status by President Theodore Roosevelt. Today the virgin forest remains much as it was in 1493, when Columbus first sighted Puerto Rico.

GETTING THERE

From San Juan, take Route 26 or the Baldorioty de Castro Expressway East to Carolina, where you will pick up Route 66 or the Roberto Sánchez Vilella Expressway. The $1.50 toll road will take you farther along Route 3, putting you in Canóvanas. Go right, east, on Route 3, which you follow east to the intersection of Route 191, a two-lane highway that heads south into the forest. Take 191 for 3 miles (4.8km), going through the village of Palmer. As the road rises, you will have entered the Caribbean National Forest. You can stop in at the El Portal Tropical Forest Center to pick up information (see below).

VISITOR INFORMATION

El Portal Tropical Forest Center, Route 191, Río Grande (© 787/888-1880), an $18-million exhibition and information center, has 10,000 square feet (929 sq. m) of exhibition space. Three pavilions offer exhibits and bilingual displays. The actor Jimmy Smits narrates a documentary called "Understanding the Forest." The center is open daily from 9am to 5pm; it charges an admission of $3 for adults and $1.50 for children 11 and under.

El Yunque is the most popular spot in Puerto Rico for hiking. Hikers will find useful information at any of the park's visitor information

are conducted Saturday to Monday every hour on the hour from
10:30am to 3:30pm; they cost $5 for adults and $3 for children 11
and under.

EXPLORING EL YUNQUE

Encompassing four distinct forest types, El Yunque is home to 240
species of tropical trees, flowers, and wildlife. More than 20 varieties
of orchids and 50 varieties of ferns share this diverse habitat with millions of tiny tree frogs, whose distinctive cry of *coquí* (pronounced
"ko-*kee*") has given them their name. Tropical birds include the lively,
greenish-blue, red-fronted Puerto Rican parrot, once nearly extinct
and now making a comeback.

El Yunque is the best of Puerto Rico's 20 forest preserves. The forest is situated high above sea level, with El Toro its highest peak. You
can be fairly sure you'll be showered upon during your visit, since
more than 100 billion gallons of rain fall here annually. However, the
showers are brief, and there are many shelters.

HIKING TRAILS   One of the best hikes, which takes 2 hours
round-trip, is called the **Big Tree Trail,** which winds through the
towering trees of the Tabonuco Forest and passes the beautiful La
Mina Falls, a great waterfall and natural pool where you can take a
dip. The mountain stream seems freezing at first but becomes abso-
lutely refreshing nearly instantaneously. Along the trail you might
spot such native birds as the Puerto Rican woodpecker, the tanager,
the screech owl, and the bullfinch.

Those with more time might opt for the **El Yunque Trail,** which
takes 4 hours round-trip to traverse. This trail—signposted from El
Caimitillo Picnic Grounds—takes you on a steep, winding path.
Along the way you pass natural forests of sierra palm and *palo colorado*
before descending into the dwarf forest of Mount Britton, which is
often shrouded in clouds. Your major goal, at least for panoramic
views, will be the lookout peaks of Roca Marcas, Yunque Rock, and
Los Picachos. On a bright, clear day, you can see all the way to the
eastern shores of the Atlantic.

DRIVING THROUGH EL YUNQUE   If you're not a hiker but you
appreciate rainforests, you can still enjoy El Yunque. You can drive
through the forest on Route 191, which is a tarmac road. This trail
goes from the main highway of Route 3, penetrating deep into El
Yunque. You can see ferns that grow some 120 feet (37m) tall, and at
any minute you expect a hungry dinosaur to peek between the fronds,
looking for a snack. You're also treated to lookout towers offering
panoramic views, waterfalls, picnic areas, and even a restaurant.

Ceiba Country Inn (Finds)   This small, well-maintained bed-and-breakfast is located 15 miles (24km) from El Yunque. The rooms, painted in tropical motifs, are on the bottom floor of a large, old family home, and each has a private shower-only bathroom. For a quiet evening cocktail, try the small lounge on the second floor.

Road no. 977 Km 1.2 (P.O. Box 1067), Ceiba, PR 00735. (📞 **888/560-2816** or 787/885-0471. Fax 787/885-0471. 9 units (shower only). $85 double. Rate includes breakfast. AE, DISC, MC, V. Free parking. **Amenities:** Bar (guests only); patio for outdoor entertainment. *In room:* A/C, fridge, ceiling fan.

2 LUQUILLO BEACH ★★★

31 miles (50km) E of San Juan

GETTING THERE
If you are driving, follow the above directions to Canóvanas and continue on Route 3 east into Río Grande. The entrance to El Yunque is on the right, and just beyond is the left turn to the Wyndham. The Gran Melía Puerto Rico is also off Hwy. 3.

HITTING THE BEACH
Luquillo Beach ★★★, Puerto Rico's finest beach, is palm-dotted and crescent-shaped, opening onto a lagoon with calm waters and a wide, sandy bank. It's very crowded on weekends but much better during the week. There are lockers, tent sites, showers, picnic tables, and food stands that sell a sampling of the island's *frituras* (fried fare), especially cod fritters and tacos. The beach is open from 8:30am to 5pm Wednesday through Sunday, plus holidays.

GOLF
Tom Kite and Bruce Besse designed two 18-hole courses for the **Trump International Golf Club Puerto Rico,** Clubhouse Dr. 100, Río Grande 00745 (📞 **787/657-2000**), adjacent to the well-recommended Gran Melia Puerto Rico (see below). You face a spectacular vista of fairways, lakes, and the Atlantic beyond. Four 9-hole loops fan out from the Caribbean's largest clubhouse. Each paspalum-grass course is imbued with its own character, including elevation changes. In the backdrop El Yunque's peaks stare at you. The Palms is a sprawling layout skirting wetlands, with the most difficult par 3 and the longest (571 yards/522m) par 5. Winter fees are $160 per 18 holes or $140 after noon. Fees include golf carts. The Paradise Bay Grill overlooks the

ocean and serves up freshly caught lobster and succulent steaks, and the locker rooms feature massages and Jacuzzis. Donald Trump announced a $600-million investment with a local partner to construct luxury vacation villas and make other improvements when he bought it in 2008.

The **Wyndham Río Mar Beach Resort** (see below) has two world-class courses, stretching out in the shadow of El Yunque rainforest along a dazzling stretch of coast. The entire 6,782 yards (6,201m) of Tom and George Fazio's Ocean Course has seaside panoramas and breezes, and fat iguanas scampering through the lush grounds. The other course, a 6,945-yard (6,351m) design by golf pro Greg Norman, follows the flow of the Mameyes River through mountain and coastal vistas. Greens fees are $165 for guests, $200 for nonresident walk-ons.

Another nice option in town is the **Bahia Beach Plantation Resort and Golf Club** (Rte. 187 Km 4.2; ✆ **787/857-5800**), with greens fees weekdays at $225 and weekends at $275. For years it was a favorite of local golfers, but Robert Trent Jones, Jr., renovated the course with a breathtaking new design that was inaugurated in April 2008. He spent 3 years working on the 7,014-yard (6,414m) course, sprawling across some 480 acres (194 hectares) of lush beachfront, running from the tip of Loiza River to the mouth of the Espíritu Santo River. Much of the course overlooks a verdant green valley of El Yunque rainforest. The new course is part of the new luxury Saint Regis resort being developed on the beautiful site with a planned opening in winter 2009.

WHERE TO STAY

Gran Melia Puerto Rico ★★★ (Kids) Checking into this pocket of posh on the Miquillo de Río Grande peninsula is the best reason for heading east of San Juan. An all-suite luxury resort, it has set new standards for comfort, convenience, and amenities along the Atlantic northeastern shoreline. Set amid gardens of 40 acres (16 hectares), it opens onto the white sands of the mile-long (1.6km) shoreline of Coco Beach. From watersports to two 18-hole golf courses, the resort has everything on-site, including whirlpool tubs and massage tables. Spa treatments revitalize and rejuvenate. You can also wander the globe in the widely varied restaurants, ranging from Italian to Southeast Asian. Naturally, the chefs also prepare locally caught seafood imbued with Creole flavor.

You will find golf, a full-service spa, a slew of watersports possibilities, and a Kids Club that will keep your young ones happy and busy. The staff is great at organizing activities, and you can take salsa and merengue dancing lessons by the pool. It's a big reason why this resort is a cut above some competitors, and why you will have so much fun here.

Coco Beach Blvd. 1000, Río Grande, PR 00745. *C* **866/436-3542** or 787/809-1770. Fax 787/809-1785. www.gran-melia-puerto-rico.com. 582 units. Winter $610–$700 suite for 2, $760–$910 Royal Service Suite; off season $264–$314 suite for 2, $344–$424 Royal Service Suite. AE, DISC, MC, V. **Amenities:** 6 restaurants; 3 bars; 2 outdoor pools; 2 golf courses; 3 lit tennis courts; fitness center; gym; spa; sauna; kids' clubs; business center; 24-hr. room service; babysitting; laundry service; dry cleaning; nonsmoking rooms; casino; medical services; rooms for those w/limited mobility. *In room:* A/C, TV, dataport, kitchenette, minibar, beverage maker, hair dryer, iron, safe.

The Río Mar Beach Resort & Spa, A Wyndham Grand Resort ★

This is a great spot to have fun in the sun and relax, but if you're expecting roaring nightlife or a cultural experience, stay elsewhere. The resort lies between the El Yunque rainforest and the Atlantic coastline. One of its championship golf courses, designed by George and Tom Fazio, crisscrosses the dramatic coastline, while the other, by Greg Norman, winds through lush tropical forest. Watersports offerings include sailing, snorkeling, scuba, parasailing, windsurfing, kite boarding, and others. There are also other sports activities like volleyball and water polo, and lots to do for children, including the Iguana Club for kids and a game room. There's a kids' pool next to the adult pool, which are both right near the beach. And you can actually fulfill a Caribbean dream and go horseback riding through the rainforest and along the beach. (We highly recommend this.)

Landscaping includes several artificial lakes situated amid tropical gardens. Guest rooms either overlook the palm-lined Atlantic or the green mountains of the rainforest. The style is Spanish hacienda with nods to the surrounding jungle; unusual art and sculpture alternate with dark woods, deep colors, rounded archways, big windows, and tile floors. In the bedrooms, muted earth tones and natural woods add to the ambience. Bedrooms are spacious, with balconies or terraces, and good mattresses, plus tub/shower combinations in the large bathrooms.

Río Mar Blvd. 6000, Río Grande, PR 00745. *C* **877/636-0636** or 787/888-6000. Fax 787/888-6600. www.wyndhamriomar.com. 600 units. Winter $359–$509 double; off season $189–$339 double; year-round from $695 suite. Children ages 5–17 staying in parent's room $85, including meals and activities; free for 4 and under. AE, DC, DISC, MC, V. 19 miles east of Luis Muñoz Marín International Airport, with entrance off Puerto Rico Hwy. 3. **Amenities:** 8 restaurants; 4 bars; outdoor pool; 13 tennis courts; health club and spa; deep-sea fishing; sailing; children's programs; 24-hr. room service; laundry; dry cleaning; nonsmoking rooms; casino; horseback

WHERE TO DINE

Brass Cactus Finds AMERICAN/REGIONAL   This amiable
spot has thrived since the early 1990s, when it was established by an
Illinois-born bartender who outfitted the interior with gringo memo-
rabilia. It's a great American-style pub, where you can hear rock 'n'
roll or catch a game on television. Menu items include king crab
salad; tricolor tortellini laced with chicken and shrimp; several kinds
of sandwiches, burgers, and wraps; and platters of churrasco, T-bone
steaks, chicken with tequila sauce, barbecued pork, and fried mahimahi. Locations in Luquillo and Loiza.

In the Condominio Complejo Turistico, Rte. 3, Marginal. © **787/889-5735.**
Another location at Rte. 3, Plaza Noreste Centro Comercial, Loíza. © **787/256-
0595.** Reservations not necessary. Sandwiches $8–$11; main courses $8–$26. MC,
V. Sun–Thurs 11am–11pm; Fri–Sat 11am–midnight.

Palio ★ ITALIAN   This richly decorated restaurant is the premier
dining outlet of the region's largest and splashiest hotel. A certain
attachment to culinary tradition doesn't preclude a modern approach
to the cookery. Dishes we've sampled have a superbly aromatic flavor
and are beautifully presented and served. The sophisticated menu
includes potato and sage gnocchi; rack of American lamb; fresh
Maine lobster; center-cut veal chops stuffed with fresh mozzarella,
tomatoes, and avocado and served with grappa-laced mashed potatoes; and baby free-range chicken, spit-roasted and served with rosemary jus.

In the Wyndham Río Mar Beach Resort and Golf Club. © **787/888-6000.** Reservations recommended. Main courses $22–$52. AE, DC, MC, V. Daily 6am–11pm.

Sandy's Seafood Restaurant & Steak House ★ Value SEA-
FOOD/STEAKS/PUERTO RICAN   The concrete-and-plate-glass
facade is less obtrusive than that of other restaurants in town, and the
cramped, Formica-clad interior is far from stylish. Nonetheless, Sandy's is one of the most famous restaurants in northeastern Puerto
Rico, thanks to the wide array of luminaries who travel from as far
away as San Juan to dine here. Set about a block from the main square
of the seaside resort of Luquillo, it was founded in 1984 by Miguel
Angel, aka Sandy. Platters, especially the daily specials, are so huge
they are discussed with fervor by competitors and clients alike.

Calle Fernandez García 276. © **787/889-5765.** Reservations recommended. Main
courses $8–$25; lunch special Mon–Fri 11am–2:30pm $5. AE, MC, V. Wed–Mon
11am to btw. 9:30 and 11pm, depending on business.

3 DORADO ★

18 miles (29km) W of San Juan

For decades, the Hyatt Cerromar and Dorado Beach put this north coast beach town west of San Juan on the world tourism map. The storied resorts had world-class facilities housed in classic quarters along a stunning coastal stretch of rolling palm groves and white-sand beaches. Currently, vacation and golf clubs are operated on the former site, and there are plans to renovate the old resort buildings and reopen as a luxury resort.

This area was originally developed in 1905 by Dr. Alfred T. Livingston (a Jamestown, New York, physician) as a 1,000-acre (405-hectare) grapefruit-and-coconut plantation. Then Livingston's daughter Clara (an aviator and friend of Amelia Earhart) built an airstrip here and sold the 1,700-acre (688-hectare) site in 1955 to the Rockefeller family. Her former house, now called Su Casa, which served as a golf clubhouse in the '70s and restaurant from 1982 to 2006, remains on the property. On May 31, 2006, 48 years after Laurence Rockefeller officially opened the hotel, the resorts that had made Dorado synonymous with upscale tourism closed their doors. It brought an end to a legendary resort—with a list of clients including former presidents John F. Kennedy, Dwight Eisenhower, Gerald Ford, and George H. Bush; as well as athletic greats Joe Namath, Mickey Mantle, and Joe DiMaggio; and actresses Joan Crawford and Ava Gardner.

GETTING THERE

If you're driving from San Juan, take Expressway 22 west. Take exit 22-A to get on Route 165 north to Dorado. Alternately, you can take the meandering coastal route along Hwy. 2 west to Route 693 north to Dorado (trip time: 40 min.). You'll pass a couple interesting beaches and coastal lookouts, as well as fine spots to eat.

HITTING THE BEACHES

There are a few fine bathing beaches along this route before getting to Dorado. The best is probably **Cerro Gordo** public beach (Rte. 690, Vega Alta; ✆ **787/883-2730**), along with the **Manuel "Nolo" Morales** public beach along Dorado's "Costa del Oro," or "Gold Coast" (✆ **787/796-2830**). Both charge $3 per car parking fee and keep the same hours as other public beaches and parks, Wednesday through Sunday and holidays, 8:30am to 5pm.

Tips

World-Class Golf at the Former Hyatt Dorado

The Hyatt Dorado Beach and Cerromar closed their doors in May 2006, but luckily their world-class golf courses and country club are still open. The former **Dorado Beach resort's professional golf courses** ★★, designed by Robert Trent Jones, Sr., match the finest anywhere. They are now operated by the **Dorado Beach Resort & Club.** The two original courses, known as East and West, were carved out of a jungle and offer tight fairways bordered by trees and forests, with lots of ocean holes. The somewhat newer and less noted North and South courses, now called the Plantation Club, feature wide fairways with well-bunkered greens and an assortment of water traps and tricky wind factors. Each is a par-72 course (call ✆ **787/796-8961** or 626-1006, the Dorado Beach Pro Shop, for tee times). The longest is the South course, at 7,047 yards (6,444m). Fees for all courses hover around $160 for nonresidents. Golf carts are included for all courses, and the two pro shops have both a bar and snack-style restaurant. Both are open daily from 7am until dusk. There are plenty of opportunities for a post-game meal in Dorado afterward, but none better than the two upscale restaurants right near the golf course that have remained open: Hacienda del Sol and Zafra (call ✆ **787/796-8999** for either). Dorado Beach Dr. 100, Ste. 1, Dorado, PR 00646. ✆ **787/796-1234.** www.doradobeachclubs.com.

WHERE TO STAY

Dorado's lodging options were severely limited when the two Hyatt properties shut their doors. Upscale resort development at the site is now taking place.

Embassy Suites Dorado del Mar Beach & Golf Resort ★

This beachfront property in Dorado lies less than 2 miles (3.2km) from the center of Dorado and has easy access to the San Juan airport. It is the only all-suite resort in Puerto Rico, and it has been a success since its opening in 2001. The property offers two-room suites with balconies and 38 two-bedroom condos.

The suites are spread over seven floors, each spacious and furnished in a Caribbean tropical motif, with artwork and one king-size bed or two double beds. Most of them have ocean views of the water. Each condo has a living room, kitchen, whirlpool, and balcony.

Although the accommodations are suites or condos, one bedroom in a condo can be rented as a double room (the rest of the condo is shut off). Likewise, it's also possible for two people to rent one bedroom in a condo, with the living room and kitchen facilities available (the other bedroom is closed off). Because condos contain two bedrooms, most of them are rented to parties of four.

The hotel attracts many families because of its very spacious accommodations. It also attracts golfers because of its Chi Chi Rodriguez signature par-72, 18-hole golf course set against a panoramic backdrop of mountains and ocean.

Dorado del Mar Blvd. 210, Dorado, PR 00646. © **787/796-6125.** Fax 787/796-6145. www.embassysuitesdorado.com. 212 units. Year-round $160–$250 suite; $260–$485 1-bedroom villa; $360–$560 2-bedroom villa. AE, DC, DISC, MC, V. **Amenities:** 2 restaurants; bar and grill; pool; golf; tennis court; limited room service; massage; laundry service; dry cleaning; rooms for those w/limited mobility. *In room:* A/C, TV, dataport, kitchenette, wet bar, hair dryer, iron, safe.

4 ARECIBO & CAMUY ★

68 to 77 miles (109–124km) W of San Juan

GETTING THERE

Arecibo Observatory lies a 1¼-hour drive west of San Juan, outside the town of Arecibo. From San Juan head west along four-lane Route 22 until you reach the town of Arecibo. At Arecibo, head south on Route 10; the 20-mile (32km) drive south on this four-lane highway is almost as interesting as the observatory itself. From Route 10, take exit 75-B and follow the signposts along a roller-coaster journey on narrow two-lane roads. First you will go right on Route 652 and take a left on Route 651. Proceed straight through the intersection of Route 651 and Route 635, and then turn left at the cemetery onto Route 625, which will lead you to the entrance of the observatory.

On the same day you visit the Arecibo Observatory, you can also visit the Río Camuy Cave Park. The caves also lie south of the town of Arecibo. Follow Route 129 southwest from Arecibo to the entrance of the caves, which are at Km 18.9 along the route, north of the town of Lares. Like the observatory, the caves lie approximately 1½ hours west of San Juan.

Dubbed "an ear to heaven," **Observatorio de Arecibo** ★ (© 787/
878-2612; www.naic.edu) contains the world's largest and most sen-
sitive radar/radio-telescope, which features a 20-acre (8-hectare) dish,
or radio mirror, set in an ancient sinkhole. It's 1,000 feet (305m) in
diameter and 167 feet (51m) deep, and it allows scientists to monitor
natural radio emissions from distant galaxies, pulsars, and quasars,
and to examine the ionosphere, the planets, and the moon using
powerful radar signals. Used by scientists as part of the Search for
Extraterrestrial Intelligence (SETI), this is the same site featured in
the movie *Contact* with Jodie Foster. This research effort speculates
that advanced civilizations elsewhere in the universe might also com-
municate via radio waves. The 10-year, $100-million search for life in
space was launched on October 12, 1992, the 500-year anniversary of
the New World's discovery by Columbus. Unusually lush vegetation
flourishes under the giant dish, including ferns, wild orchids, and
begonias. Assorted creatures like mongooses, lizards, and dragonflies
have also taken refuge there. Suspended in an outlandish fashion
above the dish is a 600-ton (544,311kg) platform that resembles a
space station.

You are allowed to walk around the platform, taking in views of
this gigantic dish. At the Angel Ramos Foundation Visitor Center,
you are treated to interactive exhibitions on the various planetary
systems and introduced to the mystery of meteors and educated about
intriguing weather phenomena. Tours are available at the observatory
Wednesday through Friday from noon to 4pm, Saturday and Sunday
from 9am to 4pm. Normal hours are Wednesday through Sunday,
9am to 4pm, but during a summer session (June 1–July 31) and a
winter session (Dec 15–Jan 15) the observatory is open to visitors
every day. The cost is $5 for adults, $3 for seniors and children.
There's a souvenir shop on the grounds. Plan to spend about 1¹/₂
hours at the observatory.

Parque de las Cavernas del Río Camuy (Río Camuy Caves) ★★★
(© 787/898-3100) contains the third-largest underground river in
the world. It runs through a network of caves, canyons, and sinkholes
that have been cut through the island's limestone base over the course
of millions of years. Known to the pre-Columbian Taíno peoples, the
caves came to the attention of speleologists in the 1950s; they were
led to the site by local boys already familiar with some of the entrances
to the system. The caves were opened to the public in 1986. Visitors
should allow about 2 hours for the total experience.

Visitors first see a short film about the caves and then descend into
the caverns in open-air trolleys. The trip takes you through a

200-foot-deep (61m) sinkhole and a chasm where tropical trees, ferns, and flowers flourish, along with birds and butterflies. The trolley then goes to the entrance of Clara Cave of Epalme, one of 16 caves in the Camuy caves network, where visitors begin a 45-minute walk, viewing the majestic series of rooms rich in stalagmites, stalactites, and huge natural "sculptures" formed over the centuries.

Tres Pueblos Sinkhole, located on the boundaries of the Camuy, Hatillo, and Lares municipalities, measures 65 feet (20m) in diameter, with a depth of 400 feet (122m)—room enough to fit all of El Morro Fortress in San Juan. In Tres Pueblos, visitors can walk along two platforms—one on the Lares side, facing the town of Camuy, and the other on the Hatillo side, overlooking Tres Pueblos Cave and the Río Camuy.

The caves are open Wednesday through Sunday from 8am to 3pm. Tickets cost $12 for adults, $7 for children 4 to 12, and $5 for seniors. Parking is $2. For more information, phone the park.

Back down in Arecibo, a fun and interesting stop, especially if you are traveling with children, is the **Arecibo Lighthouse & Historic Park** (Hwy. 655, El Muelle, Barrio Islote, Arecibo; ✆ 787/880-7540; www.arecibolighthouse.com). Housed in a lighthouse built by the Spanish in 1898, this "cultural theme park" takes visitors on a history of Puerto Rico. But it's a very tactile tour, where you can actually walk through many of the exhibits. It really hits kids; it hit the kid in us. That's how we were riveted by the slave quarters, thrilled with the mammoth pirate ship, and excited and scared at the same time upon entering the pirate's cave, with its alligators and sharks. Tickets are $9 adults, $7 children and seniors. The park is open 9am to 6pm weekdays and holidays and 10am to 7pm weekends.

WHERE TO DINE

If you want to eat before heading back to the city, Arecibo is a good place, with several fine restaurants. The hands-down best, however, is the nearby **Salitre Mesón Costero** (Rte. 681 Km 3.8, Barrio Islote, Arecibo; ✆ 787/816-2020). You can taste the salt of the sea in the breeze blowing through this charming oceanfront restaurant's terrace dining area and in the smacking-fresh seafood served here. The dining room has big windows overlooking the coast, and there's also a comfortable bar. This is a great place to watch the sunset. We love the house specialty, a kind of *criolla* version of the classic Spanish seafood paella, called *mamposteado de mariscos,* with mussels, shrimp, and freshly caught fish, octopus, or calamari. Its seafood-stuffed *mofongo* platters and the whole red snapper with *tostones* are also hard to beat.

5 KARST COUNTRY ★★

48 miles (77km) W of San Juan

One of the most interesting areas of Puerto Rico to explore is the large **Karst Country,** south of Arecibo. One of the world's strangest rock formations, karst is formed by the process of water sinking into limestone. As time goes by, larger and larger basins are eroded, forming sinkholes. *Mogotes* (karstic hillocks) are peaks of earth where the land didn't sink into the erosion pits. The Karst Country lies along the island's north coast, directly northeast of Mayagüez in the foothills between Quebradillas and Manatí. The region is filled with an extensive network of caves. One sinkhole contains the 20-acre (8-hectare) dish of the world's largest radio/radar telescope at the Arecibo Observatory (see above). South of the Karst Country looms the massive central mountain region and Utuado at the heart of the massive Cordillera Central mountain range, which rides the island's back from east to west like an elevated spine.

GETTING THERE   Leaving San Juan, take the four-lane highway, Route 22, until you come to the town of Arecibo, a 1½-hour drive, depending on traffic. Once at Arecibo, take Route 10 south, in the direction of Utuado.

If you'd like a specific goal for exploring in the Karst Country, visit the Arecibo Observatory and the Río Camuy Caves, previewed above. However, you can also spend a day driving at random, exploring lakes and forests at your leisure.

6 CENTRAL MOUNTAINS ★

Utuado marks the southern border of Karst Country at dead center of the Cordillera Central mountain range. Make sure to stop at **Lagos dos Bocas** ★, one of the most beautiful lakes of the Karst Country, a reservoir adjacent to the Río Abajo Forest. Small boats, *launches* ★, traverse the lake leaving from a dock on the west side of the lake along Route 123 every half-hour. It's a 30-minute ride across the lake to the other main dock. On weekends, modest wooden restaurants around the lake open to serve visitors, and the launch makes stops at them. To experience the island's central mountains, continue driving up into the mountains above Lago Dos Bocas, through curving country roads. Utuado is a stronghold of *jíbaro* (country folk) culture, reflecting the mountain life of the island as few other settlements do.

Take Route 111 going west to Lares to visit the **Parque Ceremonial Indígena Caguaña (Indian Ceremonial Park at Caguaña).** Built by the Taíno Indians some 1,000 years ago, the site was used for both recreation and worship, and it is encircled by mountains near the Tanama River. You can still see the outlines of the ancient *bateyes* (ball courts), which are bordered by carved stone monoliths decorated with petroglyphs. The best-known petroglyph is the much-photographed *Mujer de Caguaña,* squatting in the position of an earth-mother fertility symbol. There is a small and very minor museum of Indian artifacts and skeletons on-site. Charging no admission, the site is open daily from 8am to 4pm. For more information, call ✆ **787/ 894-7300.**

From Lares, take Route 129 south to return to Arecibo, a good spot for a meal before taking the expressway back to San Juan (p. 35).

WHERE TO STAY

Casa Grande Mountain Retreat   This parador, situated on 107 lush and steeply inclined acres (43 hectares) of a former coffee plantation in the Caonillas Barrios district, about 1½ hours from San Juan, originated in the 19th century as a hacienda. Thanks to Steve Weingarten, a retired lawyer from New York City, the isolated compound functions today as a simple, eco-sensitive hotel. The cement-sided core of the original hacienda is on view in the lobby and in the likable eatery, Jungle Jane's Restaurant, which serves an array of well-prepared international and Puerto Rican Creole-style dishes. Nonguests can eat here daily from 7:30am to 9:30pm.

Accommodations lie within five wood-sided cottages (four units to a cottage, some of them duplex) scattered throughout the surrounding acreage. Each unit has deliberately simple, spartan-looking decor with exposed wood, airy verandas, a balcony, hammock, view of the mountains, and a small bathroom with shower. None has TV, phone, or air-conditioning—as such, they're popular with urbanites who want to get back to nature, and some come here to brush up on yoga and meditation skills. A nature trail is carved out of the surrounding forest. Under separate management, a riding stable offers horseback riding a short distance away.

P.O. Box 1499, Utuado, PR 00641. ✆ **888/343-2272** or 787/894-3900. Fax 787/ 894-3900. www.hotelcasagrande.com. 20 units. Year-round $80–$90 double. AE, DISC, MC, V. From Arecibo, take Rte. 10 south to Utuado, then head east on Rte. 111 to Rte. 140; head north on Rte. 140 to Rte. 612 for ¼-mile/.4km. **Amenities:** Restaurant; bar; pool. *In room:* Ceiling fan, no phone.

THE SOUTHERN ROUTE
TO THE MOUNTAINS

A much easier way to the central mountains from San Juan, however, is to head south along the Luis A. Ferré Expressway, Hwy. 52, to **Cayey** and even farther up to **Aibonito.** You can take an afternoon drive and have dinner as the sun sets in the mountains; from some vantage points, the view goes all the way to the coast.

In fact, this path is well worn by sanjuaneros heading south with mountain air and food on their mind. Their first stop is usually **Gua-vate,** a small village outside the Carite Forest Nature Reserve, famous for its *lechoneras,* which on weekends draw a lively crowd from early on. Live bands play romantic ballads, salsa, merengue, or country music, and patrons burn up dance floors between dining rooms and food stands, in front of the open-air fire pits where whole pigs, chickens, and turkeys are slowly roasted Puerto Rican style.

The best restaurants, however, have a certain rustic charm. Some look like wooden tropical chalets with blooming flowers, while others are set in front of a stream gushing through a lush mountainside. Our favorites include **La Casa del Guanime** (Rte. 184 Km 27.8; ✆ 787/744-3921), **El Rancho Original** (Rte. 184 Km 27.5; ✆ 787/747-7296), **Los Pinos** (Rte. 184 Km 27.7; ✆ 787/286-1917), and **El Mojito** (Rte. 184 Km 32.9, ✆ 787/738-8888). The truth is, however, that we have been rarely disappointed in any of the restaurants we visited.

Cayey is also home to the Jájome sector, which also has two fine restaurants open on weekends: **Jájome Terrace** (Rte. 15 Km 18.6, Cayey; ✆ 787/738-4016) and the **Sand and the Sea Inn** (Rte. 715, Cayey; ✆ 787/738-9086). These offer a more refined dining experience, with beautiful views.

Aibonito comes alive during its annual Fiesta de las Flores in late June and early July, but it's worth a visit anytime with its cool, crisp air. **La Piedra Restaurant** (Rte. 7718 Km 0.8; ✆ 787/735-1034) has been luring diners from San Juan for decades with its gourmet, inventive local cuisine using locally grown ingredients. It has one of the best views around. Other local favorites are **El Rincón Familiar** (Rte. 14 Km 48.8; ✆ 787/735-7425) and **Tío Pepe Restaurant** (Rte. 723 Km 0.3; ✆ 787/735-9615).

Ponce & the Southwest

For those who want to see a less urban side of Puerto Rico, head south to Ponce and the breathtaking southwest, with great beaches, dramatic coastal bluffs, and green flatlands unfolding across the horizon to the foothills of the Cordillera Central mountain range.

Ponce is a great center for sightseeing, and you can take a side trip to the rare bonsai-like Guánica State Forest; visit Puerto Rico's second-oldest city and site of the oldest church in the New World, San Germán; and venture north through the island's central mountains to the lush Toro Negro rainforest. Both nature reserves are hits with hikers and bird-watchers.

Founded in 1692, Ponce is Puerto Rico's second-largest city, and its historic sectors have been beautifully restored. San Germán and Ponce are home to some of the finest historic architecture in the hemisphere.

Ponce also attracts beach lovers. No, there's no real beach in town, but to the west are the coastal towns of Guánica, La Parguera, and Boquerón, where the best swimming beaches on the island are located. The southwest is where Puerto Ricans go for holidays by the sea. This is the real Puerto Rico; it hasn't been taken over by high-rise resorts and posh restaurants.

Puerto Rico's west coast mimics the U.S. Southwest; cacti pop up from sun-baked rock crevices, while cattle graze in the rolling Lajas Valley in the shadow of the majestic central mountains. Comparisons have also been made between the peninsula of Cabo Rojo here and Baja, California. All across the region, a beautiful western sunset settles over its charming beach towns, with their white sands and aquamarine waters, bringing very much to mind the best of the California coastline.

1 PONCE ★★

75 miles (121km) SW of San Juan

ESSENTIALS

GETTING THERE Flying from San Juan to Ponce five times a day, **Cape Air** (© 800/352-0714; www.flycapeair.com), a small regional carrier, offers flights for $154 round-trip. Flight time is 25 minutes.

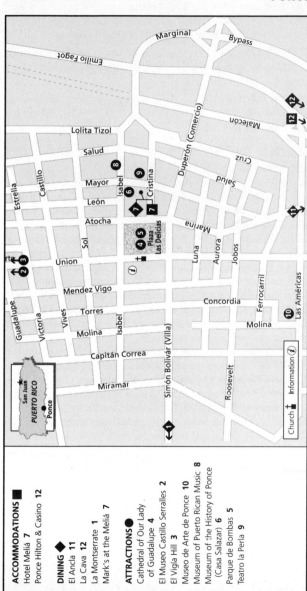

ACCOMMODATIONS ■
Hotel Meliá **7**
Ponce Hilton & Casino **12**

DINING ◆
El Ancla **11**
La Cava **12**
La Montserrate **1**
Mark's at the Meliá **7**

ATTRACTIONS ●
Cathedral of Our Lady
of Guadalupe **4**
El Museo Castillo Serrallés **2**
El Vigía Hill **3**
Museo de Arte de Ponce **10**
Museum of Puerto Rican Music **8**
Museum of the History of Ponce
(Casa Salazar) **6**
Parque de Bombas **5**
Teatro la Perla **9**

If you're driving, take Las Américas Expressway south to the Luis A. Ferré Expressway Hwy. 52, then continue south. Once you pass over the central mountain range and reach the south coast, you will continue west until you reach Ponce. The trip takes about 1¹/₂ hours.

GETTING AROUND   The town's inner core is small enough that everything can be visited on foot. Taxis provide the second-best alternative.

VISITOR INFORMATION   Maps and information can be found at the **tourist office,** Paseo del Sur Plaza, Ste. 3 (© **787/841-8044**). It's open daily 8am to 4:30pm.

SEEING THE SIGHTS
Attractions in Ponce

Most visitors go to Ponce to see the city's renovated historic section, a showcase of its whimsical architectural style. While the city dates back to 1692, its unique "Ponce Creole" architecture, mixing Spanish colonial, neoclassical, Caribbean, and contemporary influences, was mostly created from the 1850s through the 1930s. The style is marked by the use of wide balconies, distinctive masonry work, and touches like plaster garlands, punched tin ceilings, and stained glass panels, while other architectural motifs are present within specific geographic areas of the city, such as common grill work or building size. The style takes European concepts but adapts them to the city's tropical climate by using pastel colors on building facades and adding high ceilings that help keep houses cool.

There are more than 1,000 historic buildings in Ponce, and the vast majority have been restored. Many are on streets radiating from the stately **Plaza Las Delicias (Plaza of Delights).** City Hall is an 18th-century building just off the plaza. Its biggest feature, however, is the **Lion Fountain,** crafted from marble and bronze and modeled after a famous fountain in Barcelona, Spain. It was made for the 1939 New York World's Fair and later purchased by the mayor of Ponce.

Casa de la Masacre de Ponce   This small museum is a memorial to one of the bloodiest chapters of political violence in Puerto Rican history—the Ponce Massacre. Police killed 19 people and wounded 100 during a Nationalist Party march in the city on Palm Sunday, March 21, 1937, after shots rang out. The remnants of the Nationalist Party still mark the occasion with a ceremony here each year, and it is an important date for independence supporters. The museum is located at the site of the tragedy in a restored shoemaker's shop that used to be a meeting place for Nationalist Party members. The museum also documents other episodes of the political persecution of the island.

At Calle Aurora and Marina Plaza Las Delicias. ℂ **787/844-9722.** Free admission.
Daily 8am–noon.

Cathedral of Our Lady of Guadalupe In 1660 a rustic chapel
was built on this spot on the western edge of the Plaza Las Delicias,
and since then fires and earthquakes have razed the church repeatedly.
In 1919 a team of priests collected funds from local parishioners to
construct the Doric- and Gothic-inspired building that stands here
today. Designed by architects Francisco Porrato Doría and Francisco
Trublard in 1931, and featuring a pipe organ installed in 1934, it
remains an important place for prayer for many. The cathedral,
named after a famous holy shrine in Mexico, is the best-known
church in southern Puerto Rico.

At calles Concordia and Union. ℂ **787/842-0134.** Free admission. Mon–Fri 6am–
12:30pm; Sat–Sun 6am–noon and 3–8pm.

El Museo Castillo Serrallés ★ Two miles (3.2km) north of the
center of town is the largest and most imposing building in Ponce,
constructed high on El Vigía Hill (see below) during the 1930s by the
Serrallés family, owners of a local rum distillery. One of the architectural gems of Puerto Rico, it is the best evidence of the wealth produced by the turn-of-the-20th-century sugar boom. Guides will
escort you through the Spanish Revival house with Moorish and
Andalusian details. Highlights include panoramic courtyards, a baro-
nial dining room, a small cafe and souvenir shop, and a series of
photographs showing the tons of earth that were brought in for the
construction of the terraced gardens, a beautiful place to sit outside
the castle that overlooks the city.

El Vigía 17. ℂ **787/259-1774.** Admission $9 adults, $4.50 seniors, $4 children and
students. (Admission includes all attractions on El Vigía Hill.) Tues–Sun 9:30am–
5pm. Free trolley leaving from Plaza Las Delicias de Ponce. Take Ruta Norte (northern route) daily 9am–9pm.

El Vigía Hill The city's tallest geologic feature, El Vigía Hill (300
ft./91m) dominates Ponce's northern skyline. Its base and steep slopes
are covered with a maze of 19th- and early-20th-century development. In addition to the castle, as soon as you reach the summit,
you'll see the soaring Cruz del Vigía (Virgin's Cross). Built in 1984 of
reinforced concrete to replace a 19th-century wooden cross in poor
repair, this modern 100-foot (30m) structure bears lateral arms mea-
suring 70 feet (21m) long and an observation tower (accessible by
elevator), from which you can see all of the natural beauty surrounding Ponce. The cross commemorates Vigía Hill's colonial role as a
deterrent to contraband smuggling. In 1801, on orders from Spain, a
garrison was established atop the hill to detect any ships that might

try to unload their cargoes tax-free along Puerto Rico's southern coastline. Make sure to take a break in the beautifully tranquil Japanese garden, with bonsai plantings and dry areas, and elevated bridges running between ponds and streams; it's a perfect spot for a break.

At the north end of Ponce. Free trolley from Plaza Las Delicia.

Parque de Bombas Constructed in 1882 as the centerpiece of a 12-day agricultural fair intended to promote the civic charms of Ponce, this building was designated a year later as the island's first permanent headquarters for a volunteer firefighting brigade. It has an unusual appearance—it's painted black, red, green, and yellow. A tourist-information kiosk is situated inside the building (see "Visitor Information," above).

Plaza Las Delicias. ℃ **787/284-3338.** Free admission. Daily 8am–5pm.

Teatro la Perla This theater, built in the neoclassical style in 1864, remains one of the most visible symbols of the economic prosperity of Ponce during the mid–19th century. Designed by Juan Bertoli, an Italian-born resident of Puerto Rico who studied in Europe, it was destroyed by an earthquake in 1918 and rebuilt in 1940 according to the original plans; it reopened to the public in 1941. It is noted for acoustics so clear that microphones are unnecessary. The theater is the largest and most historic in the Spanish-speaking Caribbean. Everything from plays to concerts to beauty pageants takes place here.

At calles Mayor and Christina. ℃ **787/843-4322.** Prices and hours vary.

Nearby Attractions

Hacienda Buena Vista Built in 1833, this hacienda preserves an old way of life, with its whirring water wheels and artifacts of 19th-century farm production. Once it was one of the most successful plantations on Puerto Rico, producing coffee, corn, and citrus. It was a working coffee plantation until the 1950s, and 86 of the original 500 acres (35 of 202 hectares) are still part of the estate. The rooms of the hacienda have been furnished with authentic pieces from the 1850s.

Rte. 123, Barrio Magüeyes Km 16.8. ℃ **787/722-5882** (weekdays), 284-7020 (weekends). Tours $7 adults, $4 children and seniors. Reservations required. 2-hr. tours Wed–Sun at 8:30am, 10:30am, 1:30pm, and 3:30pm (in English only at 1:30pm). A 30-min. drive north of Ponce, in the small town of Barrio Magüeyes, btw. Ponce and Adjuntas.

Tibes Indian Ceremonial Center Bordered by the Río Portuguéz and excavated in 1975, this is the oldest cemetery in the Antilles. It contains some 186 skeletons, dating from A.D. 300, as well as pre-Taíno plazas from A.D. 700. The site also includes a re-created 139 Taíno village, seven rectangular ball courts, and two dance grounds. The arrangement of stone points on the dance grounds, in line with the solstices and equinoxes, suggests a pre-Columbian Stonehenge. Here you'll also find a museum, an exhibition hall that presents a documentary about Tibes, a cafeteria, and a souvenir shop.

Rte. 503, Tibes, at Km 2.2. ☎ **787/840-2255.** Admission $3 adults, $2 children. Guided tours in English and Spanish are conducted through the grounds. Tues–Sun 9am–4pm. 2 miles/3.2km north of Ponce.

BEACHES & OUTDOOR ACTIVITIES

La Guancha is a sprawling boardwalk around Ponce's bayside harbor area near the Ponce Hilton. During weekend afternoons, children and their families come here to fly kites or ride bicycles. Hundreds of yachts and pleasure craft tie up here, which is also home to the Ponce Yacht Club. A ferry runs from La Guancha to **Caja de Muertos,** or **Coffin Island,** an uninhabited cay that's covered with mangrove swamps and ringed with worthwhile beaches. It's some of the best snorkeling in the southwest. A 125-passenger ferry run by **Island Venture** (☎ 787/842-8546 or 866-7827) provides transportation daily to and from the island. Round-trip fare is $15 for adults, and $10 for children. Other private outfits will take passengers to the island, with some providing snorkeling equipment and even lunch to guests. There are hiking trails, gazebos, and basic bathrooms but no running water. The island has an old lighthouse and a nice beach.

One of the south coast's finest and newest courses is the **Costa Caribe Golf & Country Club** ★★ (☎ 787/848-1000 or 812-2650), on the site of the Ponce Hilton & Casino (see below). This 27-hole course charges from $85 ($75 for guests) to play 18 holes. The beautifully landscaped holes—with commanding views of the ocean and mountain—are laid out in former sugar-cane fields. **Club Deportivo del Oeste,** Hwy. 102 Km 15.4, Barrio Jogudas, Cabo Rojo (☎ 787/851-8880 or 254-3748), lies 30 miles (48km) west of Ponce. This course is an 18-holer, open daily from 7am to 5pm. Greens fees are $35 during the week and $40 on the weekend.

SHOPPING

If you feel a yen for shopping in Ponce, there are many shops in the renovated downtown area that have local arts and crafts. The **Atochoa Pedestrian Mall** (☎ 787/841-8044) runs along Calle Cristina just off the city's central **Plaza Las Delicias.** It's been one of Ponce's main shopping areas for decades.

The best outlet for souvenirs and artisans' work is **El Palacio del Coquí Inc.,** Calle Marina 9227 (☎ 787/812-0216), whose name means "palace of the tree frog." This is the place to buy the colorful *vejigantes* masks (viewed as collectors' items) that are crafted from papier-mâché and used at carnival time. Ask the owner to explain the significance of these masks.

Utopía, Calle Isabel 78 (② **787/848-8742**), conveniently located in Plaza Las Delicias, has the most imaginative and interesting selection of gift items and handicrafts in Ponce. Prominently displayed are more *vejigantes* masks, which sell at bargain prices of between $5 and $500, depending on their size.

WHERE TO STAY
Expensive

Hilton Ponce Golf & Casino Resort ★★ On an 80-acre (32-hectare) tract of land on the coast, this is the most glamorous hotel in southern Puerto Rico. At the western end of Avenida Santiago de los Caballeros, it's about a 15-minute drive from the center of Ponce. Designed like a miniature village, with turquoise-blue roofs, white walls, and lots of tropical plants, ornamental waterfalls, and gardens, it welcomes both conventioneers and individual travelers. The main pool behind the hotel is spacious and stretches like a wave through towering palms and gardens. The 28-hole golf course is the best in the area, and there's another set of pools by its clubhouse. The small beach is pretty, but it does not compare with those to the west. There's a large playground for kids and two children's pools. A trolley shuttles guests around the property, and the city government **Chu Chu Tren** provides transportation to downtown Ponce and the nearby La Guancha boardwalk area.

Accommodations contain tropically inspired furnishings, ceiling fans, and terraces or balconies. All the rooms are medium to spacious, with adequate desk and storage space, tasteful fabrics, good upholstery, and fine linens. The ground-floor rooms are the most expensive. Each is equipped with a generous tiled bathroom with a tub/shower combination.

The food is the most sophisticated and refined on the south coast of Puerto Rico. All the waiters seem to have an extensive knowledge of the menu and will guide you through some exotic dishes—of course, you'll find familiar fare, too.

Av. Caribe 1150 (P.O. Box 7419), Ponce, PR 00716. ② **800/HILTONS** (445-8667) or 787/259-7676. Fax 787/259-7674. www.hilton.com. 153 units. High season $279–$419 double, off season $152–$269 double; $400 suite. AE, DC, DISC, MC, V. Valet parking $10; self-parking $4.50. **Amenities:** 2 restaurants; 2 bars; nightclub; pool ringed w/gardens; 2 tennis courts; golf course; fitness center; bike rentals; playground; children's program; business center; room service (7am–midnight); babysitting; laundry service; dry cleaning; casino; rooms for those w/limited

Moderate

Meliá   A city hotel with southern hospitality, the Meliá, which has no connection with the international hotel chain, attracts business-people. The location is a few steps away from the Cathedral of Our Lady of Guadalupe and from the Parque de Bombas (the red-and-black firehouse). Although the more expensive Hilton long ago out-classed this old and somewhat tattered hotel, many people who can afford more upscale accommodations still prefer to stay here for its old-time atmosphere. The lobby floor and all stairs are covered with Spanish tiles of Moorish design. The desk clerks speak English. The small rooms are comfortably furnished and pleasant enough, and most have a balcony facing either busy Calle Cristina or the old plaza. Bathrooms are tiny, each with a shower stall. Breakfast is served on a rooftop terrace with a good view of Ponce, and Mark's at the Meliá thrives under separate management (see "Where to Dine," below). You can park your car in the lot nearby.

Calle Cristina 2, Ponce, PR 00731. (℃) **800/448-8355** or 787/842-0260. Fax 787/ 841-3602. www.hotelmeliapr.com. 73 units (shower only). Year-round $105–$115 double; $130 suite. Rates include continental breakfast. AE, MC, V. Parking $3. **Amenities:** Restaurant; bar; outdoor pool; limited room service; rooms for those w/limited mobility. *In room:* A/C, TV, free high-speed Internet, hair dryer, iron, safe.

WHERE TO DINE
Expensive

La Cava ★★ INTERNATIONAL   This hive of venerable rooms within a 19th-century coffee plantation is the most appealing and elaborate restaurant in Ponce. There's a well-trained staff, old-fashioned charm, well-prepared cuisine, and a champagne bar where the bubbly sells for around $8 a glass. Menu items change every 6 weeks but might include duck foie gras with toasted brioche, Parma ham with mango, cold poached scallops with mustard sauce, a fricassee of lobster and mushrooms in a pastry shell, and grilled lamb sausage with mustard sauce on a bed of couscous. Dessert could be a black-and-white soufflé or a trio of tropical sorbets.

In the Ponce Hilton, Av. Caribe 1150. (℃) **787/259-7676.** Reservations recommended. Main courses $26–$35. AE, DC, DISC, MC, V. Mon–Sat 6:30–10:30pm.

Mark's at the Meliá ★★★ INTERNATIONAL   Mark French (isn't that a great name for a chef?) makes international haute cuisine with a Puerto Rican flair at this landmark eatery. You'd think he'd been entertaining the celebs in San Juan instead of cooking at what is somewhat of a Caribbean backwater. French was hailed as "Chef of the Caribbean 2000" in Fort Lauderdale. With his constantly changing menus and his insistence that everything be fresh, he's still a winner. You'll fall in love with this guy when you taste his tamarind barbecued lamb with yuca mojo. Go on to sample the grilled lobster with tomato-and-chive salad or the freshly made sausage with pumpkin, cilantro, and chicken. All over Puerto Rico you get fried green plantains, but here they come topped with sour cream and a dollop of caviar. The corn-crusted red snapper with yuca purée and tempura jumbo shrimp with Asian salad are incredible. The desserts are spectacular, notably the vanilla flan layered with rum sponge cake and topped with a caramelized banana, as well as the award-winning bread pudding soufflé with coconut vanilla sauce.

In the Meliá Hotel, Calle Cristina. (C) **787/284-6275.** Reservations recommended. Main courses $16–$30. AE, MC, V. Tues–Sat noon–3pm and 6–10:30pm; Sun noon–5pm.

Moderate

El Ancla ★ PUERTO RICAN/SEAFOOD   This is one of Ponce's best restaurants, with a lovely, informal location 2 miles (3.2km) south of the city center, in the Playa del Ponce sector overlooking the Caribbean Sea. Look out at the water from the dining room and enjoy the culinary delights from the sea. Menu items are prepared with real Puerto Rican zest and flavor. A favorite here is red snapper stuffed with lobster and shrimp, served either with fried plantains or mashed potatoes. Other specialties are filet of salmon in caper sauce, and a seafood medley of lobster, shrimp, octopus, and conch. Most of the dishes are reasonably priced, especially the chicken and conch. Lobster tops the price scale. The side orders, including crabmeat rice and yuca in garlic, are delectable.

Av. Hostos Final, Playa Ponce. (C) **787/840-2450.** Main courses $13–$36. AE, DC, MC, V. Sun–Thurs 11am–10pm; Fri–Sat 11am–11pm.

La Montserrate PUERTO RICAN/SEAFOOD   This is one of a string of seaside restaurants specializing in Puerto Rican cuisines and seafood lined along the beautiful coastline about 4 miles (6.4km) west of the town center. This restaurant draws a loyal following from the surrounding neighborhood. A culinary institution in Ponce since it was established 20 years ago, it occupies a large, airy, modern building divided into two different dining areas. The first of these is slightly more formal than the other. Most visitors head for the less formal, large room in back, where windows on three sides encompass a view of some offshore islands. Specialties, concocted from the catch of the day, might include octopus salad, several different kinds of *asopao,* a

whole red snapper in Creole sauce, or a selection of steaks and grills.
Nothing is innovative, but the cuisine is typical of the south of Puerto
Rico, and is a family favorite. The fish dishes are better than the meat
selections.

Sector Las Cucharas, Rte. 2. $\textcircled{C}$ **787/841-2740.** Main courses $12–$26. AE, DISC,
MC, V. Daily 11am–10pm.

2 THE SOUTHWEST COAST

GUANICA

Guánica, on the Caribbean Sea, lies 73 miles (118km) southwest of
San Juan and 21 miles (34km) west of the city of Ponce. The Guánica
Dry Forest and adjacent area is a UNESCO-designated world biosphere reserve. The rare bonsai-like forest is home to more than 100
species of migratory and resident birds, the largest number in Puerto
Rico. The beach at Guánica is pristine, and the crystal-clear water is
ideal for swimming, snorkeling, and diving. Directly offshore is the
famed Gilligan's Island, plus six of Puerto Rico's best sites for night or
day dives. The area was once known for its leaping bullfrogs. The
Spanish conquerors virtually wiped out this species. But the bullfrogs
have come back and live in the rolling, scrub-covered hills that sur-
round the 18-acre (7.3-hectare) site of the Copamarina Beach Resort,
the area's major hotel (see below).

Guánica is adjacent to the unique Dry Forest and experiences very
little rainfall. Nearby mountains get an annual rainfall of 15 feet
(4.6m), but Guánica receives only about 15 inches (38cm). This is the
world's largest dry coastal forest region. The upper hills are ideal for
hiking. Guánica was once the haunt of the Taíno Indians, and it was
the place where Ponce de León first explored Puerto Rico in 1508.
One of his descendants later founded the nearby city of Ponce in
1692.

It is also the site of the landing of the Americans in 1898 during
the Spanish-American war that began Puerto Rico's century-long
relationship with the United States. You reach the harbor by taking
the main exit to Guánica from Route 116 to Avenida 25 de Julio. A
large rock monument on the town's *malecón,* or harbor, commemorates the landing. The Williams family, descendants of a doctor who
arrived with the troops and settled here after marrying a local girl, still
live in one of the historic wooden homes along the waterfront. The
area has lots of seafood restaurants and bars, as well as snack vendors
along a bayside promenade. It is festive on weekend evenings.

Heading directly west from Ponce, along Route 2, you reach **Guánica State Forest ★★** (© 787/821-5706) along Route 334, a setting that evokes a coastal desert. Here you will find the best-preserved sub-tropical ecosystem on the planet. UNESCO has named Guánica a World Biosphere Reserve. Some 750 plants and tree species grow in the area, as well as several rare migratory birds: the Puerto Rican emerald-breasted hummingbird and the Puerto Rican nightjar, a local bird that was believed to be extinct. Now it's estimated that there are nearly a thousand of them.

To reach the forest, take Route 334 northeast of Guánica, to the heart of the forest. There's a ranger station here that will give you information about hiking trails. The booklet provided by the ranger station outlines 36 miles (58km) of trails through the four forest types. The most interesting is the mile-long (1.6km) **Cueva Trail,** which gives you the most scenic look at the various types of vegetation. You might even encounter the endangered bufo lemur toad, once declared extinct but found to still be jumping in this area.

Scuba Diving, Snorkeling & Other Outdoor Pursuits

The best dive operation in Guánica is **Sea Venture Dive Copamarina** (© **787/821-0505,** ext. 729), part of the **Copamarina Beach Resort.** Copamarina has a long pier where fishing is permitted, and a 42-foot (13m) Pro Jet dive boat. Guánica is one of the Caribbean's best areas for day and night dives. A two-tank dive costs $119, with full diving equipment. You can also rent snorkeling gear or take a ride to one of the islands nearby. It's good to reserve in advance to assure the dive master is working that day.

Whale-watching excursions can be arranged from January to March at the hotel's tour desk, which also offers ecotours, kayaking, deep-sea fishing, and sunset sails. Horseback riding and sunset biking are also available.

At one of the local beaches, **Playa Santa,** west of town, **Pino's Boat & Water Fun** (© **787/821-6864** or 484-8083) will rent you a paddle boat or kayak at prices ranging from $13 to $22 hourly. A banana-boat ride costs $7.50 per person, while water scooters cost $45 for a half-hour.

One of the most visited sites is **Gilligan's Island,** a series of mangrove and sand cays near the Caña Gorda peninsula. Part of the dry forest reserve, it is set aside for recreational use. A small ferry departs from in front of Restaurant San Jacinto, just past Copamarina Beach

Resort, every hour daily from 10am to 5pm, weather permitting; round-trip costs $6. **Ballena Beach** is farther down Route 333, in the coastal border of the Dry Forest. This is a beautiful beach, with huge palm trees and golden sand. During winter storms, surfers flock here for rare, tubular waves.

Caña Gorda ★ is a public beach adjacent to the Copamarina, at the edge of a legally protected marsh that's known for its rich bird life and thick reeds. Caña Gorda is a sprawling expanse of pale beige sand that's dotted with picnic areas and a beach refreshment stand/bar, showers, bathrooms and other facilities.

Where to Stay

Copamarina Beach Resort ★★ (Value)

In the 1950s, Copamarina was the private vacation retreat of the de Castro family, Puerto Rican cement barons. In 1991 it was enlarged and upgraded by talented entrepreneurs. Today, charming, low-key, and discreetly elegant, it stands head and shoulders above everything else along Puerto Rico's western coast, except for the regal Horned Dorset Primavera (its strongest competitor). Situated beside a public beach (the best in the area), amid a landscaped palm grove, the resort is airy and relaxing. A favorite destination of sanjuaneros, it also draws a well-heeled crowd of clients from Europe and North America, who know good value when they see it.

The accommodations are in one- and two-story wings that radiate from the resort's central core, as well as a set of villas. The attractively decorated units have tile floors, lots of exposed wood, and louvered doors with screens that open onto large verandas or terraces. Everything is airy and comfortable. Bathrooms are larger than you might expect, and up-to-date, some with shower, others with tub.

Rte. 333 Km 6.5, Cana Gorda (P.O. Box 805), Guánica, PR 00653. (℗ **888/881-6233** or 787/821-0505. Fax 787/821-0070. www.copamarina.com. 106 units. High season $235–$285 double; low season $190–$240 double; year-round $350–$450 suite, $800–$1,000 villa. AE, DC, MC, V. From Ponce, drive west along Rte. 2 to Rte. 116 and go south to Rte. 333, then head east. **Amenities:** 2 restaurants; bar; 2 outdoor pools; tennis courts; health club; limited room service; babysitting; laundry service; dry cleaning; rooms for those w/limited mobility. *In room:* A/C, TV, dataport, fridge, coffeemaker, hair dryer, safe.

Mary Lee's by the Sea ★ (Finds)

This is an informal collection of cottages, seafront houses, and apartments. Five California-style houses are subdivided into eight living units, each suitable for one to three couples. Rooms are whimsically decorated; each has a small, tiled bathroom with a tub. The entire compound, which grew in an artfully erratic way, is landscaped with flowering shrubs, trees, and vines. Overall, the ambience is friendly and low-key. There aren't any formally organized activities here, but the hotel sits next to sandy beaches and a handful of uninhabited offshore cays. The management maintains rental boats with motors, two waterside sun decks, and several kayaks for the benefit of active guests. Hikers and bird-watchers can go north to the Guánica State Forest. Don't come here looking for nighttime activities or enforced conviviality. The place is quiet, secluded, and appropriate for low-key vacationers looking for privacy. There isn't a bar or restaurant here, but each unit has a modern kitchen and an outdoor barbecue pit. The rooms are serviced weekly, although guests can arrange daily maid service for an extra fee.

Rte. 333 Km 6.7 (P.O. Box 394), Guánica, PR 00653. © **787/821-3600.** Fax 787/821-0744. www.maryleesbythesea.com. 11 units. Year-round $80–$120 double; $100–$140 studio and 1-bedroom apt; $160–$200 2-bedroom apt; $250 3-bedroom house. MC, V. From Ponce, take Rte. 2. When you reach Rte. 116, head south toward Guánica. The hotel is signposted from the road. **Amenities:** Laundry service. *In room:* A/C, kitchen, coffeemaker, iron, safe, no phone.

Parador Guánica 1929 This charming property lies on one of the island's prettiest roads, enveloped by a canopy of trees as it winds along Ensenada Bay and a line of plantation homes atop a hill overlooking it. Guánica's Ensenada sector was once the site of one of the largest sugar mills in the Caribbean, but it's been a bit of a ghost town since it shut down in the 1980s. Shadows of its former opulence can be glimpsed in the sun-baked decaying structures throughout the area, as well as the few restored buildings, such as this immaculate hotel. A classic Spanish-style plantation home, with a wide, wraparound veranda on each of its two levels, its rooms have subdued tropical decor and are comfortable and well equipped. Breakfast is served on the downstairs side veranda overlooking the large pool area, with sun chairs on its surrounding deck. The food at the on-site restaurant is only okay. Prices at area restaurants are extremely competitive.

Rte. 3116 Km 2.5, Av. Los Veteranos, Ensenada, Guánica 00767. © **787/821-0099** or 842-0260. Fax 787/841-3602. www.tropicalinnspr.com. 21 units. Year-round $102 double. Rates include continental breakfast. AE, MC, V. **Amenities:** Coin laundry facility. *In room:* A/C, satellite TV, high-speed Internet, kitchen, coffeemaker, hair dryer, iron, safe.

Where to Dine

Alexandra ★ INTERNATIONAL   This is a genuinely excellent restaurant with a kitchen team turning out delectable dishes that include fried red snapper with Creole sauce, filet of mahimahi with pigeon peas, garlic shrimp with local rice, and beef parmigiana with red-wine sauce. The interior is air-conditioned but tropical in its feel, providing a welcome dose of relaxed glamour.

Guánica. (*C*) **787/821-0505.** Reservations recommended. Main courses $18–$36.
AE, DC, DISC, MC, V. Sun–Thurs 6–10:30pm; Fri–Sat 6–11pm.

The Blue Marlin SEAFOOD   The most established restaurant on Guánica's famous harbor, this is still the best place for local seafood. Housed in a rambling plantation-style structure overlooking the pretty bay, there is a large but relaxed quiet dining area, with some tables on balconies overlooking the harbor, serving excellent local meals, with an accent on freshly caught seafood. We love everything from the Caribbean lobster ceviche salad to the *mofongo* stuffed with mixed seafood (conch, octopus, shrimp, and red snapper) in a light tomato sauce. But culinary landlubbers can find satisfaction here with budget priced *comida criolla*. Even the pork chops are tasty. There's an adjacent bar area with a jukebox playing all sorts of local hits—from reggaeton to classic salsa—and televisions tuned to sports or music videos. The long rectangular bar not only overlooks the harborside drive, but also one of its sides is actually on the street. Tasty snacks like seafood turnovers and fried fish fritters are available as well as more substantial menu items. There's even a more informal outdoor terrace area with cafeteria-style booths perfect for families who want a quick snack after the beach.

55 Calle Esperanza Idrach, Malecón de Guánica (at the end of Calle 25 de Julío), Guánica. (*C*) **787/821-5858.** Reservations recommended. Main courses $9.50–$23. MC, V. Thurs–Mon 11am–1am.

LA PARGUERA ★

This charming fishing village lies 78 miles (126km) southwest of San Juan and 26 miles (42km) west of Ponce, just south of San Germán. From San Germán, take Route 320 directly south and follow the signposts. Note that this route changes its name several times along the way, becoming Route 101, 116, 315, 305, and then 304 before reaching La Parguera—even though it's all the same highway.

The name of the village comes from *pargos,* meaning snapper. Its main attraction, other than its beaches and diving, is **Phosphorescent Bay,** which contains millions of luminescent dinoflagellates (microscopic plankton). A disturbance causes them to light up the dark waters. For dramatic effect, they are best seen on a moonless night. Boats leave for a troll around the bay nightly from 7:30pm to 12:30am from La Parguera pier, depending on demand. The trip costs $7.50 per person.

Offshore are some 12 to 15 reefs with a variety of depths. The Beril reef goes down to 60 feet (18m), then drops to 2,000 feet (610m). This wall is famous among divers, and visibility ranges from 100 to

120 feet (30–37m). These reefs also provide some of the best snorkeling possibilities in Puerto Rico. Marine life is both abundant and diverse, including big morays, sea turtles, barracudas, nurse sharks, and manatees. **Paradise Scuba Center,** Hotel Casa Blanca Building, at La Parguera (② **787/899-7611**), offers the best diving and snorkeling. A two-tank dive costs $150; a 3-hour snorkeling jaunt goes for $35 per person. Full equipment can be rented.

Where to Stay

Parador Posada Porlamar   Developed by the Pancorbo family in 1967 as one of the first full-service hotels in town, this parador evokes life in a simple fishing village. A horseshoe-shaped compound that overlooks a narrow channel flanked by mangroves, it conducts an ongoing business with dive enthusiasts, thanks to its on-site scuba shop. Bedrooms are plain and neat but don't invite lingering. Some have balconies, minibars, and small sitting rooms, and each has a small, tiled, shower-only bathroom. All are nonsmoking. The social center here is a patio overlooking the channel. The restaurants and bars of La Parguera are within a short walk of this centrally located place. On the premises is a rather formal restaurant, La Pared. Specialties include seafood in Creole sauce, lamb chops in Dijon mustard, and sautéed shrimp in soursop-flavored butter sauce.

Rte. 304 (P.O. Box 3113), La Parguera, Lajas, PR 00667. ② **787/899-4343.** Fax 787/899-5558. www.parguerapuertorico.com. 40 units (shower only). Winter $117–$145 double; off season $80–$119 double. AE, DISC, MC, V. Drive west along Rte. 2 until you reach the junction of Rte. 116; then head south along Rte. 116 and Rte. 304. **Amenities:** Restaurant; bar; pool; rooms for those w/limited mobility. *In room:* A/C, TV, minibar, coffeemaker, hair dryer, safe.

Parador Villa Parguera (Kids)   Although the water in the nearby bay is too muddy for swimming, guests can enjoy a view of the harbor and take a dip in the swimming pool. Situated on the southwestern shore of Puerto Rico, this parador is favored by sanjuaneros for weekend escapes. It's also known for its seafood dinners (the fish are not caught in the bay), comfortable and uncomplicated bedrooms, and location next to the bay's famous phosphorescent waters. Each unit has either a balcony or a terrace. Bathrooms are rather cramped but well maintained, and each has either a shower or a tub. This place is more gregarious and convivial, and usually more fun, than the Porlamar, a few steps away.

The spacious, air-conditioned restaurant, where the occasionally slow service might remind you of Spain in a bygone era, offers traditional favorites, such as filet of fish stuffed with lobster and shrimp. Nonguests are welcome here, and there's a play area for children. Because the inn is popular with local vacationers, there are frequent specials, such as a $395 weekend (Fri–Sun) special for two that includes welcome drinks, breakfasts, dinners, flowers, and dancing, along with a free show.

There's a dock right outside the restaurant where boats tie up, which is convenient because the thing to do here is to hire a boat and explore the beautiful shallow coast replete with reefs and tropical sea life.

Main St. 304 (P.O. Box 3400), Carretera 304 Km 303, La Parguera, Lajas, PR 00667. ℂ 787/899-7777. Fax 787/899-6040. www.villaparguera.net. 74 units (all with either shower or tub). Year-round $107–$165 double. 2 children 9 or under stay free in parent's room. AE, DC, DISC, MC, V. Drive west along Rte. 2 until you reach the junction with Rte. 116; then head south along Rte. 116 and Rte. 304. **Amenities:** Restaurant; bar; pool; babysitting; rooms for those w/limited mobility. *In room:* A/C, TV.

Where to Dine

La Casita SEAFOOD   This is the town's most consistently reliable and popular restaurant. It's flourished here since the 1960s, in a simple wooden building. Inside, lots of varnished pine acts as a decorative foil for platters of local and imported fish and shellfish. Filets of fish can be served in any of seven different styles; lobster comes in five. Even the Puerto Rican starchy staple of *mofongo* comes in versions stuffed with crab, octopus, shrimp, lobster, and assorted shellfish. Begin with fish chowder, a dozen cheese balls, or fish croquettes. End with coconut-flavored flan. Don't expect grand service or decor but rather a setting where food is the focus.

Calle Principal 304. ℂ 787/899-1681. Reservations not necessary. All main courses $8. AE, MC, V. Tues–Sun 11am–10:30pm. Closed 2 weeks in Sept.

BOQUERON

Lying 85 miles (137km) southwest of San Juan and 33 miles (53km) west of Ponce is the little beach town of Boquerón. It is just south of Cabo Rojo, west of the historic city of San Germán, and near the western edge of the Boquerón Forest Preserve.

What puts sleepy Boquerón on the tourist map is its lovely public beach, one of the island's finest for swimming. It is also known for the shellfish found offshore. The beach has facilities, including lockers and changing places, plus kiosks that rent watersports equipment. Parking costs $2. On weekends the resort tends to be crowded with families driving down from San Juan.

The outfitter that offers the best scuba diving and snorkeling in the area is **Mona Aquatics,** on Calle José de Diego, directly west of the heart of town (ℂ 787/851-2185) near the town marina and Hotel Boquemar. It offers several dive packages (a two-tank dive starts at $105 per person), including trips to Desecheo and Mona Island some

50 miles (81km) out to sea, a sanctuary known for its spectacular dive opportunities. The company also rents snorkeling gear and, if enough people are interested, conducts boat tours of the Bahía de Boquerón.

From Boquerón you can head directly south to **El Faro de Cabo Rojo** at the island's southernmost corner. The century-old Cabo Rojo Lighthouse lies on Route 301, along a spit of land between Bahía Sucia and Bahía Salinas. Looking down from the lighthouse, you'll see a 2,000-foot (610m) drop along jagged limestone cliffs. The lighthouse dates from 1881, when it was constructed under Spanish rule. The famous pirate Roberto Cofresi used to terrorize the coast along here in the 19th century and was said to have hidden out in a cave nearby.

Where to Stay

Bahia Salinas Beach Resort & Spa ★ ⓕFinds   You live close to nature here. Nature lovers and bird-watchers are drawn to this intimate inn in Cabo Rojo in the far southwestern corner of Puerto Rico. At the tip of the western coast, the sanctuary is bordered by a mangrove reserve, bird sanctuaries, and salt flats in the undeveloped coastal region near the Cabo Rojo Lighthouse. Salt mineral waters, similar to those of the Dead Sea, supply water for the on-site Jacuzzi and for treatments at its Cuni Spa, which gives a full range of beauty and relaxation treatments. There is ample opportunity for jogging and hiking in the natural surroundings as well as all sorts of watersports. It is near many white-sand beaches, including the town's large public beach. Both restaurants—the fine-dining **Agua al Cuello Bistro** and **Balahoo's Bar & Grill**—are excellent. The Bistro features local music on Saturday nights. There is also a conference room and business center. Fresh seafood is a specialty. The bedrooms are midsize to large, and are furnished in the so-called "hacienda" Puerto Rican style, which means wooden colonial-style furniture and four-poster beds. The place is well run and maintained.

Rd. 301 Km 11.5, Sector El Faro, Cabo Rojo, PR 00622. ⓒ **787/254-1212.** Fax 787/254-1215. www.bahiasalinas.com. 22 units. Year-round $193–$205 double. Children 11 and under stay free in parent's room. AE, MC, V. **Amenities:** Restaurant; bar; 2 outdoor pools; high-speed Internet access; room service (noon–9pm); rooms for those w/limited mobility. *In room:* A/C, TV.

Parador Boquemar   This family favorite lies right at the heart of town by Boquerón beach. A recent renovation has spruced up the common areas and guest rooms, which gives them a more tropical feel, but the hotel still lacks character. Despite the small units here, Puerto Rican families like this place a lot, causing readers to complain that children sometimes run up and down the corridors. Rooms are simple but comfortable and clean. This is not the place to stay if you are going for ambience, but it is a good deal at a great location. Kids will enjoy the pool. Stay here only if you plan to spend most of your time outside the hotel. The hotel's restaurant, **Las Cascadas,** has good food, but again the atmosphere leaves much to be desired.

Carretera 101, Poblado de Boquerón, Cabo Rojo, PR 00622. ℂ **787/851-2158.** Fax 787/851-7600. www.boquemar.com. 75 units (shower only). Year-round $95–$115 double; $120 junior suite. AE, DC, MC, V. **Amenities:** Restaurant; bar; outside pool; babysitting; rooms for those w/limited mobility. *In room:* A/C, TV, small fridge.

Where to Dine

Boquerón has great roadside food stands. You can get everything from fresh oysters to hand-rolled burritos from vendors set up along the beach village's main drag. Open-air bars and restaurants also sell turnovers stuffed with fresh fish, lobster, or conch, as well as seafood ceviche salad in plastic cups.

Galloway's ★ CREOLE/CONTINENTAL   This is our favorite restaurant in Boquerón, right near the center of town but set back along the water. Sit in the back dining room that is on a dock over Boquerón Bay. It's a great spot for a fresh seafood meal as you watch one of those perfect western sunsets. This is a casual spot, but the food is first-rate. Being right on the water, we can't help but take our seafood straight up—such as a whole fried red snapper and boiled Caribbean lobster. While much of the menu is typical of the area, specializing in local cuisine and seafood, you'll also find great pasta dishes and pub fare like burgers and nachos. The bar near the entrance is a good spot to mix with locals and expats and pick up tips on area activities. On weekends, there's often live music.

Calle José de Diego 12, Poblado de Boquerón, Cabo Rojo. ℂ **787/254-3302.** Reservations not necessary. Main courses $8–$26. AE, MC, V. Thurs–Tues noon–midnight.

Roberto's Fish Net PUERTO RICAN   This is one of two restaurants, both named "Roberto," on the same sleepy street in the center of Boquerón. Both belong to Roberto Aviles and offer roughly equivalent versions of the same food. We prefer this spot to **Roberto's Restaurant Villa Playera** (ℂ 787/254-3163). However, the Villa Playera is still a good choice, particularly on Monday and Tuesday, when the Fish Net is closed. Within the Fish Net's simple environment, a cross between a luncheonette and a bar, you can order tender beefsteaks, well-flavored chicken breasts, or fresh fish, any of which comes with rice and beans. More unusual are the *pilones,* a combination of mashed plantains flavored with your choice of shrimp, conch, or octopus, usually served with salsa, that come in tall wooden cups with old-fashioned mortars.

Calle José de Diego s/n (without number). ✆ **787/851-6009.** Reservations not necessary. Main courses $5–$23. AE, DISC, MC, V. Wed–Sun 11am–10pm.

---

3 SAN GERMAN ★★

104 miles (167km) SW of San Juan, 34 miles (55km) W of Ponce

8

Founded in 1512, San Germán is Puerto Rico's second-oldest town and retains colorful reminders of its Spanish colonial past. The town's historic quarter mixes verdant scenery and a variety of restored buildings in a variety of architectural styles—Spanish colonial (1850s), *criolla* (1880s), neoclassical (1910s), Art Deco (1930s), and international (1960s). There are 249 historical treasures within easy walking distance of one another. Most of the city's architectural treasures lie uphill from the congested main thoroughfare (Calle Luna). One of the most noteworthy churches in Puerto Rico is **Iglesia Porta Coeli (Gate of Heaven)** ★ (✆ **787/892-0160**), which sits atop a knoll at the eastern end of a cobble-covered square, the Parque de Santo Domingo. Dating from 1606 and built in a style inspired by the Romanesque architecture of northern Spain, this is the oldest church in the New World. Restored by the Institute of Puerto Rican Culture, and sheathed in a layer of salmon-colored stucco, it contains a museum of religious art with a collection of ancient *santos,* the carved figures of saints that have long been a major part of Puerto Rican folk art. Look for the 17th-century portrait of St. Nicholas de Bari, the French Santa Claus. Inside, the original palm-wood ceiling and tough ausobo-wood beams draw the eye upward. Other treasures include early choral books from Santo Domingo, a primitive carving of Jesus, and 19th-century Señora de la Monserrate Black Madonna and Child statues. Admission is $3 for adults, $2 for seniors and children 12 and over, free for children 11 and under. The church is open Wednesday through Sunday from 8:30am to noon and 1 to 4:30pm.

San Germán's most impressive church—and the most monumental building in the region—is **San Germán de Auxerre** (✆ **787/892-1027**), which rises majestically above the western end of the Plaza Francisco Mariano Quiñones. Designed in the Spanish baroque style, it was built in 1573 in the form of a simple chapel with a low-slung thatch roof. Its present grandeur is the result of at least five subsequent enlargements and renovations. Much of what you see today is the result of a rebuilding in 1688 and a restoration in 1737 that followed a disastrous earthquake. Inside are three naves, 10 altars, three chapels, and a belfry that was rebuilt in 1939, following an earthquake in 1918. The central chandelier, made from rock crystal and imported from Barcelona in 1866, is the largest in the Caribbean. The pride of the church is the *trompe l'oeil* ceiling, which was elaborately restored in 1993. A series of stained-glass windows with contemporary designs was inserted during a 1999 restoration. The church can be visited daily from 8 to 11am and 1 to 3pm.

WHERE TO STAY & DINE

Tapas Café ★ Ⓕⁱⁿᵈˢ SPANISH   This charming restaurant is our favorite spot in the historic district of San Germán, an oasis of sophistication in the provincial countryside. The interior dining room, with mosaic tiles and blue stars on the ceiling, offers a cool respite from the heat. Portions are sizeable. The seafood paella is loaded with prawns, mussels, and lobster, and the beef medallions in blue cheese did not disappoint. Other menu items range from Spanish sausage sautéed in wine sauce to the classic soup *caldo gallego* to fried fish fritters.

50 Calle Dr. Santiago Veve, San Germán. ℂ **787/264-0610.** Reservations not necessary. Tapas $2–$15. AE, MC, V. Thurs–Fri 4:30–11pm; Sat 11am–11pm; Sun 11am–9pm.

Villa Del Rey ★ Ⓕⁱⁿᵈˢ   This is the best place to stay in historic San Germán, although you'll have to drive 15 minutes west to a good beach. The fine country inn is completely modernized and attractively furnished, mostly with picture windows. You're offered a choice of midsize-to-spacious and well-furnished accommodations—single, doubles, or suites. Both the doubles and suites are suitable for families with two children 11 years old and under. Each unit comes with a private bathroom with tub and shower. Light meals can be prepared in the suites, each equipped with kitchenette. Guests meet fellow guests at La Veranda, sheltered but in the open air, featuring three meals a day, with a focus on regional dishes.

Rte. 361 Cain Alto Ward Km 0.8, San Germán. ℂ **787/642-2627.** Fax 787/264-1579. www.villadelrey.net. 19 units. Year-round $85–$95 double; $110–$120 suite. $10 per child in parent's room. MC, V. **Amenities:** Restaurant; bar; outdoor pool; business center. *In room:* A/C, TV.

4 THE SOUTHERN MOUNTAINS

TORO NEGRO FOREST RESERVE ★★★ & LAKE GUINEO ★

North of Ponce, **Toro Negro Forest Reserve** ★★★ (ℂ 787/867-3040) lies along the Cordillera Central, the cloud-shrouded, lush central mountain chain that spans Puerto Rico's spine from the southeast town of Yabucoa all the way to outside Mayagüez on the west coast. This 7,000-acre (2,833-hectare) park, ideal for hikers, straddles the highest peak of the Cordillera Central at the very heart of Puerto Rico, quite near the midway point between east and west coasts. A forest of lush trees, the reserve also contains the headwaters of several main rivers and lakes, and has several crashing waterfalls. The reserve lies between Villalba and Jayuya, Adjuntas and Orocovis.

The lowest temperatures recorded on the island—some 40°F (4°C)—were measured at **Lake Guineo ★**, the island's highest lake, which lies within the reserve. The best trail to take here is a short, paved, and wickedly steep path on the north side of Route 143, going up to the south side of **Cerro de Punta,** which at 4,390 feet (1,338m) is the highest peak on Puerto Rico. Allow about half an hour for an ascent. Once at the top, you'll be rewarded with Puerto Rico's grandest view, sweeping across the lush interior from the Atlantic to the Caribbean coasts.

The main entrance to the forest is at the Doña Juana recreational area, which has a swimming pool filled with cold water from the mountain streams, a picnic area, and a rustic campground. An adjacent restaurant serves up Puerto Rican barbecued chicken and pork and other local delicacies. Many hiking trails originate from this area. One of the best is a 2-mile (3.2km) trek to an observation post and the impressive 200-foot (61m) Doña Juana Falls.

Jayuya, known for the relics found here from Puerto Rico's Taíno past, lies north of the reserve. Off Route 144 is La Piedra Escrita, the Written Rock, a huge boulder beside a stream, with Taíno petroglyphs carved into the stone. It's a wonderful picnic spot. Jayuya also hosts an annual Indigenous Festival in November, which combines native crafts with music and food. The **Cemi Museum,** Rte. 144 Km 9.3 (© **787/828-1241**), in town has a collection of Taíno pottery and cemís, amulets sacred to the island's indigenous peoples. The adjacent **Casa Museo Canales,** Rte. 144 Km 9.4 (© **787/828-1241**), is a restored 19th-century coffee plantation home with interesting exhibits. Both museums charge $1 for adults and 50¢ for children and are open from 9am to 3pm every day.

Where to Stay & Dine

Hacienda Gripiñas This restored plantation home is set amid 20 acres of coffee fields and nature. It's a charming respite from the 21st century. Take a walk in the cool mountain countryside, then stake out a hammock or rocking chair on the porch or one of the many balconies and relax awhile. First built in 1853 by coffee baron and Spanish nobleman Eusebio Pérez del Castillo, the former plantation home was turned into an inn in 1975 but retains the elegance and grandeur of its past. A wide porch wraps around this restored plantation home, and there are gorgeous gardens and coffee fields surrounding it. There are also reading rooms and common areas in which to lounge. The sweet song of chanting *couquís,* ubiquitous small Puerto Rican tree frogs, fills the air. There is also an excellent restaurant on the premises and a pool. A small trail from here leads to the summit of Cerro Punta, Puerto Rico's highest peak. There are frequent specials with meals included that make sense for visitors because of the parador's isolation. If you are looking for solitude, go during the week, and you will likely have the place to yourself and a few other guests. You will also save a few bucks on your tab.

Rte. 527 Km 2.5, Jayuya PR 00664. (℃) **787/828-1717.** Fax 787/828-1718. www. haciendagripinas.com. 48 units. Year-round weekdays $75 double; weekends $91 double. AE, MC, V. **Amenities:** Restaurant; bar; 2 pools; game room; library. *In room:* A/C, TV, iron.

9

Mayagüez & the Northwest

Mayagüez lies in the middle of Puerto Rico's west coast, a major fun-in-the-sun zone, but it lacks its own quality beach.

Yet Puerto Rico's third-largest city is close enough to several world-class beaches to make it worth a stay. And it can offer guests dueling visions of the Caribbean vacation.

To the north, along the northwest coast that stems from Rincón to Isabella, lie the Caribbean's best surfing beaches, which compare favorably to those of California when conditions are right. These are the beaches we'll focus on in this chapter. And to the south are equally attractive beaches with among the calmest waters in the Caribbean, offering excellent snorkeling, scuba, and sailing opportunities (see chapter 8).

The city is not as renowned for its historic sites, architecture, and attractions as San Juan or Ponce, but it has all three.

Mayagüez is also close to the western mountains, especially Maricao, perhaps the prettiest of the mountain towns in Puerto Rico. You can stay here in a renovated coffee plantation house or just have lunch on its charming veranda. Or you may prefer to rent a cabin at the Monte del Estado national park, or just spend the day in its swimming pool fed by mountain streams.

Throughout the calm southwestern coastal villages and the northwest beach towns, there are a few top-level properties, several modestly priced and attractive hotels and guesthouses, and a few noteworthy paradores, privately operated country inns approved by the Puerto Rico Tourism Company that choose to participate in its joint promotion program.

This western part of Puerto Rico contains the greatest concentration of paradores, which are both along the coast and in the cool mountainous interior of the west, a wonderful escape from pollution and traffic on a hot day.

One of the biggest adventure jaunts in Puerto Rico, a trip to Mona Island, can also be explored from the coast near Mayagüez

1 MAYAGÜEZ ★

98 miles (158km) W of San Juan, 15 miles (24km) S of Aguadilla

Mayagüez is a convenient stopover for those exploring the west coast. Big-wave beaches with dramatic coastal cliffs lie to the north, while a string of white-sand beaches with palms and tranquil aquamarine water are to the south.

The city was destroyed in a great fire in 1841 and then again in 1918 during an offshore quake and ensuing tsunami that sent 20-foot waves crashing over Mayagüez. The rebuilding efforts, which used a conglomeration of styles popular at the time of the reconstructions, have created a unique architectural style in Mayagüez, whose elegance and charm reached its zenith during the mercantile and agricultural prosperity of the 19th century.

Today, the city is getting ready to host the 2010 Caribbean and Central American Games, with a slew of new construction projects, including new sports facilities, underway. Some $400 million is being invested.

ESSENTIALS

GETTING THERE **Cape Air** (© 800/352-0714; www.flycapeair. com) flies from San Juan to Mayagüez twice daily (flying time: 40 min.). Round-trip passage is $132 per person.

If you rent a car at the San Juan airport and want to drive to Mayagüez, it's fastest and most efficient to take the northern route that combines sections of the newly widened Route 22 with the older Route 2. Estimated driving time for a local resident is about 90 minutes, although newcomers usually take about 30 minutes longer. The southern route, which combines the modern Route 52 with transit across the outskirts of historic Ponce, and final access into Mayagüez via the southern section of Route 2, requires a total of about 3 hours and affords some worthwhile scenery across the island's mountainous interior.

GETTING AROUND **Taxis** meet arriving planes. If you take one, negotiate the fare with the driver first because cabs are unmetered here.

There are branches of **Avis** (© 787/832-0406), **Budget** (© 787/832-4570), and **Hertz** (© 787/832-3314) at the Mayagüez airport.

VISITOR INFORMATION The **Mayagüez Municipal Tourism Development Office** (© 787/832-5882) can help orient visitors. In Aguadilla, there is also a **Puerto Rico Tourism Company** office

(© 787/890-3315). If you're starting out in San Juan, you can inquire there before you set out (see "Visitor Information" under "Orientation," in chapter 3).

EXPLORING THE AREA
Mayagüez Attractions

The area surrounding the city's elegant central Plaza Colón is among the prettiest in the city, with several restored historic buildings. A bronze monument of Christopher Columbus atop a globe surrounded by 16 female statues dominates the plaza, which is also marked by mosaic-tiled walkways and gurgling fountains, blooming tropical gardens, and squat, leafy trees.

The neo-Corinthian **Mayagüez City Hall** and the **Nuestra Señora de la Candelaria,** which has gone through several incarnations since the first building went up in 1780, are noteworthy buildings right off the plaza.

Make sure to stroll down nearby **Calle McKinley,** home to the fabulous, recently restored **Yaguez Theater.** The neoclassical jewel served as both an opera and a silent movie house and is still in active use today. The city's smashing Art Deco post office is also located here.

Mayagüez's historic waterfront district, with a restored 1920s Custom House and rows of neat warehouses, is also worth a look. The century-old **University of Puerto Rico Mayagüez Campus** is also beautiful.

To soak in the magical sunsets of the Puerto Rican west coast, either head to the hills surrounding the city or try a room with a view on the waterfront.

Juan A. Rivero Zoo   This 14-acre (5.7-hectare) zoo recently underwent a $14-million renovation. The African safari exhibit has lions, elephants, zebras, and rhinos, and jaguars are part of a Caribbean exhibit. There's also a butterfly and lizard exhibit and gorgeous grounds. The birdhouse has this fantastic elevated walkway where you look down on colorful tropical birds such as parrots. There are also eagles, hawks, and owls. You can see the entire zoo in 2 hours.

Rte. 108, Barrio Miradero, Mayagüez Union. © **787/834-8110.** Admission $6 adults, $4 ages 11–17, $2 ages 5–10, free for age 4 and under. Wed–Sun and holidays 8:30am–5pm.

The Tropical Agricultural Research Station   This is not a botanical garden but a working research facility of the U.S. Department of Agriculture. It's located on Route 65, between Post Street and Route 108, adjacent to the University of Puerto Rico at Mayagüez

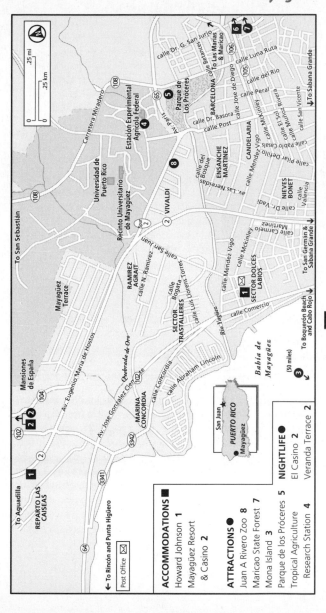

ACCOMMODATIONS ■

Howard Johnson **1**

Mayagüez Resort
& Casino **2**

ATTRACTIONS ●

Juan A Rivero Zoo **8**

Maricao State Forest **7**

Mona Island **3**

Parque de los Próceres **5**

Tropical Agriculture
Research Station **4**

NIGHTLIFE ●

El Casino **2**

Veranda Terrace **2**

Mona Island: The Galápagos of Puerto Rico

Off Mayagüez, the unique **Isla Mona** ★★★ teems with giant iguanas, three species of endangered sea turtles, red-footed boobies, and countless other seabirds. It features a tabletop plateau with mangrove forests and cacti, giving way to dramatic 200-foot-high (61m) limestone cliffs that rise above the water and encircle much of Mona.

A bean-shaped pristine island with no development at all, Mona is a destination for the hardy pilgrim who seeks the road less traveled. It lies in the middle of the Mona Passage, about halfway between Puerto Rico and the Dominican Republic. A pup tent, backpack, and hiking boots will do fine if you plan to forego the comforts of civilization and immerse yourself in nature. Snorkelers, spelunkers, biologists, and ecotourists find much to fascinate them in Mona's wildlife, mangrove forests, coral reefs, and complex honeycomb, which is the largest marine-originated cave in the world. There are also miles of secluded white-sand beaches and palm trees.

Mona can be reached by organized tour from Mayagüez. Camping is available at $10 per night. Everything needed, including water, must be brought in, and everything, including garbage, must be taken out. For more information, call the

campus and across the street from the **Parque de los Próceres (Patriots' Park).** At the administration office, ask for a free map of the tropical gardens, which have one of the largest collections of tropical plant species intended for practical use, including cacao, fruit trees, spices, timbers, and ornamentals. There are lots of trees and a wide variety of plants. A hacienda-style building houses the visitor's office. The area is divided into fruit trees, a palm plantation, a bamboo forest, and a botanical garden. There are labs, greenhouses, and other research facilities throughout the area.

2200 Av. Pedro Albizu Campos. ✆ **787/831-3435.** Free admission. Mon–Fri 9am–5pm.

Puerto Rico Department of Natural and Environmental Resources at (C) 787/999-2200. The Puerto Rico government invested $1.7 million on a new visitor center on Mona, which includes living quarters for researchers and park rangers.

To reach the island, contact **Adventures Tourmarine,** Rte. 102 Km 14.1, Playa Joyuda, Cabo Rojo ((C) **787/375-2625**). Captain Elick Hernández operates boat charters to Mona with a minimum of 10 passengers, each paying $135 for a round-trip day adventure. **Acampa Nature Adventures,** Av. Piñero 1221, San Juan ((C) **787/706-0659**), runs a 4-day, 3-night trip to Mona, which includes all equipment, meals, and guides. The trips are run in groups with a 10-person limit. Price depends on how many people are in the group.

Warning: The passage over is extremely rough, and many passengers prone to seasickness take Dramamine the night before the boat ride. There is no bottled water on the island, so bring your own. Also bring food, mosquito repellent, and even toilet paper. Alcoholic drinks are forbidden. While Mona's uninhabited landscape and surrounding turquoise waters are beautiful, this can also be a dangerous, unforgiving place. In 2001, a Boy Scout got lost and died from hypothermia; in 2005, a psychologist suffered the same fate.

WHERE TO STAY

Howard Johnson Downtown Mayagüez This converted monastery is a charming historic hotel right near Plaza Colón. With its wide tiled walkways wrapped around an interior courtyard and Spanish colonial furnishings, this hotel is at home in the city's prettiest neighborhood. The construction allows the breeze in and affords nice vistas of historic Mayagüez. A pool is located in one courtyard. The hotel is outfitted with high-speed Internet and other modern amenities. There's no restaurant on premises but there are several nearby, including the delectable Ricomini Café across the street, where you'll have your free continental breakfast. It can get noisy on weekends.

Calle Mendez Vigo Este 57, Mayagüez, PR 00680. ℭ **787/832-9191.** Fax 787/832-9122. www.hojo.com. 35 units. Year-round $85–$125 double; $140 suite. Rates include continental breakfast at neighboring bakery. AE, MC, V. Parking $4. **Amenities:** Pool; 1 room for those w/limited mobility. *In room:* A/C, TV, Internet access (in some), fridge, hair dryer.

Mayagüez Resort & Casino ★   This is the largest and best general hotel resort in western Puerto Rico, appealing equally to business travelers and vacationers. Set atop a hill, it benefits from a country-club format spread of 20 acres (8 hectares) of tropical landscaping with trees and gardens. The landscaped grounds have been designated an adjunct to the nearby Tropical Agriculture Research Station. Five species of palm trees, eight kinds of bougainvillea, and numerous species of rare flora are set adjacent to the institute's collection of tropical plants, which range from a pink torch ginger to a Sri Lankan cinnamon tree. The river pool is also set among palms and boulders. There is high-speed Internet access throughout the property.

The hotel's well-designed bedrooms open onto views of the swimming pool, and many units have private balconies. Guest rooms tend to be small, but they have good beds. The restored bathrooms are well equipped with makeup mirrors, scales, and tub/shower combinations.

For details about El Castillo, the hotel's restaurant, see "Where to Dine," below. The hotel is the major entertainment center of Mayagüez. Its casino has free admission and is open 24 hours a day. You can also drink and dance at the Victoria Lounge.

Rte. 104 Km 0.3 (P.O. Box 3781), Mayagüez, PR 00680. ℭ **888/689-3030** or 787/832-3030. Fax 787/265-3020. www.mayaguezresort.com. 140 units. Year-round $189–$259 double; $335 suite. AE, DC, DISC, MC, V. Parking $4.50. **Amenities:** 2 restaurants; 3 bars; Olympic-size pool; children's pool; 3 tennis courts; small fitness room; Jacuzzi; steam room; playground; 24-hr. room service; massage; babysitting; laundry service; casino; rooms for those w/limited mobility. *In room:* A/C, TV, high-speed Internet, minibar, coffeemaker, iron.

WHERE TO DINE

El Castillo INTERNATIONAL/PUERTO RICAN   This is one of the best large-scale dining rooms in western Puerto Rico, as well as the main restaurant for the largest hotel and casino in the area. The food has real flavor and flair, unlike the typical bland hotel fare so often dished up. Known for its generous lunch buffets, El Castillo serves only a la carte items at dinner, including seafood stew served on a bed of linguine with marinara sauce, grilled salmon with a mango-flavored Grand Marnier sauce, and filets of sea bass with a cilantro, white-wine, and butter sauce. Steak and lobster are served on the same platter, if you want it.

2 RINCON

100 miles (161km) W of San Juan, 6 miles (9.7km) N of Mayagüez

Rincón is no longer a sleepy coastal village attracting surfers and bohemian travelers. They, of course, are still coming, but a building boom has brought a wave of new condo, hotel, and luxury vacation residence projects, which has attracted more and more visitors here over the last decade.

The town dates from the 16th century when a landowner allowed poor families to set down roots on his land. It eventually gained fame as the Caribbean's best surfing spot, a fact reinforced by its hosting the World Surfing Championship in 1968. It remains the surfing capital of the Caribbean, a center for expatriate North Americans, and a tourist magnet.

With over a dozen beaches in town, great surfing, sailing, and snorkeling, and an ever better nightlife and cultural scene, it's not hard to see why. It continues evolving as a destination, reinforcing the fact it's one of the best stops to make in Puerto Rico.

There was a time when nonsurfers visited Rincón for only one reason: the Horned Dorset Primavera hotel, not only one of the finest hotels in Puerto Rico, but one of the best in the entire Caribbean. Now there are several reasons for them to come.

SURFING & OTHER OUTDOOR PURSUITS

Rincón has been the Caribbean's surfing capital since hosting the World Surfing Championship in 1968. Part of the town's appeal, however, is that its 8 miles of beaches include both rough surfing beaches along the North and tranquil Caribbean coastal areas along its south.

The best surfing beaches include **Las Maria's, Spanish Wall,** and **Domes** near the town lighthouse on the north side. **Córcega** is probably the best of the Caribbean beaches. Some beaches, meanwhile, can show different faces at different times of the year. For instance, **Steps,** which is also named **Tres Palmas,** is a great surfing beach in winter, but in summer it is calm and one of the best spots for snorkeling.

Visitors need to proceed with caution during winter when venturing into the surf off Rincón, which can be particularly strong, with powerful riptides and undertows that routinely cause drownings. This should not stop visitors from coming here, however. The town has beaches with both tranquil and strong surf. Just proceed with caution and ask locals about surf conditions.

Windsurfing, and increasingly kite-boarding, is also extremely popular here, with **Sandy Beach** a favored site because it does not have the rocks found on the ocean floor that some of the other beaches in the area have. Excellent scuba, snorkeling, parasailing, and sailing are also available in Rincón, making it one of the most active of Caribbean destinations.

Endangered humpback whales winter here, attracting a growing number of whale-watchers from December to March. The lighthouse at El Faro Park is a great place to spot these mammoth mammals.

As a surf mecca, Rincón is also a great spot to learn the sport or improve your technique. The **Rincón Surf School,** P.O. Box 1333, Rincón (© **787/823-0610**), offers beginners lessons or can teach surfers how to improve their performance. One lesson costs $95, and there are also 2-day ($180), 3-day ($260), and 5-day ($390) packages. A private 2-hour lesson is $150, $75 each for two people. The school also arranges surf vacation packages in conjunction with the Casa Verde Guesthouse. **Puntas Surf School,** P.O. Box 4319, HC-01 Calle Vista del Mar (© **787/823-3618** or 207/251-1154), is another great option. It's run by Melissa Taylor and Bill Woodward, whose love of the sport is infectious, and they say they can teach would-be surfers of any age, from 5 to 105. Private lessons cost $40 per hour, $60 for 2 hours. Group rates and package deals are also available. A professional photographer takes photos of the lessons, which you can purchase.

There are many surfing outfitters in town, and one of the most established is the **West Coast Surf Shop,** Muñoz Rivera 2E, Rincón (© **787/823-3935**), open daily 9am to 6pm. The shop rents surfing equipment and gives lessons. The **Hot Wavz Surf Shop,** Maria's Beach (© **787/823-3942**), also rents long boards, as well as boogie boards. Prices for board rentals start at around $25 daily. Snorkeling gear can also be rented at these shops.

Good snorkeling can be found just off the beach. When conditions are right, **Tres Palmas–Steps** is a great spot. Scuba divers and snorkeling enthusiasts will also want to head out to **Desecheo Island,** the large mass of land seen offshore from Rincón looking west. A quick half-hour boat trip, the small island is a nature reserve with great coral formations and large reef fish. Visibility is 100 feet plus (30m), and average water temperature is between 80° and 86°F (27°–30°C).

A good scuba outfitter is **Taíno Divers,** Black Eagle Marina at Rincón (© **787/823-6429**), which offers local boat charters along

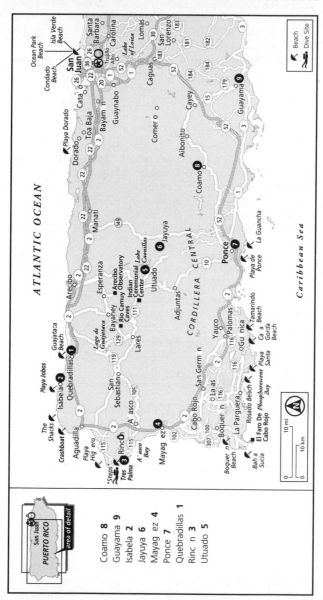

ATLANTIC OCEAN

Caribbean Sea

Beach
Dive Site

N

10 mi
0
10 km
0

PUERTO RICO

San Juan

area of detail

Coamo **8**
Guayama **9**
Isabela **2**
Jayuya **6**
Mayagüez **4**
Ponce **7**
Quebradillas **1**
Rincón **3**
Utuado **5**

with scuba and snorkeling trips. The Desecheo day trip departs at 8am and returns at 2pm. Snorkeling costs $75 while a two-tank dive is $109. Prices include gourmet sandwiches and drinks. The outfit also runs half-day fishing charters for $725 and whale-watching expeditions and sunset cruises for $35.

Makaira Fishing Charters, P.O. Box 257, Rincón (ⓒ **787/823-4391** or 299-7374), offers fishing charters from a no-frills, tournament-rigged, 35-foot 2006 Contender that fits six comfortably. Half-day rates are $575 and full-day $850. **Moondog Charters** (ⓒ **787/823-3059**) also runs fishing excursions and dive charters aboard a 32-foot Albermarle Express Sport Fisherman.

Katarina Sail Charters (ⓒ **787/823-SAIL** [7245]) gives daily sailing trips aboard a 32-foot catamaran. The day sail (from around 10:20am–2:30pm) consists of some fine cruising, a stop for a swim and snorkel, and then lunch. It costs $60, $30 for children 11 and under. The sunset sail leaves at 4:30pm and returns after dark, about 2 hours later. Watching the western sunset while sailing and listening to great music is wonderful, with rum punch, beer, and nonalcoholic drinks.

The most visible and sought-after whale-watching panorama in Rincón is **Parque El Faro de Rincón (Rincón Lighthouse Park),** which lies on El Faro Point peninsula at the extreme western tip of town. Within its fenced-in perimeter are pavilions that sell souvenirs and snack items, rows of binoculars offering 25¢ views, and a stately looking lighthouse built in 1921. The park is at its most popular from December to March for whale-watching and in January and February for surfer gazing.

WHERE TO STAY
Very Expensive

Horned Dorset Primavera ★★★　This is the most sophisticated hotel on the west coast of Puerto Rico, and one of the most exclusive small properties anywhere in the Caribbean. Set on 8 acres (3.2 hectares), it opens onto a secluded semiprivate beach. It was built on the massive breakwaters and seawalls erected by a local railroad many years ago. The hacienda evokes an aristocratic Spanish villa, with wicker armchairs, hand-painted tiles, ceiling fans, seaside terraces, and cascades of flowers. Accommodations are in a series of suites that ramble amid lush gardens. The decor is tasteful, with four-poster beds and brass-footed tubs (with showers) in marble-sheathed bathrooms. Rooms are spacious and luxurious, with Persian rugs over tile floors, queen-size sofa beds in the sitting areas, and fine linens and tasteful fabrics on the elegant beds. The eight-suite Casa Escondida villa, set at the edge of the property, adjacent to the sea, is decorated with an accent on teakwood and marble. Some of the units have private plunge pools; others offer private verandas or sun decks. Each contains high-quality reproductions of colonial furniture by Baker.

The hotel's restaurant, also called Horned Dorset Primavera, is one of the finest on Puerto Rico (see "Where to Dine," below). Rates do not include meals. The Modified American Plan, or MAP (breakfast and dinner), is available at the price of $200 per night per couple.

Apartado 1132, Rincón, PR 00677. © **800/633-1857** or 787/823-4030. Fax 787/823-5580. www.horneddorset.com. 55 units. Winter $496–$1,070 double, $1,385 ocean suite; holidays $696–$1,270 double, $1,385 ocean suite; summer $260–$670 double, $800 ocean suite. AE, MC, V. Children 11 and under not accepted. **Amenities:** 2 restaurants; bar; 3 outdoor pools (1 infinity); fitness center; kayaking (free); limited room service; massage; laundry service; library. *In room:* A/C, hair dryer, safe.

Expensive

Rincón Beach Resort   Everybody from romantic lovebirds to hipsters in logo T-shirts to families with young children checks into this secluded hideaway. At this beachfront resort, an open-air deck stretches along the coastline at the end of an "infinity pool." It's perhaps the most welcoming place along the western coastline. The staff can help you arrange everything from watersports to golf. Guests meet fellow guests in the lobby bar, and later enjoy a savory Caribbean cuisine in Brasas Restaurant, with its open-air terrace. You're given a choice of oceanview or poolside-view units, and can also rent well-furnished one- and two-bedroom apartments. The decor is tropical throughout, with vibrant colors.

Rte. 115 Km 5.8, Añasco, PR 00610. © **866/598-0009** or 787/589-9000. Fax 787/589-9040. www.rinconbeach.com. 118 units. Winter $240–$280 double, $355 junior suite, $459 1-bedroom suite, $650 2-bedroom suite; off season $205–$245 double, $315 junior suite, $405 1-bedroom suite, $570 2-bedroom suite. Rates include continental breakfast. AE, DISC, MC, V. **Amenities:** Restaurant; grill; 3 bars; outdoor pool; gym; babysitting; laundry service; nonsmoking rooms; rooms for those w/limited mobility. *In room:* A/C, TV, Internet, kitchenettes in suites, fridge, hair dryer, iron, safe.

Moderate

Casa Isleña Inn ★ (Finds)   "Island House" is created from a simple oceanfront former home right on the beach. Behind its gates, away from the water, is a private and tranquil world that offers a series of medium-size and comfortably furnished bedrooms decorated in bright Caribbean colors and designs. Each room has a neatly maintained shower-only bathroom. A natural tidal pool formed by a reef is an 8-minute stroll from the inn. At the tidal pool and from the inn's terraces guests can enjoy views of Aguadilla Bay and Mona Passage. In winter, while standing on the terraces, you can often watch the migration of humpback whales. There is a large Olympic-size swimming pool surrounded by a nice sun deck with lounge chairs. This area overlooks the adjacent beach. The inn is built in a Spanish style, with several balconies and a tiled veranda where breakfast is served. The fine tapas restaurant operates Wednesday through Sunday afternoons and evenings.

Barrio Puntas Carretera Interior 413 Km 4, Rincón, PR 00677. ℂ 888/289-7750 or 787/823-1525. Fax 787/823-1530. www.casa-islena.com. 9 units (shower only). Year-round $115–$165 double. Extra person $15. MC, V. **Amenities:** Tapas restaurant and bar; 1 room for those w/limited mobility. In room: A/C, TV, no phone.

Lemontree Waterfront Suites ★ (Finds)

Right on a good, sandy beach, these spacious apartments with kitchenettes are for those who don't want to limit themselves to hotel rooms and meals. With the sound of the surf just outside your private back porch, these well-furnished seaside units can provide a home away from home, with everything from ceiling fans to air-conditioning, from paperback libraries to custom woodworking details. The suites have been refreshed recently with new furnishings and tropical colors. The property is well maintained. Families enjoy the three-bedroom, two-bathroom oceanfront suite called "Papaya;" "Mango" and "Pineapple" are ideal for two persons. Each unit contains a midsize shower-only bathroom. The least expensive units, "Banana" and "Coconut," are studio units for those who want a kitchen but don't require a living room. Spa treatments are available as well as scuba-diving lessons. The cottages lie a 10-minute drive west of Rincón.

Rte. 4290 (P.O. Box 3200), Rincón, PR 00677. ℂ 888/418-8733 or 787/823-6452. Fax 787/823-5821. www.lemontreepr.com. 6 units (shower only). Year-round $165–$195 double; $265 quad; $295 for 6. AE, MC, V. In room: A/C, TV, kitchenette, coffeemaker.

Inexpensive

Beside the Pointe Guesthouse This tiny guesthouse sits on a lovely spot on the beach and has a popular tavern, restaurant, and shop on the grounds. With only a handful of rooms, though, this is probably not for everyone. We recommend the more expensive oceanfront double and the oceanview suites on the upper deck, which are removed enough from the public areas to maintain a sense of privacy. The view is also beautiful, and there's a great sun deck.

Carretera 413 Km 4, Sandy Beach, Rincón, PR 00677. ℂ 888/823-8550. Fax 787/823-8550. www.besidethepointe.com. 21 units. High season $120–$140 double, $170 oceanfront double, $185–$210 suites; low season $80–$120 double, $140 oceanfront double, $165–$190 suites. AE, MC, V. **Amenities:** Restaurant; bar; Wi-Fi; gift shop w/local crafts. In room: A/C, TV, kitchenette (suites), fridge.

The Lazy Parrot   Set within an unlikely inland neighborhood, this place is nonetheless one of the best spots in Rincón to stay. It's one of the only hotels on Route 413, the so-called "road to happiness" because it's the main road to town from the rest of Puerto Rico. "Value" rooms are located on the first floor. They are clean, well-organized, and comfortable, if not overly large. They have no view, but each has either a deck, patio, or balcony, and an attractive decor of light, natural colors. The upstairs "panoramic" rooms have a view to the pretty Cadena Hills and the coast and overlook the pool area. These are also larger and have upgraded facilities like flatscreen TVs. Definitely pay the extra cost for an upstairs room if privacy is important to you. The other rooms are close to the lobby, pool, and restaurant. Smilin' Joes is one of the best eateries in Rincón, while the Rum Shack serves light fare and drinks poolside, and can be a lot of fun at night. This is one of the better-managed properties in town. Though its inland location is a drawback, you should have a car rental to explore several of the area's beaches anyway, and the pool area is quite nice.

Rd. 413 Km 4.1, Barrio Puntas, Rincón, PR 00677. ⓒ **800/294-1752** or 787/823-5654. Fax 787/823-0224. www.lazyparrot.com. 21 units. Year-round $125 double value rooms; $165 double panoramic rooms. The smallest room goes for $99 single or double. Rates include continental breakfast. AE, DISC, MC, V. **Amenities:** 2 restaurants; bar; pool; Wi-Fi; gift shop w/local crafts; limited room service; babysitting. *In room:* A/C, TV, fridge.

Villa Cofresi (Kids)   About a mile (1.6km) south of Rincón's center, this is a clean, family-run hotel with a view of the beach. Thanks to the three adult children of the Caro family, the place is better managed than many of its competitors. Bedrooms are comfortable and airy, with well-chosen furniture that might remind you of something in southern Florida. Each unit has a white-tile floor and a small bathroom with a tub and shower. Most rooms have two double beds; some have two twin beds. All are nonsmoking. The two units that tend to be reserved out long in advance are nos. 47 and 55, which have windows opening directly onto the sea.

The in-house restaurant, La Ana de Cofresi, is named after the ship that was captained by the region's most famous 18th-century pirate, Roberto Cofresi. Hand-painted murals highlight some of his adventures. Open Monday through Friday from 5 to 10pm and Saturday and Sunday from noon to 10pm, it charges $8 to $30 for well-prepared main courses that are likely to include fish consommé, four kinds of *mofongo*, breaded scampi served either with Creole sauce or garlic, and very good steaks, including a 12-ounce New York sirloin.

Rd. 115 Km 12.0, Rincón, PR 00677. ☎ **787/823-2450.** Fax 787/823-1770. www.
villacofresi.com. 80 units. Winter $135–$155 double, $160 suite; off season $115–
$135 double, $160 suite. AE, DC, MC, V. **Amenities:** Restaurant; bar; outdoor pool;
room service; rooms for those w/limited mobility. *In room:* A/C, TV, fridge, hair
dryer, iron.

WHERE TO DINE
Very Expensive
Horned Dorset Primavera ★★ FRENCH/CARIBBEAN   This
is the finest restaurant in western Puerto Rico—so romantic that
people sometimes come from San Juan just for an intimate dinner. A
masonry staircase sweeps from the garden to the second floor, where
soaring ceilings and an atmosphere similar to that in a private villa
awaits you.

The menu, which changes virtually every night based on the inspi-
ration of the chef, might include chilled parsnip soup, a fricassee of
wahoo with wild mushrooms, grilled loin of beef with peppercorns,
and medallions of lobster in an orange-flavored beurre blanc sauce.
The grilled breast of duckling with bay leaves and raspberry sauce is
also delectable. Mahimahi is grilled and served with ginger-cream
sauce on a bed of braised Chinese cabbage. It's delicious.

In the Horned Dorset Primavera hotel, Apartado 1132. ☎ **787/823-4030.** Reservations recommended. Fixed-price dinner $68 for 5 dishes, $92 for 8 dishes. AE,
MC, V. Daily 7–9:30pm.

Expensive
Smiling Joe's ★ CARIBBEAN ASIAN FUSION   With an inventive menu and beautiful but laid-back setting, this is one of Rincón's
best restaurants. Worldwide flavors are brought together for optimal
impact, and diners sit in an open-air terrace with panoramic views of
a tropical garden. The restaurant's takes on such local classics as churrasco and red snapper are a delicious mix of Puerto Rican *sabor*,
down-island flavorings, and Asian herbs, and we love the way it kicks
up classic Jamaican jerk with a bit of tamarind and mango salsa and
then targets grilled mahimahi rather than chicken. But the plates that
really wowed us were the pork tenderloin, filled with chorizo–red
pepper stuffing and glazed in guava and rum, and the almond crusted
chicken with a goat cheese–veggie filling. We got off to a roaring start
with the spicy red coconut curry mussels and the tempura pepper
stuffed with lobster risotto.

Rd. 413 Km 4.1, Barrio Puntas, Rincón, PR 00677. ☎ **787/823-0101.** Reservations
not necessary. Main courses $19–$33 dinner only. AE, DISC, MC, V. Daily 5:30–
10pm.

Tamboo Tavern and Seaside Grill Restaurant AMERICAN-CARIBBEAN This tavern and restaurant at Beside the Pointe Guesthouse on Sandy Beach is the favored hangout for the young and beautiful beach crowd and surfing enthusiasts from the island and across the planet. It's a great place to eat, offering good food and a beautiful setting, no matter who you are. Beachfront dining does not get better than this. Tables are stretched along a deck running along the beach sands and palm trees. It's basic steaks, ribs, and lots of seafood, but it's well prepared and tastes extra great while you're breathing in the sea and the salt. The mahimahi in caper sauce and grilled Caribbean lobster are both recommended, and you might want to start out with a platter of Puerto Rican appetizers. Burgers, wraps, and salads are also available for lunch and dinner.

Carretera 413 Km 4, Sandy Beach, Rincón. ℂ **888/823-8550** or 787/823-8550. Reservations not accepted. Main courses $16–$26 dinner; lunch items $6–$10. MC, V. Restaurant Thurs–Tues noon–9:30pm. Bar daily noon–2am.

A NEARBY PLACE TO STAY & DINE IN AGUADA

J. B. Hidden Village Hotel ★ Named using the initials of its owners (Julio Bonilla; his wife, Jinnie; and their son, Julio, Jr.), this is a well-maintained and isolated hotel launched in 1990. Half a mile (.8km) east of Aguada, on a side street that runs off Route 4414, it's nestled in a valley between three forested hillsides, almost invisible from the road. The hotel is a quiet and simple refuge to vacationers who enjoy exploring the area's many beaches. There are two restaurants on the premises (one with a view of a neighboring ravine). Each comfortable bedroom offers views of the pool and has a small tiled bathroom with tub/shower combination. Nice place but not near any beach.

Carretera 2, Intersection 4416, Km 1, Punta Nueve, Barrio Piedras Blancas, Sector Villarrubia, Aguada, PR 00602. ℂ **787/868-8686.** Fax 787/868-8701. 42 units. Year-round $72–$120 double; $125 suite. AE, MC, V. **Amenities:** Restaurant; bar; 2 outdoor pools; rooms for those w/limited mobility. *In room:* A/C, TV, no phone.

RINCON AFTER DARK

Join the surfers for a "sundowner" at **Calypso's Tropical Bar,** Maria's Beach (ℂ **787/823-1626**), which lies on the road to the lighthouse. Locals gather to watch the sunset in the outdoor courtyard. Happy-hour specials are daily 5 to 7pm. Live music takes place Friday and Saturday nights, and the bar is open daily from 11am until the last customer leaves (usually long after midnight). The Calypso Café has grilled seafood and pub fare. If you decide to eat something here, go for the grilled seafood, with main courses costing from $4 to $12.

One of the best *simpático* bars is **Rock Bottom,** adjoining Casa Verde Guest House along Sandy Beach Road (℃ 787/823-3756). It serves burgers and other stateside food. The upstairs surfer bar is decorated with dozens of graffitied surf boards and has a treehouse feel to it. You'll find great piña coladas and daily drink specials. The bar is open until midnight, at least. Wednesdays are acoustic jam nights, and Sundays are dedicated to movies and surf videos.

A young crowd gathers at **Tamboo Tavern** (℃ 787/823-8550), another surfer's bar in a tropical dream location right on Sandy Beach. The action percolates throughout the day, and really takes off as the sun begins to set. Watch it from the terrace or sit at the bar inside tapping your feet to rock *en español* and progressive American music. There's live music most weekend nights. The **Rum Shack** (℃ 787/823-0101) is a good place to rub shoulders with local expats and a diverse group of travelers. Don't miss the full-moon party or reggae nights if one is occurring while you are in town. There's also a weekly movie night.

3 AGUADILLA & THE NORTHWEST

Aguadilla is the biggest town on Puerto Rico's northwest corner, which is filled with great beaches and other natural blessings for an active vacation experience. And it makes a good base from which to explore the area, with lots of hotels, restaurants, good infrastructure, a fairly large mall, and lots of attractions, such as a water park and golf course. Several airlines now run direct flights to the town's **Rafael Hernández Airport,** especially during the high season. It's the island's second international airport after Luis Muñoz Marín in San Juan.

ESSENTIALS

GETTING THERE & GETTING AROUND   Both JetBlue and Continental have nonstop flights from East Coast destinations, particularly from New York and Florida, direct to the **Rafael Hernández Airport,** Antigua Base Ramey, Hangar 405, Aguadilla (℃ 787/891-2226). Many other flights offer connections from San Juan onto Aguadilla.

There are branches of **Avis** (℃ 787/890-3311), **Budget** (℃ 787/890-1110), and **Hertz** (℃ 787/833-3170) at the Aguadilla airport.

If you're driving from San Juan, travel west on Hwy. 22, then Route 2 (trip time: 2 hr.).

WATERSPORTS & OTHER OUTDOOR PURSUITS

While Rincón has wider name recognition, Aguadilla and Isabela have equally good surf spots. In fact, the Puerto Rican Pipeline is actually composed of beaches in the three towns. **Gas Chambers, Crash Boat,** and **Wilderness** rule in Aguadilla, while the preferred spots in **Isabela** include **Jobos** and **Middles.** The best time to surf is from November through March, but summer storms can also kick up the surf. In the summer season, however, when the waves diminish, these northwest beaches double as perfect spots for windsurfing and snorkeling, with calm waters filled with coral reefs and marine life. The towns are quite close together, and the string of beaches through both really forms a single destination.

Crash Boat is popular; vendors sell street food from stands by its parking lot while a local restaurant serves freshly caught seafood (brightly colored wooden fishing boats are often parked on the beach). One-half of the beach is protected, with the aquamarine water kissing the white sand, while the other side faces the open water and is much rougher. **Shacks** draw both snorkelers and scuba divers, who converge on one section of the large beach filled with reefs and coral caverns that teem with rainbow-hued fish. It's also the best spot in the area for kite-boarding and windsurfing.

The **Isabela** coastline is also beautiful. In some places dirt roads still weave between cliffs and white beaches, set off by dramatic rock formations and submerged coral reefs that send surf crashing skyward. This is an area of saltwater wells and blowholes, through which dramatic eruptions of salt water spew from submerged sea caves. Several are found in the area known as **La Princesa,** and **Jobos** beach is home to one of the most famous saltwater wells, **El Pozo de Jacinto.**

Jobos is a large beach with a famed surf break at its western end, but kids can frolic along more protected areas along this mammoth shore. There are also guesthouses and restaurants here, and on summer and holiday weekends it's got a party atmosphere. The **Ocean Front Hotel and Restaurant** (© 787/872-3339), right at the beach, is a good spot for a drink and seafood. **Montones Beach** has rock outcroppings and reefs that make a beguiling seascape and also protect the water from the raging surf in this area. You won't find the restaurants and bars here that you will in Jobos, but you can find your own secluded spot on the beach.

Steep cliffs drop in flat jagged lines to the rough surf along the rugged Atlantic coastline of **Quebradillas. Guajataca Beach,** named after a powerful Taíno Indian chief, is a great spot, but think twice about swimming here. The currents are extremely powerful and dangerous, and while surfers love it, casual swimmers should proceed with caution. The beach is also called **El Tunel** because there's a large abandoned railroad tunnel carved out of a mountain at the entrance to the beach. There is a parking area here and a no-frills, open-air restaurant and bar.

Aquatica Dive, Bike and Surf Adventures, Rte. 110 Km 10, outside gate 5 of Rafael Hernández Airport, Aguadilla (© 787/890-6071), is a full-service dive and surf shop, but it also rents equipment and gives lessons in scuba and surfing. The outfit also runs mountain-bike excursions to the Guajataca Forest. Prices depend on season and group size, but surf lessons cost from $45 to $65 for 1½ hours, and a two-tank scuba dive is from $60 to $85. Bicycle tours cost between $45 and $65 per person and last up to 3 hours. Surf and scuba equipment rentals run from $20 to $45 per day, while bicycles are $25 per day.

The **Hang Loose Surf Shop,** Rte. 4466 Km 1.2, Playa Jobos, Isabela (© 787/872-2490; Tues–Sun 10am–5pm), is well stocked with equipment. It gives surf lessons ($55/hour private lesson) and rents boards for $25 daily. The shop is owned by Werner Vega, a great big-wave rider, who is one of Puerto Rico's premier board shapers.

Punta Borinquén Golf Club, Route 107 (© 787/890-2987), 2 miles (3.2km) north of Aguadilla's center, across the highway from the city's airport, was originally built by the U.S. government as part of Ramey Air Force Base. Today, it is a public 18-hole golf course, open daily from 7am to 7pm. Greens fees are a bargain at $20 per round; a golf cart that can carry two passengers rents for $30 for 1 8 holes. A set of clubs can be rented for $15. The clubhouse has a bar and a simple restaurant. It's also a nice course with coastal views. **Parque Aquatica Las Cascadas,** Hwy. 2 Km 126.5, Aguadilla (© 787/819-0950 or 819-1030), is a water park run by the municipality that the kids will love. There are giant slides and tubes and the Río Loco rapids pool. A big drawback is that it is only open in the summer, from May through September (10am–5pm weekdays, 10am–6pm weekends). Tickets are $16 for adults and $14 for kids (ages 4–12) plus a $5 tube-rental fee. You probably did not come to Puerto Rico to go ice-skating, but you can do it at the **Aguadilla Ice Skating Rink,** Hwy. 442 (© **787/819-5555,** ext. 221). This is another city-run facility, open from 9:30am to 11pm. It's popular with kids and is a training facility for island figure skaters. Cost is $10 an hour during the day and $13 in the evening (including skates).

Where to Stay & Dine

Marriott Courtyard Aguadilla (Kids)   The whole family will love this hotel with pool, aquatics playground, and spacious guest rooms near some of the prettiest beaches on the island, and right around attractions like the Camuy Caves, Arecibo Observatory, local water park, and ice-skating rink. Beautiful beaches ring the coast here from Isabela to the east and Rincón to the west. It's built on the old Ramey Air Force Base near a coastal suburb. Great location and facilities make a good base to explore the northwest.

West Parade/Belt Rd., Antigua Base Ramey, Aguadilla, PR 00603. © **800/321-2211** or 787/658-8000. Fax 787/658-8020. www.marriott.com. 152 units. Year-round $169–$199 double. AE, MC, V. **Amenities:** 2 restaurants; 2 bars; 2 pools; fitness center; business services; Wi-Fi; beauty shop; room service; babysitting; dry cleaning. *In room:* A/C, TV, Internet, coffeemaker, iron.

Parador Vistamar   In the Guajataca area, this parador, one of the largest in Puerto Rico, sits like a sentinel surveying the scene from high atop a mountain overlooking greenery and a seascape. There are gardens and intricate paths carved into the side of the mountain, where you can stroll while enjoying the fragrance of the tropical flowers. For a unique experience, visitors can try their hand at freshwater fishing just down the hill from the hotel (bring your own gear). Flocks of rare tropical birds are frequently seen in the nearby mangroves.

Bedrooms (all nonsmoking) are comfortably furnished in a rather bland motel style. Bathrooms with either shower or tub are functional but without much decorative zest. There's a dining room with an ocean view where you can have a typical Puerto Rican dinner or choose from the international menu.

Rte. 113N 6205, Quebradillas, PR 00678. © **787/895-2065.** Fax 787/895-2294. www.paradorvistamar.com. 55 units (each with either shower or tub). Year-round $76–$125 double. Up to 2 children 11 and under stay free in parent's room. AE, DISC, MC, V. At Quebradillas, head northwest on Rte. 2, then go left at the junction with Rte. 113 and continue for a mile/1.6km. **Amenities:** Restaurant; bar; pool; limited room service; rooms for those w/limited mobility. *In room:* A/C, TV, coffeemaker (in some).

MAYAGÜEZ & THE NORTHWEST

9

AGUADILLA & THE NORTHWEST

Villas del Mar Hau ★ (**Kids**) Opening onto a long, secluded beach, this family-friendly parador complex is peppered with typical Puerto Rican country cottages in vivid Caribbean pastels with Victorian wood trim. The location is midway between the west coast cities of Arecibo in the east and Aguadilla in the west, right outside the smaller town of Isabela. Under the shelter of casuarina pine trees, most guests spend their days lying on Playa Montones. The huge tidal "wading" pool is ideal for children. The place is unpretentious but not completely back-to-nature, as the beachfront cottages are well furnished and equipped, each with a balcony and with capacities for two to six guests. Some have ceiling fans, others have air-conditioning, and all units are equipped with small, tiled, shower-only bathrooms. Since 1960 the Hau family has run this little beach inn. The on-site restaurant is well known in the area for its creative menu featuring fresh fish, shellfish, and meats.

Carretera 4466 Km 8.3, Playa Montones, Isabela, PR 00662. © **787/830-8315.** Fax 787/830-4988. 42 units (shower only). High season $110–$160 double, $185–$260 cottage; low season $90–$140 double, $175–$200 cottage. AE, MC, V. From the center of Isabella, take Rte. 466 toward Aguadilla. **Amenities:** Restaurant; bar; barbecue area; pool w/snack bar; tennis; beach toy rental; photocopy and fax; convenience store; babysitting; laundry service; horseback riding. *In room:* A/C, TV (in most rooms), kitchenette, coffeemaker.

Villa Montana Beach Resort ★ (**Finds**)

This breathtaking property is set on a 35-acre (14-hectare) beachfront plot. The rooms and villas are spread across Caribbean-style plantation buildings with large verandas and balconies. The buildings have cathedral ceilings, peaked tin roofs, and interior courtyards. The facades use muted pastel colors, and rooms are beautifully decorated with a subdued tropical aesthetic and have large terra-cotta tile. There are two beautiful pools and a 3-mile (4.8km) beach, where every watersport you can imagine is possible to practice. You can also hike through tropical forests, ride horses, go biking, or use the climbing wall on the property. There's a health club, spa, and sports facilities like basketball courts. Both restaurants, Eclipse and O, have quality food but are on the expensive side. The grounds are lush and beautiful, and there are numerous tropical birds. This is a place to kick way back.

Carretera 4466 Km 1.9, Barrio Bajuras, Isabela, PR 00662. © **888/780-9195** or 787/872-9553. Fax 787/872-9553. 60 units. $200–$400 double; $400–$600 villas. AE, MC, V. **Amenities:** 2 restaurants; bar; 2 pools; tennis court; basketball court; volleyball court; climbing wall; spa; watersports rentals; business center; store; babysitting; laundry service; horseback riding. *In room:* A/C, TV, kitchenette (in villas), ceiling fans.

The west is also a good area to head up into the mountains, and Maricao, west of Mayagüez, is one of the prettiest of Puerto Rico's mountain towns. You can reach Maricao from Mayagüez, but you'll have to take a number of routes heading east. It's quicker to head south along Hwy. 2 until Sabana Grande, then take Hwy. 120 directly to Maricao.

Monte del Estado National Park, Rte. 120 Km 13.2 (© 787/873-5632), is a picnic area and campground in the Maricao Forest, with wonderful pools fed by mountain streams. The stone observation tower, at 2,600 feet (792m) above sea level, provides a panoramic view across the green mountains up to the coastal plains, and you can see clear out to Mona Island. Nearly 50 species of birds live in this forest, including the Lesser Antillean pewee and the scaly naped pigeon. There are 280 tree species in this reserve and 18 rivers and creeks running through the forest.

Marciao is coffee country, and there are several plantations and historic plantation houses in the town.

From Isabela, you can visit **Lago de Guajataca** and the **Guajataca Forest Reserve,** which are located in the mountains south of town. The **Dept. de Recursos Naturales Oficina,** Rte. 446 Km 9, Barrio Llanadas (© 787/872-1045 or 999-2000), which is open daily 7am to 3:30pm, has maps and other information. Guajataca Forest sprawls across nearly 2,400 acres (971 hectares) of forestland, rising and falling at various elevations, ranging from 500 to 1,000 feet (152–305m) or more. It's punctuated by mogotes and covered with 25 miles (40km) of hiking trails. Check out the Cueva del Viento, the "Cave of the Wind." The 4-mile long **Lago de Guajataca** ★, is one of Puerto Rico's most majestic lakes.

Where to Stay & Dine

Parador Hacienda Juanita ★   Named after one of its long-ago owners, a matriarch named Juanita, this pink stucco building dates from 1836, when it was a coffee plantation. Situated 2 miles (3.2km) west of the village of Maricao, beside Route 105 heading to Mayagüez, it has a long veranda and a living room furnished with a large-screen TV and decorated with antique tools and artifacts of the coffee industry. Relatively isolated, it's surrounded by only a few neighboring buildings and the jungle. Situated on 24 acres (9.7 hectares) of plantation, the parador is a beautiful spot to hike around. It has a fine restaurant, and both breakfast and dinner are included with the room.

There's a swimming pool, billiards table, and Ping-Pong table on the premises. Its restaurant, **La Casona de Juanita,** serves tasty, hearty Puerto Rican fare. The best spot to dine is on the veranda overlooking the verdant grounds. The bedrooms are simple and rural, with ceiling fans, rocking chairs, and rustic furniture, plus small tub-and-shower bathrooms. All are nonsmoking. None of the rooms has air-conditioning (ceiling fans suffice in the cool temperatures of this high-altitude place). It sits at 1,600 feet (488m) above sea level.

Rte. 105 Km 23.5 (HC01 Box 8200), Maricao, PR 00606. ℂ **787/838-2550.** Fax 787/838-2551. www.haciendajuanita.com. 21 units. $125 double. Rate includes breakfast and dinner. Children 11 and under stay free in parent's room. AE, MC, V. Free parking. **Amenities:** Restaurant; bar; pool; tennis; 1 room for those w/limited mobility. *In room:* TV, Internet, ceiling fan, no phone.

10

Eastern Puerto Rico

The northeast corner of the island, only about 45 minutes from San Juan, contains the island's major attractions: El Yunque rainforest, two of the world's rare bioluminescent bays whose waters glow at night, and several great beaches, including Luquillo Beach (see chapter 7). There are a variety of landscapes, ranging from miles of forest to palm groves and beachside settlements. Here you will find one of the best resorts on the island, El Conquistador Resort and Country Club, which literally sits on the northeast corner of Puerto Rico, where the Atlantic Ocean and the Caribbean Sea meet.

This is the site of Fajardo, a preeminent sailor's haven, where you can catch ferries to the nearby island municipalities of Vieques and Culebra. The east coast city is actually part of a hub of islands, weaving through the neighboring Spanish Virgin Islands, and on to the U.S. and British Virgin Islands. Not for nothing, as there are at least seven marinas in town, which also has its share of gorgeous beaches, snorkeling spots, and untamed forest.

Farther down the east coast is the **Palmas del Mar,** an ever-growing resort and upscale vacation home community on a wildly gorgeous beachfront. There's a hotel and another on the way, and visitors can also rent private vacation homes and villas throughout the resort, which has marinas, golf, tennis, stores, restaurants, and bars. There are several pools and a great beach, with all watersports activities available. Palmas also has its own school and post office.

The coast has small fishing towns, rural farmland, and quaint historic plazas surrounded by beautiful Spanish colonial architecture.

The southeast corner of Puerto Rico is still relatively undiscovered, despite the beauty of its untarnished coastline and traditional towns.

1 FAJARDO

35 miles (56km) E of San Juan

A huge submerged reef off Fajardo's coast protects its southeastern waters, which are also blessed by trade winds. The sea here is run through with coral and marine life, from barracudas and nurse sharks to shimmering schools of tropical fish. It adds up to a diving, snorkeling, and sailing paradise. There are dozens of small islands off the coast of this eastern town, which also has a bioluminescent bay and other natural wonders.

With seven marinas in town, Fajardo is the first of a string of ports extending to Vieques and Culebra, the U.S. and British Virgin Islands, and the Windward island chain, the pleasure boating capital of the Caribbean.

Las Croabas, a village within the municipality, is the site of the El Conquistador Resort and Golden Door Spa, which sprawls across a dramatic cliff and down along a harbor area. The buildings are wrought with Mediterranean motifs, from blooming Spanish court-yards to elegant neoclassical facades and fountains.

Las Croabas is a charming fishing village, with boats tied up at harbor and open-air seafood restaurants. Many are clustered along Route 987 at the entrances of the Seven Seas public beach and Las Cabezas de San Juan Nature Reserve.

GETTING THERE

El Conquistador staff members greet all guests at the San Juan airport (p. 34) and transport them to the resort. Guests can take a taxi or a hotel shuttle to the resort ($68, for hotel guests only). The cost of a taxi from the San Juan airport is about $60.

If you're driving from San Juan, head east along the new Route 66 Corridor Noreste highway and then Route 3 toward Fajardo. At the intersection, cut northeast on Route 195 and continue to the intersection with Route 987, at which point you turn north.

OUTDOOR ACTIVITIES

Fajardo's public beach, **Playa Seven Seas,** is an attractive and shel-tered strip of sand. For even better snorkeling, walk to the western end of this beach and along a dirt path cutting though a wooded mount. After about a half-mile (.8km), you'll come to another path heading to **Playa Escondida (Hidden Beach),** a small white-sand cover with coral reefs in aquamarine waters right off this beach. If you continue straight for another mile, you will come to the gorgeous **El Convento Beach,** stretching out along the miles-long undeveloped coastline between Fajardo and Luquillo. The area has managed to ward off development despite the building craze taking place across much of the rest of Puerto Rico. There are only a few unmarked dirt roads providing access, or there are paths like the one from Seven Seas.

The area is a nesting ground for endangered sea turtles, and its waters team with reefs and fish. A small forest runs along much of the

El Yunque	5
Fajardo	4
Humacao	7
Las Cabezas de San Juan Nature Reserve	2
Las Croabas	3
Luquillo Beach	1
Naguabo	6
Palmas del Mar	8
Yabucoa	9

beach, and behind it stands the imposing El Yunque rainforest, looming over the white sand beach and pristine blue waters. About a mile down the beach is the governor's official beach house, El Convento, a rustic wooden cottage. Just beyond the cottage is a great spot to snorkel. The water plunges steeply just offshore, and it is pocked with large reefs, which draw even large fish to the brink of the beach.

Environmentalists have pushed to protect this area from development, while developers want to build two large resorts. Legislation to name a nature reserve here failed to win legislative approval, but the governor signed a less binding executive order doing so, which would only permit low-impact tourism in the area.

WATERSPORTS Several operators offer day sailing trips (10am–3pm) from Fajardo marinas, which include sailing, snorkeling, swimming, and a stop at one of the island beaches, where lunch is usually served. It's the easiest way to really experience the Caribbean marine world while in Puerto Rico. Prices, including lunch and equipment, start from $69 per person. The trips are aboard luxury catamarans, with plush seating, a

To the Lighthouse: Exploring Las Cabezas de San Juan Nature Reserve

Las Cabezas de San Juan Nature Reserve, better known as El Faro or "The Lighthouse," has seven ecological systems and a restored 19th-century Spanish colonial lighthouse with views to St. Thomas in the U.S. Virgin Islands.

Surrounded on three sides by the Atlantic Ocean, the 316-acre (128-hectare) site encompasses forestland, mangroves, lagoons, beaches, cliffs, offshore cays, and coral reefs. Boardwalk trails wind through the fascinating topography. Ospreys, sea turtles, and an occasional manatee are seen from the windswept promontories and rocky beach.

The nature reserve is open Wednesday through Sunday. Reservations are required; for reservations during the week, call (C) **787/722-5882,** and call 860-2560 for reservations on weekends (weekend reservations must be made on the day of your visit). Admission is $7 for adults, $4 for children under 13, and $2.50 for seniors. Guided 2½-hour tours are conducted at 9:30am, 10am, 10:30am, and 2pm (in English at 2pm).

Laguna Grande, within the reserve, is one of the world's best bioluminescent bays. The presence of multitudes of tiny organisms, called dinoflagellates, in the protected bay is responsible for the nocturnal glow of its waters. They feed off the red mangroves surrounding the water. Kayaking through the bay at night should be on your bucket list. We highly recommend **Las Tortugas Adventures,** P.O. Box 1637, Canóvanas 00729 ((C) **787/636-8356** or 809-0253; http://kayak-pr.com). Gary Horne is one of the most experienced guides in Puerto Rico; he's a certified dive master and Coast Guard veteran. There are two nightly tours of the bay at 6pm and 8pm Monday through Saturday, which cost $45 per person—or daytime kayak and snorkel adventures for $65, which we highly recommend as well. Another option is a kayak adventure through the Río Espirtu Santo, a beautiful river through El Yunque rainforest.

sound system, and other comforts, such as a bar. Among the local operators are **Traveler Sailing Catamaran** ((C) 787/853-2821), **East Island Excursions** ((C) 787/860-3434), and **Catamaran Spread Eagle**

(© 787/887-8821). **Erin Go Bragh Charters** (© 787/860-4401)
offers similar day trips aboard a 50-foot sailing ketch.

For scuba divers, **La Casa del Mar** (© 787/863-1000) is one good
option operating out of El Conquistador. You can go for ocean dives
on the outfitter's boats; a two-tank dive goes for $150, including
equipment. A PADI snorkel program, at $65 per person, is also avail-
able. **Sea Ventures Dive Center,** Rte. 3 Km 51.4, Puerto del Rey
(© 787/863-3483), has a $95 offer for a two-tank dive.

Fajardo's seven marinas are proof that it is a sailor's paradise. The
most renowned is the **Puerto del Rey Marina,** Rte. 3 Km 51.4
(© 787/860-1000 or 801-3010), with 1,100 slips, the largest in the
Caribbean. **Villa Marina Yacht Harbour,** Rte. 987 Km 1.3 (© 787/
863-5131 or 863-5011), is another big marina in town, with the
shortest ride to the offshore cays and isolated white-sand beaches on
the mainland.

WHERE TO STAY
Very Expensive
El Conquistador Resort & Golden Door Spa ★★ (Kids) El
Conquistador is a destination unto itself, sprawling across 500 acres
(202 hectares) of forested hills sloping down to the sea. Accommodations are divided into five separate sections united by their Mediterranean architecture and lush landscaping. Most lie several hundred
feet above the sea. A faux Andalusian hamlet, Las Casitas Village, is
its exclusive self-contained enclave.

All the far-flung elements of the resort are connected by serpentine,
landscaped walkways, and by a railroad-style funicular that makes
frequent trips up and down the hillside.

One of the most comprehensive spas in the Caribbean, the Golden
Door maintains a branch in this resort. The hotel is sole owner of a
"fantasy island" (Palomino Island), with caverns, nature trails, horseback riding, and watersports such as scuba diving, windsurfing, and
snorkeling. Free private ferries at frequent intervals connect the
island, which is about a half-mile (.8km) offshore, to the main hotel.
There's also a 25-slip marina. The hotel operates an excellently run
children's club with activities planned daily. The resort has opened up
a water park that's a hit with the kids (and the young at heart) with
water slides, a lazy river, and a large pool. It's on the harbor level, right
by the water, below the pool's main deck.

Av. Conquistador 1000, Las Croabas, Fajardo, PR 00738. © **866/317-8932** or 787/
863-1000. Fax 787/863-6500. www.elconresort.com. 918 units. Winter $299–$558
double, $499–$2,000 Las Casitas Village suites; off season $179–$399 double,
$350–$1,700 Las Casitas suites. MAP (breakfast and dinner) packages are available.
Children ages 16 and under stay free in parent's room. AE, DC, DISC, MC, V.

Self-parking $16 per day; valet parking $21. **Amenities:** 12 restaurants; 8 bars; nightclub; 7 pools; golf course; 7 Har-Tru tennis courts; health club; spa; 35-slip marina; dive shop; fishing; sailing; children's programs; tour desk; business center; limited room service; massage; laundry service; dry cleaning; nonsmoking rooms; casino; rooms for those w/limited mobility. *In room:* A/C, TV, minibar, fridge, coffeemaker, hair dryer, iron, safe.

Moderate

The Fajardo Inn ★ (Finds) A good base for those visiting El Yunque, this inn is ideal for those who are seeking a location in the east and don't want to pay the prices charged at the El Conquistador (above). Lying on a hilltop overlooking the port of Fajardo, this parador evokes a Mediterranean villa with its balustrades and grand staircases. The midsize bedrooms, most of which open onto good views, are spotless, and each has a small shower-only bathroom. The inn and its pool are handsomely landscaped. The on-site Star Fish restaurant specializes in Creole and Continental cuisine, especially fresh fish, with indoor and outdoor dining. The Blue Iguana Mexican Grill & Bar is a casual pub with good food. Coco's Park is a new pool area with activities like a beach pool, slide, Jacuzzi, tennis, basketball, and miniature golf. It's separated from the rest of the hotel so as not to disturb the relative tranquillity of the rest of the grounds.

Parcela Beltrán 52, Fajardo, PR 00740. (C) **787/860-6000.** Fax 787/860-5063. www. fajardoinn.com. 105 units (shower only). Year-round $100–$132 double; $150–$300 suite. AE, DISC, MC, V. A 15-min. walk east of the center of Fajardo. **Amenities:** 2 restaurants; 2 bars; pool; snorkeling and diving arranged; limited room service; 1 room for those w/limited mobility. *In room:* A/C, TV, hair dryer, iron.

WHERE TO DINE
Expensive

Otello's ★ NORTHERN ITALIAN Here you can dine by candlelight either indoors or out. The decor is neo-Palladian. You might begin with one of the soups, perhaps pasta fagioli, or select one of the zesty Italian appetizers, such as an excellently prepared clams Posillipo. Pastas can be ordered as a half portion for an appetizer or as a main dish, and they include homemade gnocchi and fettuccine with shrimp. The chef is known for his superb veal dishes. A selection of poultry and vegetarian food is offered nightly, along with several shrimp and fish dishes. The salmon filet in champagne sauce has beautiful accents, as does the veal chop in an aromatic herb sauce.

Rte. 987 Km 3.4, in the El Conquistador Resort. (C) **787/863-1000.** Reservations required in winter, recommended in off season. Main courses $26–$43. AE, DC, DISC, MC, V. Daily 6–10:30pm.

Stingray Café ★★ CARIBBEAN FUSION We loved this
resort's harborside restaurant, with a deliciously crafted seafood menu
and views of the Caribbean and Palomino Island. The modern decor
is inconsequential compared to the view and the Latin, down-island,
and Asian-infused Continental classics. Flavors float in the air with
the smell of the sea—saffron clams and chorizo and the cilantro
conch chowder, seared tuna in a Szechuan au poivre and the lemon
sole filet lobster beurre blanc. But the filet mignon in roasted bacon
shallot sauce and the pistachio-crusted veal medallions also command
attention. Fruit sorbets are the dessert specialty. Really, it's all about
the food and the view.

In the El Conquistador Resort. ℰ **787/863-1000.** Reservations recommended.
Main courses $29–$50. AE, DISC, MC, V. Daily 6–10:30pm.

2 PALMAS DEL MAR

46 miles (74km) SE of San Juan

Halfway down the east coast, south from Fajardo, lies the resort and
luxury residential community of Palmas del Mar in the municipality
of Humacao. Here you'll find one of the most action-packed sports
programs in the Caribbean, offering golf, tennis, scuba diving, sailing,
deep-sea fishing, and horseback riding. Sprawling across 2,700 acres
(1,092 hectares) of beautifully landscaped coast, it is a self-contained
resort and residential community with several different luxury neighborhoods, ranging from Mediterranean-style villas to modern marina
town houses.

GETTING THERE

Humacao Regional Airport is 3 miles (4.8km) from the northern
boundary of Palmas del Mar. It accommodates private planes; no
regularly scheduled airline currently serves the Humacao airport.
Palmas del Mar Resort will arrange minivan or bus transport from
Humacao to the San Juan airport. Two persons can book the van for
$40. If five or more passengers book the van, the cost is only $20 per
person. The bus can accommodate up to 10 passengers. At night the
price goes up to $45 per person for two. That is lowered to $22 per
person if five or more share the ride. For reservations, call ℰ **787/
285-4323.** Call the resort if you want to be met at the airport.

If you're driving from San Juan, take Hwy. 52 south to Caguas,
then take Hwy. 30 east to Humacao. Follow the signs from there to
Palmas del Mar. A van ride to San Juan is $90 for the first three pas-
sengers, and $25 per person for four or more.

BEACHES & OUTDOOR ACTIVITIES

BEACHES Palmas del Mar Resort has 3 exceptional miles (4.8km) of white-sand beaches (all open to the public). Nonguests must park at the hotel parking ($2 per hour), and there are showers and bathrooms near the beach. The waters here can get rough in winter but are generally calm, and there's a watersports center and marina (see "Scuba Diving & Snorkeling," below).

FISHING Some of the best year-round fishing in the Caribbean is found in the waters just off Palmas del Mar. **Capt. Bill Burleson,** based in Humacao (© 787/850-7442), operates charters on his customized, 46-foot sport-fisherman, *Karolette,* which is electronically equipped for successful fishing. Burleson prefers to take fishing groups to Grappler Banks, 18 nautical miles (33km) away, which lie in the migratory paths of wahoo, tuna, and marlin. A maximum of six people are taken out, costing $800 for $4^1/_2$ hours, $960 for 6 hours, or $1,280 for 8 hours. Burleson also offers snorkeling charter expeditions starting at $640 for up to six persons.

GOLF Few other real-estate developments in the Caribbean devote as much attention and publicity to their golf facilities as the **Palmas del Mar Country Club ★★** (© 787/285-2256). Today, both the older course, the Gary Player–designed Palm course, and the newer course, the Reese Jones–designed Flamboyant course, have pars of 72 and layouts of around 2,250 yards (2,057m) each. Crack golfers consider holes 11 to 15 of the Palm course among the toughest five successive holes in the Caribbean. The pro shop that services both courses is open daily from 6:30am to 6pm. To play the course costs $85 for guests of Villas at Palmas of Four Points by Sheraton or $100 for nonguests.

SCUBA DIVING & SNORKELING Some of the best dives in Puerto Rico are right off the eastern coast. Two dozen dive sites south of Fajardo are within a 5-mile (8km) radius offshore. **Palmas Dive Center ★,** Anchors Village, 110 Harbor Dr. (© 787/863-3483), owns a 44-foot-long dive boat with a 16-foot (4.9m) beam to make it stable in rough seas. They offer both morning and afternoon sessions of two-tank dives (for experienced and certified divers only), priced at $99 each. Half-day snorkeling trips, priced at $60 per participant and departing for both morning and afternoon sessions, go whenever there's demand to the fauna-rich reefs that encircle Monkey Island, an offshore uninhabited cay.

TENNIS The **Tennis Center at Palmas del Mar ★★** (© 787/852-6000, ext. 51), the largest in Puerto Rico, features 13 hard courts, two Omni courts, and four clay courts, open to resort guests and nonguests. Fees for guests are $20 per hour during the day and $25 per hour at night. Fees for nonguests are $25 per hour during the day and $33 per hour at night. Within the resort's tennis compound is a **fitness center,** which has the best-equipped gym in the region; it's open Monday to Friday 6am to 9pm, and Saturday and Sunday 6am to 8pm.

WHERE TO STAY

It's still possible to rent either a studio or villa from the **Villas at Palmas del Mar,** 295 Palmas Inn Way, Ste. 6, Carretera no. 3, Km 86.4, Candelero, Humacao, PR 00791 (© **800/468-3331;** fax 787/ 852-0927). Some 40 studios and villas are available. Renting year-round for $245 to $340, studios come with one bedroom, a kitchenette, and full bathroom. Air-conditioning and cable TV are available. Villas rent year-round from $290 to $595, come with anywhere from one to three bedrooms, and have full kitchens and dining rooms. On the grounds are six pools, two golf courses, 20 tennis courts, a fitness center, and a dive shop. Fishing, bike or car rentals, babysitting, and horseback riding can be arranged.

Four Points by Sheraton Palmas del Mar Resort ★ Completely restored and imbued with a post-millennium update, the resort offers bedrooms that are spacious and handsomely furnished. The junior suites are especially comfortable and inviting. Furnishings are tasteful and exceedingly comfortable, typical of Sheraton's deluxe hotels. Available extras include private balconies, luxury bathrooms, and work desks. The hotel also offers business services for commercial travelers, plus a special pool for kids. The hotel restaurant offers a varied international menu (some dine here every night), and you'll also find a wine and cigar bar.

Candelero Dr. 170, Humacao, PR 00791. © **787/850-6000.** Fax 787/850-6001. www.starwoodhotels.com. 107 units. Year-round $160–$240 double; winter $355 suite; off season $270 suite. AE, MC, V. Self-parking $12; valet parking $15. **Amenities:** Restaurant; 2 bars; outdoor pool; kids' pool; golf; tennis; fitness center; scuba diving; business services; 24-hr. room service; laundry service; dry cleaning; non-smoking rooms; casino; rooms for those w/limited mobility. *In room:* A/C, TV, dataport, fridge, beverage maker, hair dryer, iron, safe.

WHERE TO DINE

Thanks to the kitchens that are built into virtually every unit in Palmas del Mar, many guests prepare at least some of their meals "at home." This is made relatively feasible thanks to the on-site general store at the Palmanova Plaza, which sells everything from fresh lettuce and sundries to liquor and cigarettes.

Blue Hawaii CHINESE   This is the best Chinese restaurant in the region. It combines Polynesian themes (similar to a toned-down Trader Vic's) with an Americanized version of Chinese food that's flavorful and well suited to Puerto Rico's hot, steamy climate. Menu items include lobster with garlic-flavored cheese sauce; blackened salmon or steaks reminiscent of styles in New Orleans; and a superb house version of honey chicken. You'll find the place within the dignified courtyard of the resort's shopping center, with tables for alfresco dining. Your host is Tommy Lo, former chef aboard the now-defunct ocean liner SS *United States.*

La Brochette, in the Palmanova Shopping Center. ✆ **787/285-6644.** Reservations recommended. Main courses $13–$39. AE, MC, V. Daily noon–10:30pm.

Chez Daniel ★ FRENCH   It's French, and it's the favorite of the folks who tie up their yachts at the adjacent pier. Normandy-born Daniel Vasse, the owner, along with his French Catalonian wife, Lucette, maintain a dining room that is the most appealing in Palmas del Mar. Chez Daniel shows a faithful allegiance to the tenets of classical French cuisine, placing emphasis on such dishes as bouillabaisse, onion soup, and snails as well as lobster and chicken dishes. For dessert, consider a soufflé au Cointreau.

Marina de Palmas del Mar. ✆ **787/850-3838.** Reservations required. Main courses $23–$36 at dinner, $8–$19 at lunch; $42 Sun brunch (includes 1st drink). AE, DISC, MC, V. Wed–Mon 6:30–10pm; Fri–Sun noon–3pm. Closed June.

3 THE SOUTHEAST

More and more visitors are discovering the bewitching allure of Puerto Rico's wild and wooly southeast coast, with deep sand beaches, powerful waves, and cliffs cutting across the landscape straight down to the coast. There are still empty beaches with lighthouses, but now there are more restaurants and lodging options than just a few years ago. In Yabucoa, you can also catch the start of the Panoramic Route, a tangle of narrow country roads crisscrossing Puerto Rico's mountainous interior from the east to west coasts. Roadways climb oceanfront cliffs, cutting back and forth in switchbacks that afford outstanding views of the Caribbean and the islands in the distance.

WHERE TO STAY & DINE
Moderate
Hotel Parador Palmas de Lucía ★ (Finds)   Just steps from the pleasant sands of Playa Lucía, this is one of the newest hotels in eastern Puerto Rico, filling a vast gap in accommodations in this remote

part of the island. The López family is your host, and their complex combines colonial styling with tropical decoration. Each midsize bedroom is well furnished and has a pool-view balcony and an efficiently organized, tiled, shower-only bathroom. The López family, under its Tropical Inns Puerto Rico company, also runs two nearby small hotels we also recommend, **Parador Costa del Mar** in Yabucoa and **MaunaCaribe** in nearby Maunabo. All are clean, well managed, and surprisingly affordable for what you get.

Palmas de Lucía, routes 901 and 9911, Camino Nuevo, Yabucoa, PR 00767. © **787/ 893-4423.** Fax 787/893-0291. www.palmasdelucia.com. 34 units (shower only). Year-round $102 double. AE, MC, V. From Humacao, take Rte. 53 south to Yabucoa, to the end of the highway, where you connect with Rte. 901 to Maunabo. After a 2-min. drive, turn left at the signposted Carretera 9911, which leads to Playa Lucía. **Amenities:** Restaurant; bar; pool; basketball court. *In room:* A/C, TV.

El Nuevo Horizonte (Finds) PUERTO RICAN/SEAFOOD With

the best view in southeast Puerto Rico and great food, this restaurant in the coastal hills of Yabucoa is probably our favorite of the typical Puerto Rican eateries on the island. Seafood is the star here. The house special is the paella rey, or king paella, prepared to moist perfection and loaded with lobster, clams, shrimp, and mussels. The stuffed *mofongo* with seafood is among the island's best, and the restaurant has a great stuffed lobster dish as well. While the restaurant is simple, the view is outstanding. The dining room is perched on a cliff overlooking the Caribbean, and you can see clear out to Vieques and the other islands. The restaurant has an outdoor deck that serves drinks and food in a more informal environment.

Rte. 901 Km 8.8, Yabucoa. © **787/893-5492.** Reservations not necessary. Main courses $12–$45. AE, MC, V. Thurs–Sat 11am–9pm; Sun 11am–8pm.

Appendix A:
Puerto Rico
Fast Facts

AIRPORT See "Arriving by Plane" and "Getting from the Airport to the City," in chapter 3.

AMERICAN EXPRESS Call the company's local toll-free customer service line: © **800/327-1267.**

BANKS Local banks have branches with ATMs in San Juan that function on U.S. networks. Branches are open Monday to Friday 8:30am to 4pm. Bank branches in malls are open Saturday 8:30am to 6pm and Sunday 9am to 3pm.

BUS INFORMATION See "Getting Around" in chapter 3. For information about bus routes in San Juan, call © **787/767-7979.**

CAMERA & FILM Foto One (© 787/722-1949), located at Calle Fortaleza 259 in Old San Juan, offers a wide variety of photographic supplies. Open Monday through Saturday from 9am to 6pm.

CAR RENTALS See "Getting Around" in chapter 3. If you want to reserve after you've arrived in Puerto Rico, try **Avis, Budget,** or **Hertz.**

CONSULATES Many countries maintain honorary consulates here, mostly to try to drum up mutually beneficial trade on the island, but they can be of assistance to travelers. **Britain** has a consulate at Av. Chardón 350 (© **787/758-9828**) at Hato Rey, open Monday to Friday 9am to 1pm and 2 to 5pm. The consulate for **Canada** is at Av. Ponce de León 268 (© **787/759-6629**), also at Hato Rey and open only by appointment.

CURRENCY EXCHANGE The unit of currency is the U.S. dollar. Most banks provide currency exchange, and you can also exchange money at the **Luis Muñoz Marín International Airport.** See "Money" in chapter 2.

DRUGSTORES One of the most centrally located pharmacies is **Puerto Rican Drug Co.,** Calle San Francisco 157 (© **787/725-2202**), in Old San Juan. It's open Monday to Friday from 7:30am to

9:30pm, Saturday 8am to 9:30pm, and Sunday 8:30am to 7:30pm. **Walgreens,** Av. Ashford 1130, Condado (© **787/725-1510**), is open 24 hours. There are also other Walgreens throughout the city, one in practically every neighborhood. There are other locations in Old San Juan, Miramar, Isla Verde, and on Calle Loiza near Ocean Park.

EMERGENCIES   In an emergency, dial © **911.** Or call the local police (© **787/343-2020**), fire department (© **787/343-2020**), ambulance (© **787/766-2222**), or medical assistance (© **787/754-2550**).

EYEGLASSES   Services are available at **Pearle Vision Express,** Plaza Las Americas Shopping Mall (© **787/753-1033**). Hours are Monday to Saturday from 9am to 9pm and Sunday from 11am to 5pm. **Tropical Vision,** La Fortaleza St. 308 (© **787/723-5488**), is located in Old San Juan.

HOSPITALS   **Ashford Presbyterian Community Hospital,** Av. Ashford 1451 (© **787/721-2160**), maintains a 24-hour emergency room.

INTERNET ACCESS   Try **CyberNet Café,** Av. Ashford 1128 (© **787/724-4033**), on the Condado; it charges $5 for 35 minutes or $7 for 50 minutes. Open Monday to Saturday 9am to 11pm, Sunday 10am to 11pm. There is another branch in Isla Verde. If you have a laptop or other wireless device, there are Internet hotspots throughout the city at food courts in malls, Starbucks, Burger King and McDonald's, and historic plazas in Old San Juan.

POLICE   Call © **787/726-7020** for the local police.

POST OFFICE   In San Juan, the **General Post Office** is at Av. F.D. Roosevelt 585 (© **787/622-1758**). If you don't know your address in San Juan, you can ask that your mail be sent here "c/o General Delivery." This main branch is open Monday to Friday from 5:30am to 6pm, Saturday from 6am to 2pm. A letter from Puerto Rico to the U.S. mainland will arrive in about 4 days.

RESTROOMS   Restrooms are not public facilities accessible from the street. It's necessary to enter a hotel lobby, cafe, or restaurant to gain access to a toilet.

SAFETY   At night, exercise caution when walking along the back streets of San Juan, and don't venture onto the unguarded public stretches of the Condado and Isla Verde beaches at night. All these areas are favorite targets for muggings.

SALONS   Most of San Juan's large resort hotels, including the Condado Plaza, the Marriott, and the Sheraton Old San Juan Hotel, maintain hair salons. **Los Muchachos** in Old San Juan has an army of stylists cutting and sprucing walk-in traffic as well as appointments.

TAXIS See "Getting Around" in chapter 3.

TELEPHONE & FAX There are many public telephone centers for international callers around the cruise-ship docks (catering mostly to crew). Most have fax and Internet service as well. Long distance calling cards are widely available in drugstores and variety shops.

Appendix B: Useful Terms & Phrases

1 BASIC VOCABULARY

ENGLISH-SPANISH PHRASES

English	Spanish	Pronunciation
Good day	**Bucn día**	bwchn *dee*-ah
Good morning	**Buenos días**	*bweh*-nohss *dee*-ahss
How are you?	**¿Cómo está?**	*koh*-moh ehss-*tah?*
Very well	**Muy bien**	mwee byehn
Thank you	**Gracias**	*grah*-syahss
You're welcome	**De nada**	deh *nah*-dah
Good-bye	**Adiós**	ah-*dyohss*
Please	**Por favor**	pohr fah-*vohr*
Yes	**Sí**	see
No	**No**	noh
Excuse me	**Perdóneme**	pehr-*doh*-neh-meh
Give me	**Déme**	*deh*-meh
Where is . . . ?	**¿Dónde está . . . ?**	*dohn*-deh ehss-*tah?*
the station	**la estación**	lah ehss-tah-*syohn*
a hotel	**un hotel**	oon oh-*tehl*
a gas station	**una gasolinera**	*oo*-nah gah-soh-lee-*neh*-rah
a restaurant	**un restaurante**	oon res-tow-*rahn*-teh
the toilet	**el baño**	el *bah*-nyoh
a good doctor	**un buen médico**	oon bwehn *meh*-dee-coh
the road to . . .	**el camino a/ hacia . . .**	el cah-*mee*-noh ah/ *ah*-syah
To the right	**A la derecha**	ah lah deh-*reh*-chah
To the left	**A la izquierda**	ah lah ees-*kyehr*-dah
Straight ahead	**Derecho**	deh-*reh*-choh

English	Spanish	Pronunciation
I would like	**Quisiera**	key-*syeh*-rah
I want	**Quiero**	*kyeh*-roh
to eat	**comer**	koh-*mehr*
a room	**una habitación**	*oo*-nah ah-bee-tah-*syohn*
Do you have . . . ?	**¿Tiene usted . . . ?**	tyeh-neh oo-*sted*?
a book	**un libro**	oon *lee*-broh
a dictionary	**un diccionario**	oon deek-syow-*nah*-ryo
How much is it?	**¿Cuánto cuesta?**	*kwahn*-toh *kwehss*-tah?
When?	**¿Cuándo?**	*kwahn*-doh?
What?	**¿Qué?**	keh?
There is (Is there . . . ?)	**(¿)Hay (. . . ?)**	eye?
What is there?	**¿Qué hay?**	keh eye?
Yesterday	**Ayer**	ah-*yer*
Today	**Hoy**	oy
Tomorrow	**Mañana**	mah-*nyah*-nah
Good	**Bueno**	*bweh*-noh
Bad	**Malo**	*mah*-loh
Better (best)	**(Lo) Mejor**	(loh) meh-*hohr*
More	**Más**	mahs
Less	**Menos**	*meh*-nohss
No smoking	**Se prohibe fumar**	seh proh-*ee*-beh foo-*mahr*
Postcard	**Tarjeta postal**	tar-*heh*-ta pohs-*tahl*
Insect repellent	**Repelente contra insectos**	reh-peh-*lehn*-te *cohn*-trah een-*sehk*-tos

More Useful Phrases

English	Spanish	Pronunciation
Do you speak English?	**¿Habla usted inglés?**	*ah*-blah oo-*sted* een-*glehs*?
Is there anyone here who speaks English?	**¿Hay alguien aquí que hable inglés?**	eye *ahl*-gyehn ah-*kee* keh *ah*-bleh een-*glehs*?
I speak a little Spanish.	**Hablo un poco de español.**	*ah*-bloh oon *poh*-koh deh ehss-pah-*nyohl*
I don't understand Spanish very well.	**No (lo) entiendo muy bien el español.**	noh (loh) ehn-*tyehn*-doh mwee byehn el ehss-pah-*nyohl*

English	Spanish	Pronunciation
The meal is good.	**Me gusta la comida.**	meh *goo*-stah lah koh-*mee*-dah
What time is it?	**¿Qué hora es?**	keh *oh*-rah ehss?
May I see your menu?	**¿Puedo ver el menú (la carta)?**	*pueh*-do vehr el meh-*noo* (lah *car*-tah)?
The check, please.	**La cuenta, por favor.**	lah *quehn*-tah pohr fa-*vorh*
What do I owe you?	**¿Cuánto le debo?**	*kwahn*-toh leh *deh*-boh?
What did you say?	**¿Mande?** (formal)	*mahn*-deh?
	¿Cómo? (informal)	*koh*-moh?
I want (to see) . . .	**Quiero (ver) . . .**	*kyeh*-roh (vehr)
a room	**un cuarto** or **una habitación**	oon *kwar*-toh, *oo*-nah ah-bee-tah-*syohn*
for two persons	**para dos personas.**	*pah*-rah dohss pehr-*soh*-nahs
with (without) bathroom	**con (sin) baño**	kohn (seen) *bah*-nyoh
We are staying here only . . .	**Nos quedamos aquí solamente . . .**	nohs keh-*dah*-mohss ah-*kee* soh-lah-*mehn*-teh
one night.	**una noche.**	*oo*-nah *noh*-cheh
one week.	**una semana.**	*oo*-nah seh-*mah*-nah
We are leaving . . . tomorrow.	**Partimos (Salimos) . . . mañana.**	pahr-*tee*-mohss (sah-*lee*-mohss) mah-*nya*-nah
Do you accept . . . ?	**¿Acepta usted . . . ?**	ah-*sehp*-tah oo-*sted*
traveler's checks?	**cheques de viajero?**	*cheh*-kehss deh byah-*heh*-roh?
Is there a laundromat . . . ? near here?	**¿Hay una lavandería . . . ? cerca de aquí?**	eye *oo*-nah lah-*vahn*-deh-*ree*-ah *sehr*-kah deh ah-*kee*
Please send these clothes to the laundry.	**Hágame el favor de mandar esta ropa a la lavandería.**	*ah*-gah-meh el fah-*vohr* deh mahn-*dahr* ehss-tah *roh*-pah a lah lah-*vahn*-deh-*ree*-ah

1	**uno** (*ooh*-noh)	18	**dieciocho** (dyess-ee-*oh*-choh)
2	**dos** (dohss)		
3	**tres** (trehss)	19	**diecinueve** (dyess-ee-*nweh*-beh)
4	**cuatro** (*kwah*-troh)		
5	**cinco** (*seen*-koh)	20	**veinte** (*bayn*-teh)
6	**seis** (sayss)	30	**treinta** (*trayn*-tah)
7	**siete** (*syeh*-teh)	40	**cuarenta** (kwah-*ren*-tah)
8	**ocho** (*oh*-choh)	50	**cincuenta** (seen-*kwen*-tah)
9	**nueve** (*nweh*-beh)	60	**sesenta** (seh-*sehn*-tah)
10	**diez** (dyess)	70	**setenta** (seh-*tehn*-tah)
11	**once** (*ohn*-seh)	80	**ochenta** (oh-*chehn*-tah)
12	**doce** (*doh*-seh)	90	**noventa** (noh-*behn*-tah)
13	**trece** (*treh*-seh)	100	**cien** (syehn)
14	**catorce** (kah-*tohr*-seh)	200	**doscientos** (do-*syehn*-tohs)
15	**quince** (*keen*-seh)	500	**quinientos** (kee-*nyehn*-tohs)
16	**dieciseis** (dyess-ee-*sayss*)		
17	**diecisiete** (dyess-ee-*syeh*-teh)	1,000	**mil** (meel)

Transportation Terms

English	Spanish	Pronunciation
Airport	**Aeropuerto**	ah-eh-roh-*pwehr*-toh
Flight	**Vuelo**	*bweh*-loh
Rental car	**Arrendadora de autos**	ah-rehn-da-doh-rah deh ow-tohs
Bus	**Autobús**	ow-toh-*boos*
Bus or truck	**Camión**	ka-*myohn*
Lane	**Carril**	kah-*reel*
Nonstop	**Directo**	dee-*rehk*-toh
Baggage (claim area)	**Equipajes**	eh-kee-*pah*-hehss
Intercity	**Foraneo**	foh-rah-*neh*-oh
Luggage storage area	**Guarda equipaje**	gwar-dah eh-kee-*pah*-heh
Arrival gates	**Llegadas**	yeh-*gah*-dahss
Originates at this station	**Local**	loh-*kahl*
Originates elsewhere	**De paso**	deh *pah*-soh
Stops if seats available	**Para si hay lugares**	*pah*-rah see eye loo-*gah*-rehs

English	Spanish	Pronunciation
First class	**Primera**	pree-*meh*-rah
Second class	**Segunda**	seh-*goon*-dah
Nonstop	**Sin escala**	seen ess-*kah*-lah
Baggage claim area	**Recibo de equipajes**	reh-see-boh deh eh-kee-*pah*-hehss
Waiting room	**Sala de espera**	*sah*-lah deh ehss-*peh*-rah
Toilets	**Sanitarios**	sah-nee-*tah*-ryohss
Ticket window	**Taquilla**	tah-*kee*-yah

INDEX

See also Accommodations and Restaurant indexes, below.

ACCOMMODATIONS

RESTAURANTS